A ROSENBERG BY ANY OTHER NAME

THE GOLDSTEIN-GOREN SERIES IN AMERICAN JEWISH HISTORY

General editor: Hasia R. Diner

A Rosenberg by Any Other Name

A History of Jewish Name Changing in America

Kirsten Fermaglich

NEW YORK UNIVERSITY PRESS

New York

NEW YORK UNIVERSITY PRESS
New York
www.nyupress.org

References to Internet websites (URLs) were accurate at the time of writing. Neither the author nor New York University Press is responsible for URLs that may have expired or changed since the manuscript was prepared.

Library of Congress Cataloging-in-Publication Data
Names: Fermaglich, Kirsten Lise, author.
Title: A Rosenberg by any other name : a history of Jewish name changing in America / Kirsten Fermaglich.
Description: New York : New York University press, [2018] | Includes bibliographical references and index.
Identifiers: LCCN 2018012205 | ISBN 9781479867202 (cl : alk. paper)
Subjects: LCSH: Names, Personal—Jewish—United States—History.
Classification: LCC CS3010 .F47 2018 | DDC 929.4089/924—dc23
LC record available at https://lccn.loc.gov/2018012205

New York University Press books are printed on acid-free paper, and their binding materials are chosen for strength and durability. We strive to use environmentally responsible suppliers and materials to the greatest extent possible in publishing our books.

Manufactured in the United States of America

10 9 8 7 6 5 4 3 2 1

Also available as an ebook

CONTENTS

Introduction

Sean Ferguson, Winona Ryder, and Other Jewish Names

A Jewish immigrant entered America at Ellis Island. The procedures were confusing to him; he was overwhelmed by the commotion. When one of the officials asked him, "What is your name?" he replied, "Shayn fergessen." (in Yiddish, "I've already forgotten.") The official then recorded his name as Sean Ferguson.
—*A Treasury of American-Jewish Folklore* (1996)

Winona Ryder drinks Manischewitz wine
Then spins a dreidel with Ralph Lauren and Calvin Klein
—Adam Sandler, "The Chanukah Song, Part Two" (1999)

When I have told people I was writing a book about Jewish name changing, they have always wanted to tell me a story or joke. (It has frequently been the Sean Ferguson joke in the epigraph.) They have sometimes asked me about the name changes of Jewish celebrities, such as Winona Ryder. Although they have never sung Adam Sandler's "Chanukah Song" to me, I have sometimes felt as though his novelty piece, filled with references to the unexpected and hidden Jews in popular culture, was playing softly in the background. Some people have asked why I decided to write about name changing, and I have always responded with yet another joke: "With a name like Kirsten Fermaglich, how could I not write about name changing?"

There is no shortage of humor related to this topic, but, as is always the case, serious meaning lies just below the surface. Images of lonely, confused immigrants such as Sean Ferguson losing their authentic selves or of glamorous celebrities such as Ralph Lauren shedding their past suggest that name changing was an individual experience, one that reflected isolation and disconnection from the Jewish community. Because our culture associates name changing with humor and celebrity, some people may think that the practice was a superficial or insignificant part of American Jewish life. Even my own personal joke about name changing hints at our cultural expectations. With a given name easily mistaken for others and a long, unusual surname that no one can spell, *of course* I should want to change my name without a second thought or a word to my family. What else is there to say?

In fact, there is a great deal. As I began researching name changing in the United States, I found thousands of name-change petitions housed at the New York City Civil Court, offering compelling personal details and sometimes heartbreaking stories from men, women, and children who sought to abandon their names and find new ones. In 1929, Eli Simonowitz was promoted to assistant manager at his workplace. His employer required him to display a wooden plaque with his name on it—and "requested [Simonowitz] adopt the shorter name of "Simmons."[1] In 1946, Hedwig Steinberg, a refugee from Hitler's Germany, petitioned to change her son Ronald Philip's last name to Stanton, testifying that he wanted to "remove as much as possible all associations with or thoughts of the German regime from his mind and also to give up the surname which is of German origin and association."[2] And in 1957, Charles Moskowitz petitioned to change his 16-year-old son Ira Steven's surname to Miller, saying that "both teachers and fellow students" had "ridiculed petitioner's son for having such a name, stating that the name is un-American."[3] These untold stories and others were buried in the New York City Civil Court records.

I also found, to my surprise, that no historian had yet explored this subject—for any ethnic group—seriously or in depth. I have come to believe that the casual jokes and the glamorous images we circulate about name changing have discouraged us from truly understanding a practice that has been fundamental to many Americans' understandings of themselves, their families, their communities, and their identities. As the first historical book about name changing in the United States, *A Rosenberg by Any Other Name* recasts our standard images and questions popular assumptions in order to restore these people's experiences to our understanding of American life.

My research makes clear that, for large numbers of Jews, name changing was neither an isolated nor an individual act. Far from being merely a punch line, name changing was an important and widely-practiced phenomenon among New York Jews in the 20th century. Between 1917 and 1967, thousands of American-born New York Jews submitted name-change petitions as families in order to combat antisemitism, find jobs, and receive an education. In fact, Jewish names are represented in the New York City Civil Court name-change petitions far out of proportion to their numbers in the city, suggesting that legal name changing was a Jewish behavior during this era.

The New York Jews who changed their names represented a minority of the New York Jewish community, but they had a powerful impact on American Jewish communal life. For one thing, their neighbors, friends, and relatives in the city, and indeed all over the country, had to confront the practice and its implications: should they too change their own names? Would a new, less ethnic name improve their lives? Did changing their names mean that they were deserting their religion or their family? For the most part, fears of abandonment were unfounded. Name changers did not typically convert out of the religion, leave the Jewish community, or abandon their families, yet these fears shaped Jews' interactions with one another throughout the 20th century.

American Jewish communal leaders, like other members of the community, struggled with name changing. Name changers complicated the efforts of Jewish agencies to count Jews and provide them services, and some leaders were indeed convinced that name changers betrayed their community. Yet the urgency of defending Jews against antisemitism in the middle of the 20th century led important organizations to include name changers as integral parts of the American Jewish community.

American Jewish culture too was profoundly shaped by name changing, as writers, filmmakers, comedians, and social scientists all incorporated name changing into their work, considering the practice alternately as a symbol of Jewish social inclusion, Jewish marginality, or even American corruption and decadence. As New York witnessed a local phenomenon of Jewish name changing, Jews and non-Jews throughout the country confronted images of isolated, ambivalent, or even antisemitic name changers in such popular films as *The Jazz Singer* (1927), *Gentleman's Agreement* (1947), and *My Favorite Year* (1982).

Far from serving simply as a humorous punch line, then, or a prerogative of the Hollywood elite, name changing and our cultural discussions of the practice offer a window into American Jewish economic, social, cultural, and political life throughout the 20th century. Historical debates about immigration, antisemitism and race, class mobility, gender and family, the boundaries of the Jewish community, and the power of government all look different when name changing becomes a part of the conversation.

First, let us consider how name changing changes our thinking about immigration. It is surprising how underexplored the history of name changing is in the United States, particularly given its central place in our imagination of the immigrant experience. When it is mentioned at all, name changing is typically taken for granted, used as a simple shorthand for immigrants' assimilation into American social and cultural life.[4] These brief mentions are inadequate for a few reasons.

For one, scholars have long rejected simple portraits of immigrant assimilation into American life. Historians no longer believe that immigrants were simply uprooted from their past, shedding all elements of the Old World to become absorbed into a new American culture. Nor do they still believe that there is a natural cycle of immigration, in which individuals automatically progress through stages of forgetting their past and "becoming American." For decades, most scholars of immigration and ethnicity have pointed out instead the complex and uneven ways that first- and second-generation Americans integrated into mainstream culture.[5] Immigrants and their children constructed new ethnic identities, with elements of both the Old and New World blended together, as part of an elaborate network of ethnic families, neighborhoods, and institutions.

Rather than a step on the way to forgetting the past, name changing was a part of Jews' ethnic networks, strategies, and values. Jews did not typically change their names to "John Smith" or "Margaret Washington." They selected new names with the same initials as their former names, they frequently amputated their Jewish names to recognizable roots, such as "Rose," "Berk," and "Lebow," and they typically eschewed names that "sounded" too Christian or that had specific Christian or American connotations, such as "John" or "Christopher," "Washington" or "Jefferson." Perhaps most strikingly, Jews changed their names as families, while living in Jewish neighborhoods and supported by Jewish institutions. For many New York Jews, name changing was a part of their ethnic identity and community, not an escape from it.

Additionally, large numbers of name changers were not immigrants at all. Roughly three-quarters of all individuals who changed their name in the City Court in Manhattan in 1945 were actually second-generation Americans who had been born in the United States, attended public schools, and spoke English as their native language with accents that, more often than not, reflected Brooklyn, not Poland. Name changing for these individuals was not a means of "becoming American": they were, by virtually every measure, already American.

This is not to say that immigrants did not change their names. Indeed, countless numbers of immigrants did change their names as they traveled to the United States and established new lives. After the passage of the 1906 Naturalization Act, petitions to naturalize gave immigrants a space to record a new name, and recent research suggests that many Jewish immigrants, along with immigrants of many other backgrounds, took advantage of this option.[6] Moreover, memoirs and novels from the turn of the century make clear that unofficially taking on a new American name was a typical and accepted part of immigrants' experience in the New World. "With our despised immigrant clothing we shed also our impossible Hebrew names," Mary Antin wrote, describing a "committee of our friends, several years ahead of us in American experience" who "concocted American names for us."[7] It is likely that thousands of Jewish immigrants changed their names using these formal and informal methods.

Even so, it is striking that the New York City Civil Court has so few petitions from immigrants and so many from immigrants' children and grandchildren. Why would fairly comfortable American-born Jews living in New York—the city with the largest, most established Jewish population in the Western Hemisphere—choose to change their names in such large numbers?

One simple answer to this question is that they sought to avoid antisemitism. Jewish-sounding names could expose them to ridicule and discrimination. But antisemitism is not a simple phenomenon.

Throughout the years, American Jewish historians have done much to outline and explore the contours of antisemitism in the United States, especially in the twentieth century. Beginning in the late nineteenth century, hotels and resorts restricted Jews from registering as guests. Elite Americans began excluding Jews from their social clubs and working to halt the immigration of Jews and other "undesirables." In the 1920s, universities and colleges instituted quotas on Jewish students and refused to hire Jewish faculty. Employers posted "help wanted" ads that specified "Christians only," and homeowners signed covenants promising not to sell their homes to Jews. In public forums on radio and in the press, prominent individuals such as Henry Ford and Father Charles Coughlin attacked Jews for the threat they posed to the country—as both capitalists and communists. In the 1930s, pro-Nazi groups openly spouted hatred against Jews, distributing literature throughout the nation and sometimes targeting Jewish individuals for violent attacks. Angry rhetoric charged Jews with bringing the country into World War II and profiting from it. Antisemitism declined after the war, but perceptions of Jews as clannish or possessing control of certain industries still remained a part of many Americans' worldview.[8]

This narrative emerges from a host of important works by American Jewish historians. But these historians have rarely addressed in depth the private nature of the American antisemitism they describe. In comparison to Europe's murderous state antisemitism and the brutal racism directed at nonwhites by the US government, American antisemitism has been mostly exercised by private citizens and companies that have operated quietly, through rumor, innuendo, and informal policy, rather than government violence or decree.[9] How has the unofficial, private, *insidious* nature of American antisemitism affected American Jews?[10]

For one thing, private and unofficial limitations significantly affected Jews' status in American social and economic life. Although Jews were neither officially identified nor segregated by American state policy, private institutions—especially universities, employment agencies, and professional boards—developed unofficial but powerful mechanisms to identify and segregate Jews in social and economic life. The most important of these mechanisms was the modern application form, which asked extensive questions about nationality and ancestry in an effort to identify and thereby exclude Jews.

Both names and name changing played a crucial role on application forms. Large numbers of New Yorkers who petitioned to change their names were certain that their Jewish names, listed at the top of their application forms, had been a liability for them with employers and admissions officials: "[Golding] is foreign sounding, cumbersome, difficult to remember and easily confused with other names," Pauline Golding explained in 1937 in her petition to change her name to Pauline Bennett Gould, continuing, "Petitioner's foreign-sounding name has hindered her in her work, in obtaining employment, and in her social life. . . . Your petitioner's present name has consequently resulted in great loss to her both in business and socially."[11]

In response to name changing such as Gould's, employers and universities also used application forms to ask applicants questions about their family names in order to determine their ancestry: What was their father's surname? What was their mother's maiden name? Had they or anyone else in their family changed their names? In a society where Jews' racial status was uncertain, these subtle bureaucratic questions marked Jews as different and undesirable. To be sure, antisemites did not think Jews' racial status was in doubt: they believed they could identify Jews by their dark hair or hook noses. But most Jews in the United States were descended from European ancestors, with a skin color and eye shape that matched most white Americans; their physical appearance was frequently indistinguishable from other white Americans, making questions about religion, ethnicity, and names all the more insidious for their successful efforts to identify Jewish applicants' identity. And unlike today's voluntary affirmative-action questions on employment applications, applicants were *required* to answer these questions and thus either identify themselves as Jewish or lie about their identity. By making these questions standard on application forms, bureaucrats actually helped to construct Jews' inferior status in American social and economic life— either intentionally or unintentionally.

Then, too, bureaucracy shaped Jews' perceptions of themselves and their capacity to resist discrimination. What did it mean for Jews to live in a world that was quietly, politely, and privately laced with questions designed to mark them as different? How could they be sure they were facing discrimination? How did they understand rejections from schools, employers, and social organizations? How did shadowy, unacknowledged limitations shape their daily lives? And how did these limitations shape their identities as Jews?

The insidious nature of American antisemitism may have limited ordinary Jews' understanding of themselves as victims, as well as their capacity to protest openly. Pauline Golding's petition did not state that she had been the victim of prejudice or antisemitism, and Golding was not alone. Of the thousands of petitions found in the New York City Civil Court, virtually none mentioned antisemitism. They may have been uncertain of what they were facing—they had no proof of discrimination—or they may have been embarrassed by and ashamed of rejections that could be interpreted as personal and individual, rather than racially motivated. The unofficial nature of American antisemitism encouraged many Jews to resist discrimination by using bureaucratic name-change petitions to reshape their personal identity, rather than civil rights activism to change an unfair society. Name changing thus offers us a window into the corrosive nature of American antisemitism.

Name changing also shows us how deeply intertwined race has been with Jewish economic and social mobility in the United States. Employers and universities tried to weed out Jews precisely because they believed there were too many of them in workplaces and on campuses. As Jews achieved economic success, moving into the middle class faster than other white immigrant groups did in the early 20th century, their efforts at social mobility were severely scrutinized. And it is this interplay between Jewish success, antisemitic restriction, and Jewish name changing that needs to be considered.[12] Historians have typically focused on Jews' economic success in the United States without much consideration of the obstacles that stood in their way.[13] But the petitions found in New York City Civil Court testify to the significant obstacles Jews faced when they sought middle-class jobs. Dora Sarietzky, a secretary, described her frustratingly long search for work before a name change with a phrase that was repeated in petition after petition: "My name proved to be a handicap." Petitions also detail the effectiveness of name changing as a strategy. "Immediately [after changing his name to Edmund Cronin] petitioner did obtain a position," the engineer Melvin Applebaum reported.[14] Jews often felt that their success in the middle class required them to tailor their names to present a more acceptable outward appearance on the job.[15]

Name-change petitions also require us to consider the importance of women and children in stories of Jews' economic success. The most recent, complicated, and nuanced portraits of Jewish economic life in America have mostly been stories of men.[16] But Jews, far more than any other group in New York City then or since, developed a pattern of family name changing, in which husbands and wives changed their names together, parents changed their names with their sons and daughters, and adult brothers brought their wives and children together to change names on one petition. By the middle of the 20th century, the vast majority of Jewish name-change petitions were filed by family members working together to help one another find jobs or get an education. Sometimes it was children who pushed their mothers and fathers to change their name, as they faced hostility at school or feared that they would not be admitted to college. "For me, a change to Nuland meant that I would never have to get up on the first day of class each semester and announce to a pimply multitude that I was Sherwin Nudelman," remembered Sherwin Nuland in 2003.[17] At other times, it was women—either alone or with family members—who instigated the name change. Melanie Kaye/Kantrowitz's mother remembered that she threatened to call her first child Forsythia Kantrowitz until her husband changed their surname in 1942.[18] The intense stigma that Jewish women faced as they sought to become secretaries or saleswomen led surprisingly large numbers of single Jewish women, such as Pauline Golding, to change their names—even when they knew they might change them again upon marriage. Of course, in some ways, this may not be as surprising as we imagine: changing last names was a normal practice for women, who were always required to reshape their identities upon marriage.[19] Nonetheless, women and children played a crucial and often forgotten role in confronting antisemitism and shaping Jewish economic success. Name changing helps us remember how important they were in this process.

Indeed, name changing may have actually shaped Jews' middle-class status itself. Although only a small percentage of Jews in New York City changed their names legally, name changing was concentrated in mostly Jewish neighborhoods where residents earned a solid income, such as Washington Heights and the Upper West Side, and possessed white-collar professions and careers: doctors and dentists, secretaries and business people, writers and musicians. Scholars suggest that class is a complicated category, something we should see as being constructed, rather than taken for granted or assumed.[20] If that is the case, then name changing (and the cultural pressure that surrounded it) can be seen as one way that Jews made themselves into members of the middle class.

Name changing can also be seen as one way that Jews made themselves "white" in American social life. Although Jews of European descent have always been understood legally as white citizens in the United States, as antisemitism rose in the late 19th and early 20th centuries, their racial identity became uncertain. A number of historians have charted the ways that Jews ultimately came to be defined as white through both economic mobility and cultural integration. Eric Goldstein's work, in particular, has rightly noted the complications of this journey and the pain that it caused for many American Jews.[21]

These historians' discussions of whiteness, however, do not address one of the central elements that sociologists and theorists have identified in white identity: invisibility, the ability of white people to travel through life unmarked and unseen as a race.[22] Another related hallmark of whiteness for many theorists is ethnic options: individuals' ability to select when and where they identify their ethnic origins.[23]

Name changing adds these important dimensions of whiteness into our consideration of American Jews' lives. Name changers sought to shed the markers that identified them as Jewish to the outside world, hoping to fall under the radar screen of antisemites in the workforce and education system. Yet name changers typically continued to identify themselves as Jews in both private and public settings—when they chose to do so. Invisibility—and the ethnic options it provided—were crucial to Jews' successful redefinition as white people in the United States at the end of the 20th century.

Ironically, civil rights organizations in the middle of the 20th century similarly sought to erase Jewish racial markers—which included questions about names and name changing—in order to eliminate antisemites' power to label and exclude Jews. Unintentionally, then, Jewish civil rights lawyers' strategies mirrored the work of name changers and helped to construct Jewish identity as a white identity. While historians who study Jews and civil rights have tended to take for granted that Jews are white, our focus on name changing illustrates that the civil rights movement actually allowed Jews to redefine themselves racially.[24]

The cultural pressure for Jews to change names was intense in mid-20th-century New York City. Many reported being encouraged or pressured to change their names by employers, friends, or family members eager for advancement or success: "Dismay was my first reaction," the writer Elias Tobenkin reported in 1930, after a well-known editor offered him a meaty assignment on the condition that he change his name.[25] Fred L. Israel, a graduate student at Columbia University in the mid-1950s, remembered that the prominent historian Richard Morris took him aside and encouraged him to change his name: "so I could reach my full potential as a historian."[26] The belief that new names were essential for economic and professional advancement permeated Jewish neighborhoods and workspaces.

Yet Israel and Tobenkin ultimately chose not to change their names, reflecting countervailing pressures within the Jewish community. Many reported disdain and anger for those who changed their names: "that's not the act of a self-respecting man," Nathaniel Zalowitz argued in the *Jewish Daily Forward*.[27] A good number of Jews during this era actually identified themselves as Jewish solely because they were unwilling to escape their background, as they believed name changers did. In 1944, for example, the critic Clement Greenberg described his parents having little connection to Judaism, other than "an insistence upon specifying themselves as Jews—i.e. to change one's name because it is too Jewish is shameful."[28] Many Jews believed that name changers had essentially betrayed their people. The phenomenon of name changing triggered communal battles among New York Jews, encouraging some to find more neutral names as an economic strategy, while others kept their Jewish names as proof of their identity.

The belief that name changers abandoned the Jewish community played into the larger fears of American Jewish leaders. As the Holocaust ravaged the European Jewish community, many American Jewish leaders worried that their own society, where Jews were conditionally accepted but dogged by quiet hatred, led Jews to hate themselves. By the end of World War II, Jewish leaders had designated "self-hatred" as the chief scourge of the American Jewish community, and they devoted energy and resources to shoring up children's Jewish identities. For these leaders, one of the central indicators of self-hatred was name changing, an act they felt marked Jews' abandonment of the Jewish community.[29]

Historians have not looked closely, however, at the actual experiences of name changers to see whether these fears were realized. Did Jews such as Ronald Philip Steinberg or Eugene Martin Greenberg abandon the Jewish community when they changed their surnames to Stanton and

Grant in the 1940s?[30] Did they seek to escape their Jewish backgrounds and families? Their life trajectories do not seem to suggest any kind of abandonment. As the founder and CEO of the agrochemical corporation Transammo, one of the largest privately owned companies in the country, the philanthropist Ronald P. Stanton gave large sums of money to his synagogue, Shearith Israel, and to Yeshiva University. In 2006, he pledged $100 million to Yeshiva, after having turned down a scholarship to study there to become a rabbi when he was young: "I believe in giving to the arts, education, health care and also my synagogue, religious things," Stanton told a *Forbes* reporter in 2011.[31] Similarly, as the founder and president of a major real estate investment and development firm, Eugene M. Grant became a major philanthropist and donor for Jewish causes, including UJA/Federation, the Jewish Museum, the Westchester Holocaust Commission, the National Cabinet of the State of Israel Bonds, the American Israel Chamber of Commerce, the American Jewish Committee, and Big Tent Judaism.[32] Neither of these men seemed to have left the Jewish community at all.

What about other name changers, who were less wealthy or prominent? A closer look at the petitions and the experiences of other ordinary name changers in the years after World War II suggests that Stanton's and Green's continued engagement in the Jewish community was more typical than we might imagine and that the story of name changing is far more complicated than charges of "self-hatred" suggest. Jews such as Beverly Winston, who had changed her name from Weinstein, explained that their former names had interfered with their daily lives, but they never intended to abandon their families, religion, or community: "I never pretend that I'm not Jewish nor have I ever had the desire to do so," Winston told one writer.[33] A journalist in 1948 interviewed 25 randomly selected name changers and found that all of them continued to identify as Jews.[34] And the Bronx resident Reva Blum remembered the Rosborne family in her socialist Jewish neighborhood as the most religiously observant Jews in the community, despite their name change from Rosenberg.[35] The continuing Jewish identification of people with names such as Merrick Garland or Larry King make it clear, even in our own era, that caricatures of name changers who "escaped" or "passed" or were "self-hating" do not illustrate the complexity of real people's lives and decisions.[36]

Indeed, a close look at Jewish name changing offers us a richer portrait of the American Jewish community and of the United States as a whole. Rather than a traditional historical examination of Jews inside the organized Jewish world—members of synagogues or communal institutions—focusing on name changing allows us to look at the complicated and changing meaning of Jewishness for Jews who may not have affiliated with any Jewish organizations at all.[37] Indeed, this book examines Jews who actually chose to erase one of the markers that outwardly identified them as members of the community. Name changing allows us to reconsider the very boundaries of the American Jewish community—and by extension, the boundaries of ethnic identity in the United States more broadly. The men and women in this book reshaped what it meant to be Jewish in the United States by forcing Americans—both Jews and non-Jews—to reconsider their assumptions about Jewishness.

That reshaping of identity was not merely an individual or communal act—it was an act intimately bound up with the state. Mid-20th-century Jewish name changing was a public phenomenon closely intertwined with local, state, and federal governments. Because we are accustomed to seeing our names as the most private and individual elements of our selves, or perhaps as reflections of our immediate or extended family ties, we tend to think less about the crucial roles that names play in our official identities. But the history of names, and of name changing, is closely tied to the government.

For many groups in the United States, names and name changing have been intimately linked with state control. In the 1890s, Native Americans were compelled to abandon their traditional names and take on consistent family names that would ensure the inheritance of newly allotted parcels of land, as part of a broader effort to assimilate Native Americans into Anglo-American society and to extinguish Native culture.[38] By 1909, almost all Chinese Americans were required to carry identification cards with them, thereby allowing the federal government to police their names and identities.[39] And women's right to retain their birth surnames after marriage, although permitted in Anglo-American common law, was abrogated consistently by judges throughout the 19th and 20th centuries, requiring married women who wished to vote, inherit property, or get a business or driver's license to use their husband's surname.[40]

Jews throughout world history have faced similar state demands. Political dictates have required Jews to change their names (both surnames and given names) throughout the world, in settings as varied as Spain and Portugal in the 14th and 15th centuries to Germany in the 19th century to Israel in the 20th. At times, the threat of physical violence was a factor. Many Spanish and Portuguese Jews, for example, took on Christian names when they were forced to convert during the Inquisition.[41] At other times, governments used less physical, but no less successful, means of coercion to require Jews to change their names. In eastern and central Europe in the 19th century, adopting new surnames became a part of life for Ashkenazic Jews. With the rise of Emancipation, a political movement whose goal was to incorporate Jews as citizens of new European nation-states, states began to require Jews to take on stable, unchanging surnames so the state might tax them and require them to serve in the military.[42] Jews frequently viewed those names as nuisances or dangers and sometimes sought to subvert or change them in order to preserve control over their own lives.[43] And then, in 1938, the Nazi regime required all Jews to take on the biblical names "Israel" and "Sara" as a means of isolating, humiliating, and ultimately destroying them.[44] In all of these cases, the state's interest in Jewish names was a means of control—unsurprising given Jews' position as marginalized outsiders throughout much of the world.

In Israel in the 20th century, too, although Jews were no longer marginalized outsiders, the government still attempted to assert control over Jewish names. During the War of Independence in 1947, the Israeli Defense Forces (IDF) released a pamphlet titled "Choose a Hebrew Name for Yourself," encouraging new immigrants to Hebraize their names. After the establishment of the state, Israeli policy strongly encouraged political leaders and party officials to change their names. In 1955, President David Ben-Gurion issued a memorandum insisting that military personnel representing the IDF abroad change their European names to Hebrew ones.[45] Although individuals defied Ben-Gurion's pronouncement without penalty, there is no question that the Israeli state actively encouraged and even at times required name changing as a means of shaping its citizens' Jewish identities.

Strikingly, however, in the United States, Jewish names were barely regulated at all. To be sure, American popular culture and folklore is dominated by images of Ellis Island officials foisting unwanted American names on Jewish and other immigrants, such as Sean Ferguson. Most genealogists and immigration historians, however, argue that this Ellis Island name changing did not take place.[46] Ellis Island officials were explicitly prohibited from changing immigrants' names, and there is very little documentary evidence of official Ellis Island name changing.

Government surveillance of the identities of European Americans in the early 20th century was far more lax than that of Chinese Americans or Native Americans. The Anglo-American legal tradition has mostly understood names to be personal property and thus generally free from state intervention. Most state laws in the United States—including New York State law—do not even require that individuals change their names formally at all; so long as you use a name consistently for a period of time, it is considered to be your name, so long as you are not trying to defraud anyone.[47] Jews, as well as other European immigrants, were able to take advantage of these broad freedoms. Rather than having their names changed for them (or even policed) by state officials, immigrants from Russia, Italy, and Romania typically chose new names voluntarily, easily, and unofficially, without a second thought.

By the middle of the 20th century, however, as a growing government bureaucracy began to track individuals who needed to pay taxes, serve in the military, or receive welfare benefits, names came to take on much more social, political, and economic significance even for European-descended, native-born Americans. Ordinary individuals increasingly found it necessary or desirable to change their names officially in order to receive benefits and avoid penalties.[48] The phenomenon of New York City Jewish name changing took place right at this moment, as the federal government and the welfare state expanded their reach into ordinary Americans' lives during the Depression, World War II, and the Cold War.

Scholars have traditionally described the United States as a "weak" state, comparing it to European governments whose laws and policies regularly intervened in their citizens' personal lives.[49] But the phenomenon of thousands of New York City Jews going to City Court to change their names in the middle of the 20th century does not suggest a weak government: why would Jews in Manhattan have bothered going to court to make their names official at all if the state were truly weak? It was a combination of the private, unofficial antisemitism that Jews faced and the growing federal demand for citizens to be easily identified through one consistent name that pushed Jewish New Yorkers to take advantage of their easy access to name-change petitions at a local city court. Name changing shows us how decentralized the US government is, how interconnected it is with private interests, and how it has increasingly become powerful by subtly encouraging voluntary action from its citizens. The federal government did not demand anyone change his or her name, but private, unofficial antisemitism led Jews to use tools of the state—name-change petitions in the local New York City court—to reshape their identities officially, frequently for federal purposes, such as joining the military.[50]

The story of *A Rosenberg by Any Other Name* is, in some ways, a distinctive New York story. That is, in part, because it is a Jewish story. By 1945, almost two million of the city's residents were Jewish, more than a quarter of the city's population, making them the largest ethnic group in the city and giving New York the largest Jewish population in the United States. As the principal port where Jewish immigrants from Russia and eastern Europe first entered the United States at the end of the 19th century, it also became the predominant city in which they settled, married, and raised their children in the first half of the 20th century. Jewish contractors, architects, and workers built neighborhoods with synagogues, schools, and restaurants that catered to Jewish families' needs and tastes.[51] In Manhattan, it was neighborhoods such as these where name changing clustered, with new names showing up on storefronts, on apartment building mailboxes, and on school attendance sheets. Name changing was a part of the fabric of Jewish neighborhood life in New York City in the 20th century. And indeed, as Jews left the city for the suburbs in the 1960s and 1970s, the number of name-change petitions in New York City began to decline sharply. New York City had the largest Jewish population in the country throughout the 20th century, and its name changes were closely connected to that Jewish population.

This story is also a New York story because it is a story of the white-collar middle class. By the middle of the 20th century, the city had begun to move slowly and unevenly from a manufacturing to a service economy, with finance, real estate, and insurance, as well as the cultural and entertainment industries, gradually making up more and more of the city's labor force. And although this trend was a national one, these industries became increasingly important, especially for women, in the economic landscape of New York, as the emerging financial capital and the predominant cultural center of the country. It was those white-collar "service" jobs that propelled the New York economy as the century advanced; it was those jobs (along with the professions and retail trades) that Jews sought in large numbers, and it was those employers that were most sensitive to Jewish names.[52]

Finally, *A Rosenberg by Any Other Name* is a New York story because it is, in part, a story of progressive political activism. As the home of the headquarters of major communal defense agencies—the American Jewish Committee, the American Jewish Congress, the National Jewish Welfare Board, and, by 1946, the B'nai B'rith Anti-Defamation League—New York was the center of Jewish political activism in the middle of the 20th century. Moreover, beginning in the 1930s, the city's Jews became strong supporters of the Democratic Party and developed a liberal political style that played an important role in the fight for civil rights legislation in the 1940s and 1950s. This political and communal structure, along with a large Jewish voting population, enabled the first civil rights bill in the country to be passed into law in New York in 1945, prohibiting employers from asking job applicants about their race, religion, or ancestry.[53] As we will see, both the language of the law itself and its administration grappled specifically and consistently with the concerns of name changers—a result of the Jewish name-changing phenomenon of New York City in midcentury.

There is evidence, however, that Jews elsewhere in the country changed their names in ways similar to New York Jews. In California, for example, sociologists found disproportionate numbers of upwardly mobile Jews seeking new names in the Los Angeles County Superior Court files after World War II: Jews were only 6 percent of the Los Angeles population, but they represented 46 percent of the name-change petitions from 1946 to 1947.[54] A study of Jews in Minneapolis in the 1950s found that 28 percent of the wealthier, higher-status Jews in the city had changed their surnames.[55] And oral histories and correspondence from cities as diverse as New Haven, Chicago, Houston, San Francisco, Washington, D.C., Baltimore, Detroit, and Toronto suggest that Jews throughout North America responded to economic and social discrimination in the middle of the 20th century by changing their names: "My three brothers never were crazy about the name Cohn. . . . One has changed his name to Cole as he said there was prejudice before people even met him," reported Mrs. R. Brown, a Jewish woman from St. Louis in 1939.[56]

And even if Jewish name changing did not reach the extraordinary numbers everywhere in the nation that it did in New York City, the popularity of name changing as a theme in mainstream fiction, film, journalism, and humor affected both Jews and non-Jews throughout the country. Readers from Louisiana to Colorado to New Jersey were deeply touched by essays about Jewish name changing featured in *Reader's Digest*, even if they were offended by name changing as a strategy: "I am a strong believer that you are what you are and nothing can change you, not even changing your name," declared Mrs. Hubert H. Lowe, a Jewish woman from Corinth, Mississippi.[57]

Similarly, people all over the country reacted powerfully to Laura Z. Hobson's novel *Gentleman's Agreement*, which featured a Jewish name changer as a prominent character. First serialized in the popular magazine *Cosmopolitan*, then turned into a best-selling book, and then finally made into an Academy Award–winning film, *Gentleman's Agreement* inspired both rage and excitement from readers and viewers from Iowa City to Buffalo, Wyoming to Hollywood. Some correspondents specifically lambasted the name changing they had witnessed in their own communities, while others commented more specifically on Jewish names and antisemitism. "When a Jew becomes successful . . . he is condemned by all non-Jews," objected Michael J. Collier, a non-Jew from Grand Rapids, Michigan. "It doesn't arise because of success, but because the Jew is 'slippery,' 'sneaky,' has a Jewish name, or some other damned fool reason."[58] Cultural works that highlighted Jewish names and name changing touched ordinary Americans—both Jews and non-Jews—who witnessed both antisemitism and name changing in their own communities all over the country.

Artists from all over the country portrayed name changing (or opposition to name changing) as a part of their communities. In the middle of the 20th century, chroniclers of Jewish life, such as Meyer Levin in Chicago and Budd Schulberg in Los Angeles, incorporated Jewish name changing as a matter-of-fact part of their worlds, while southern authors such as Burke Davis and Jack Ansell made Jewish name changing a central dark secret in their fictional, and sometimes semifictional, accounts of southern life.[59] By the 1970s and 1980s, the filmmaker Barry Levinson from Baltimore, the Atlanta playwright Alfred Uhry, and the author Allegra Goodman from Honolulu all used name changing as a signal of Jewish inauthenticity. "None of those people tried to change their names or pass themselves off as something they weren't," Uhry said, testifying to the Jewish identities of the characters in his play *Last Night at Ballyhoo*.[60] Jewish name changing occurred throughout the country, and it had wide-ranging cultural impact on both Jews and non-Jews all over the United States. Although the story of *A Rosenberg by Any Other Name* is primarily a story of Jews in New York, it has profound implications for American Jewish history and American history more broadly.

The research for this book has taken me to many places: from the archives of Jewish communal organizations and New York State agencies to published fiction, film, comedy, social science, and journalism, to legal cases that have stretched from lower courts to the Supreme Court, to conversations with people whose families changed their names. The most important venue for my research, however, has been the Civil Court of New York City, which currently houses thousands of name-change petitions from the 20th and 21st centuries.[61] I systematically reviewed these petitions, examining the petitions submitted every five years (1912, 1917, 1922, etc.), and gathering one in ten petitions from each year from 1887 through 2012; this methodology ensured that I looked at thousands of petitions throughout the course of the research. I also gathered additional petitions that I thought were interesting or that illustrated larger trends I saw in the files: I did not include those additional petitions in any of the statistical analysis in this book.[62]

These petitions offer fascinating details into individuals' family lives, but of course, they have limitations. As legal documents, their language is frequently formulaic and somewhat stilted. Sometimes petitioners are referred to in the first person and sometimes in the third person. It is unclear how much control petitioners had over the language and how much was constructed by lawyers. The documents include statements listing petitioners' ages, residential addresses, occupations, and nationalities, allowing me to amass a good amount of quantitative data from the petitions, such as gender, age, residential address, occupation, and nationality, but qualitative analysis required me to read between the lines, to consider the petitions' silences, as well as their vocal claims.

One important example of this silence is that the documents did not ask for or record individuals' ethnic or religious background. Moreover, because these petitions were city documents, they were available to all New York City residents, of all ethnic backgrounds. How, then, can I be sure that Jews were actually disproportionate in the records?

If the surname was a distinctive Jewish name (see chapter 2: Goldberg, for example) or if both given and surnames were names common to Jews (Louis Schwartz, for example), I counted a petitioner and his or her family as Jewish. If only one name was common to Jews (Gerhard Schwartz, for example), I cautiously used a host of different clues, including birthplaces, residential addresses, and occupations, in order to make educated guesses about the ethnic identities of my petitioners. When in doubt, I did not count individuals as Jews. In the end, I believe this methodology had much greater potential to undercount, rather than overcount, Jews.

Perhaps the most important markers of Jewish identity in my research were petitioners' names. As is clear from my foregoing description, I used Jewish names—both given names and surnames—as indicators of Jewishness. But of course, the notion of "Jewish names" is a highly problematic one. Jews have lived in non-Jewish cultures for so long that they have borrowed (or have been required to take) both surnames and given names from their host cultures, and their hosts, in turn, have taken on Jewish-sounding names, particularly biblical ones. Intermarriage, conversion, and patterns of secular belief, moreover, have further ensured that "Jewish names" do not inherently identify Jews. Nonetheless, that does not mean that it is not worthwhile to consider "Jewish names" as indicators of identity.

Historically, names have been important features of Jewish difference in both Europe and the United States throughout the modern era. This was particularly true for Ashkenazic Jews, who originated from central and eastern Europe and formed the vast majority of American Jews in the 20th century. Sephardic Jews, who hail from the Middle East and Spanish-speaking world, represent a minority of Jewish Americans, and their names have typically not marked them as Jews in the United States.[63]

As described earlier, Ashkenazic Jews took on their surnames later than did most other Europeans and under far more restrictive circumstances. The fact that Jewish surnames were taken on belatedly, and frequently under compulsion, ensured that many Jews' names would be distinct from traditional Christian names, even if Jews' new surnames had no basis in traditional Jewish religion or culture at all.[64] Sometimes Jews' names suggested specific religious meaning (as in Cohen, a member of the priestly caste), but other times, Jews created new German names, which typically combined two words together to make names such as "Gold mountain" (Goldberg).[65] Jews did take on other types of names, and many of those names could be held by either Jewish or non-Jewish individuals (for example, the German name Kaufman). Frequently, however, states forbade (or strongly discouraged) Jews from taking on surnames commonly held by Christians, and encouraged (indeed sometimes required) Jews to take on names that would identify them as Jews.[66] After Emancipation, then, certain surnames became recognized as Jewish names, forming a basis for Jewish communal recognition as well as antisemitic labeling and humiliation in much of Europe, as well as in the United States.

Given names were a slightly different matter, but they too could convey a Jewish identity to both Jews and non-Jews. Jewish parents have traditionally given a male child a biblical name, as well as a secular name (*kinnui*) for him to use in non-Jewish state and society; girls were not included in religious services and thus typically did not receive sacred names. Sacred biblical names were used for religious services, but they could also be used outside of Jewish society; the secular and sacred names, moreover, were frequently linguistically linked and used together.[67] Biblical names such as Abraham thus became linked with Jewish identity among both Jews and antisemitic non-Jews in Europe and in the United States. "Abie" became a catchphrase of antisemites, just as surely as "Goldberg." In the United States, moreover, Jewish immigrants who had arrived during the years of mass migration, 1880–1920, developed a distinctive subculture of naming that created new Jewish first names in the United States. Searching for the most American names they could find for their children, Jewish immigrant parents selected English surnames such as Irving and Stanley for their children's first names. Over time, both in Jewish and in non-Jewish communities, those names became associated with Jews in the United States.[68]

As Jews became less distinctive in their dress, economic activity, and lifestyle in the 19th and 20th centuries, Jewish names became important badges of difference throughout much of Europe and in the United States. Indeed, European governments, troubled by the ease with which Jews could be confused with non-Jews in a post-Emancipation world, passed laws that limited or prevented Jewish name changes in an effort to preserve Jewish difference.[69] As noted earlier, however, the United States passed no such restrictive name laws for Jews. Although some name changing could and did occur in Europe, the United States offered American Jews extraordinary opportunities to change the names that marked them as Jewish.[70]

Whether or not individuals who bore Jewish-sounding names were Jewish, names with historical connections to the Jewish community became avenues for Jews to bond with one another and for antisemites at the same time to discriminate. As antisemitism swelled in the United States in the first half of the 20th century, "Jewish names" had tangible meaning for many individuals attempting to get an education, find work, join the military, or avoid social ostracism. Ultimately, rather than viewing names as inherently Jewish, it is important that we understand names as historically Jewish: at important moments in history, both Jews and non-Jews shared the belief that certain names were Jewish, and both groups used those names as stand-ins for Jewish identity.[71] By understanding Jewish names as historical entities, we can understand better the antisemitism that shaped American Jews' lives in the first half of the 20th century, as well as Jews' efforts to respond to that hatred.

There is still a place for name-change jokes in my life. Posted above my desk is a 2009 cartoon from the *New Yorker* that makes me smile every day (although it gives me no desire to change my name). In the cartoon, a teacher stands at the front of a classroom with her attendance sheet and asks, "Will Kristen, Kirsten, and Kiersten please choose new names?"[72] Although I love it, the joke also gives me pause. The artist, William Haefeli, illustrates that our names (and my name in particular!) are shaped by family, fashion, and culture, as well as the bureaucratic needs of civil servants, and he highlights (even as he satirizes) our culture's assumptions about names as superficial and easily changeable. In the pages that follow, I hope to highlight what has been fascinating and fun—but also what is serious and deeply meaningful—about name changing in the United States.

PART I

The Rise of Jewish Name Changing in New York City
after World War I

1

"My Name Proved to Be a Great Handicap"

*Developing a Pattern of Jewish Family Name Changing
in the Interwar Years*

In 1932, a man named Max Greenberger petitioned the City Court of the
City of New York to allow himself, as well as two of his four children, to
change their last name to Greene. One of Greenberger's reasons was that
"the name Greenberger is a foreign sounding name and is not conducive
to securing good employment as a musician"—the desired profession
of his daughter, Augusta. Another ground was that "the name Greenberger . . . is not helpful towards securing an appointment as interne in
a hospital"—the desired profession of his son, Irving.[1]

Max Greenberger was not a young, single man seeking to escape his
Jewish past—one of the classic images of name changers in American
film and fiction. He was instead a middle-aged father seeking to improve his family's economic status. And his petition was not unusual:
the court houses hundreds of other petitions from mothers, fathers, husbands, wives, brothers, sisters, sons, and daughters, all of whom submitted petitions together to abandon Jewish-sounding names during the
1920s and 1930s. The years between World War I and World War II saw
Jewish families pioneering a new strategy to find jobs and get an education in the face of growing antisemitism. Ironically, this strategy illustrated Jews' economic comfort in the United States—the Greenberger
children were not searching for manual labor—as much as it illustrated
Jewish weakness: an identifiable Jewish name was "not conducive to securing good employment" in an era of rampant and growing antisemitism. Ultimately, name changing permitted Jewish families to attain and
strengthen their position in the American middle class, but the practice
carried with it psychological and communal cost.

Before World War I, official name changing was a minor and fairly
limited activity in New York, with roughly 100 people each year chang-

ing their names in City Court. Beginning in World War I, however, the numbers of name-change petitioners more than doubled, so that over 250 petitions were submitted for name change in 1917. And those higher numbers remained steady throughout the interwar years: in the 1920s and 1930s, between 200 and 300 name-change petitions were submitted each year. After World War I, then, name changing became a much more broad-based activity, not limited to a handful of relatively well-off individuals.

As filing a name-change petition became a more common behavior in New York after World War I, the reasons that individuals gave for changing their names concentrated on the "foreignness" of their names. Since the beginning of the City Court records, New Yorkers had changed their names for a number of different reasons, and eliminating an ethnic-sounding name was only one of those reasons. Throughout the 20th century, for example, some people were responding to family discontent or dissolution: deaths, abandonment, and divorce all prompted individuals to change their names.[2] By the 1930s, however, the vast majority of name changers—between 75 and 85 percent—wanted to abandon "foreign" names that were "difficult to pronounce and spell" and to adopt instead more "American" names.[3] These individuals were hoping to shed the ethnic markers that disadvantaged them in American society by taking on unmarked, ordinary names that would go unnoticed.

Although New Yorkers of many different ethnic backgrounds—including those with Italian-, Slavic-, Armenian-, Greek-, and German-sounding names—petitioned to replace their ethnic names between 1917 and 1942, Jewish-sounding names predominated in the City Court files, far out of proportion to Jews' actual numbers in the city. In 1932, for example, roughly 65 percent of the total pool of petitioners had Jewish-sounding names. By way of comparison, during that same year, the number of petitioners with Italian-sounding surnames (the next largest ethnic group in the petitions during these years) represented roughly 11 percent of the petitioners. The large number of Jewish name-change petitioners cannot be explained by the large presence of Jews in New York City. In the 1920s and 1930s, the Jewish population in New York City was roughly 26 to 29 percent.[4] The Italian population at the same time was roughly 14 to 16 percent.[5] Given those numbers, one might expect Jews to change their names at roughly double the rate of Italians (that is,

29:16), not six times the rate of Italians, as was actually reflected in the petitions (that is, 65:11).

New York State law in the middle of the 20th century—just like today—made clear that one did not have to file legal papers in order to change one's name: all one had to do was use a new name consistently and without any intent to commit fraud, and one's new name was legal.[6] The decision to file an official petition signaled concern that someone would be or had been scrutinizing one's name on paper.

And that was primarily a middle-class concern. For one thing, it was expensive to change a name officially: it cost money to file a petition, to hire a lawyer, and to put an announcement in a newspaper advertising the change (a requirement of the law). More subtly and more significantly, in the first half of the 20th century, it was primarily white-collar workers and businessmen who worried that someone might be scrutinizing their names. Working-class jobs, such as domestic service or loading cargo, were more typically given to individuals on the basis of recommendations of family members or appraisals of their bodies, rather than a valuation of their names on job applications.[7] There were, to be sure, a few blue-collar workers who petitioned for official name changes—a handful of bakers, building superintendents, and chauffeurs—but most working-class men and women who sought to change their names probably did so unofficially.[8] It was white-collar workers—students seeking to get into professional school, businessmen hoping to impress clients, and secretaries applying to employment agencies—who sought to make their name changes official. Jews' unusual position among immigrants, having moved in large numbers from blue-collar to white-collar work by the time of the Depression, made them the immigrant group with the most money available for filing name-change petitions and, more importantly, the most concerned about their names' official appearance on paper.[9]

While Jewish middle-class strength was reflected in name-change petitions, however, the fact that roughly 65 percent of name-change petitioners had Jewish-sounding names in the 1930s also reflects the rise of institutionalized antisemitism during the interwar years, a rise that had its origins in the late 19th century. The entry into the country of nearly three million Jews from eastern Europe between 1880 and 1920, at a time when racial science was in its heyday, impelled new constructions of racial thought about Jews in the United States. Although antisemitism had existed in the United States before this era, it had not been a significant feature of American institutional, social, or political life, and Jews had been classified as "white" for legal purposes. In an era of exploding racial categories and fears at the turn of the century, however, Jewish difference became a far more important part of American society.[10]

Antisemitism soared in American life by the 1920s and 1930s, infecting popular discourse, shaping public policy, and affecting Jews' economic and social possibilities. During this era, negative images of Jews circulated widely in literature and journalism, while discrimination became institutionalized among employers, in higher education, and in the professions. In 1936, *Fortune* magazine, for example, reported that 50 percent of applications to medical school were from Jewish candidates, while only 17 percent of those admitted were Jewish.[11] According to a 1937 report, 89 percent of large New York companies declared that they "preferred Christians" as employees.[12] And employment advertisements throughout the 1920s and 1930s increasingly noted that employers were "Christian" or "Anglo-Saxon."[13]

Names were an important part of this anti-Jewish discrimination. The corrosive humor in *Puck* and *Judge* regularly relied on monikers such as Rosenberg and Moses. Colleges and employers screened names in their efforts to avoid selecting Jewish applicants: "Names such as Aaronson, Weinberg, Lipshutz, Levinsky or Cohen fall more harshly upon the ears of employers than Schmidt, Wise, Meyer, and Schwab," reported Heywood Braun and George Britt in their 1931 exposé of antisemitism, *Christians Only*. "By the same token, German-descended Gentiles who have names such as Schmidt, Wise, Meyer, and Schwab tell of being kept waiting until they establish that . . . they are free from Jewish association."[14] Although certainly not the only badges of Jewishness or the only means of excluding Jews from employment or education, names played a crucial role in identifying and discriminating against Jews as members of a distinct racial group (see chapter 4 for more on application forms as means of identifying Jews).

Petition after petition lodged at the City Court darkly hinted at the forces of antisemitism that limited petitioners' livelihoods. Dora Sarietzky, a stenographer and typist, testified, "My name proved to be a great handicap in securing a position. . . . In order to facilitate securing work,

I assumed the name Doris Watson."[15] Bertram Levy, the president of a mail-chute corporation, found that "his name [had] been a hindrance to him in his efforts to gain an entrance to various firms and to secure business from them." He sought permission from the court to adopt "an American name": Bertram Leslie.[16] And the traveling salesman Lawrence Lipschitz sought to change his name to Lipson, explaining that "people out west find it hard to pronounce as well as spell petitioner's name and petitioner is at times subject to ridicule and embarrassment."[17]

A few of the petitions spoke openly of the antisemitism of the era. An engineer named Julius Kaminsky petitioned the court to allow him to change his name to George Joseph Kaley because, he said, although he was a Hungarian Roman Catholic, employers consistently assumed he was a Jew, making it hard for him to keep a job. "While petitioner has the highest of respect for people of the Jewish race, he finds that other people in the City of New York have not that respect and that a good many employers under whom he has worked have discriminated against the Jewish race."[18] Another Roman Catholic man, Leo Goldkopf, claimed that his friends and family members had urged him to file a petition to change his name to Leo Dawson because of his difficulties in finding jobs: "I have had many opportunities of obtaining employment in organizations where Christians were preferred, but my name precluded favorable consideration of my application. Upon occasions friends of mine declined to give me a written recommendation solely on the ground that my name would make it impossible to obtain the position in question."[19] Kaminsky's and Goldkopf's petitions shed a powerful light on the veil of antisemitism that shrouded many Jews' efforts to find jobs in the 1920s and 1930s.

That antisemitism also affected the language used in name-change petitions. Most petitioners used obscure legal language that evaded any discussion of antisemitism or discrimination. In contrast with the avowed Roman Catholic petitioners just described, most petitioners with Jewish names typically used vague legal language that downplayed any discrimination they faced.[20] Many simply used formulaic reasons such as "employers found my name difficult to pronounce, spell and remember," even when the name was pronounced and spelled phonetically.[21] In Rose Lefkowitz's petition to change her name to Rose Lynford, for example, the housewife and widow testified that her name "is difficult to pronounce."[22] Others, such as Max Greenberger, called their names "foreign-sounding" or asked the court to grant them permission to use an "American" name.[23] The physician Belle Sheinberg did explain that she had unofficially changed her name to Isabel Beaumont because of the virulent antisemitism she experienced while a student in France and Austria; she said nothing, however, about American antisemitism.[24] For the most part, petitioners with Jewish-sounding names never referred to their names as Jewish and never openly described antisemitism on American soil. To be sure, this veiled language was probably constructed by lawyers, rather than individual petitioners, and it was designed to appeal to judges' standards. Much of the language on name-change petitions was too formulaic and repetitive to have emerged naturally from petitioners' personal experiences alone. Nonetheless, the fact that large numbers of men and women with Jewish-sounding names used the vague terminology of "foreign" or "difficult to pronounce," while Catholic men were much more willing to describe prejudice, suggests that Jews were uncomfortable talking about antisemitism and may have even been ashamed of their experiences with discrimination.

It is worth noting, moreover, that it is likely that many of the lawyers who constructed the veiled language in these petitions were Jewish and that at least some of them had changed their own names. Names such as Friedman and Levy appear frequently as lawyers in name-change petitions in 1922, for example, as do names typical to Jewish name changers, such as Kent and Lane.[25] In the beginning of the 20th century, Jews flooded the legal profession but were unable to get jobs with prestigious corporations and frequently limited to work within the Jewish community.[26] These lawyers often lived in the same Jewish neighborhoods, communities, and families as their clients. Like their clients, they had experienced significant social and economic antisemitism, and indeed, many of them chose to change their names.[27] Limited evidence suggests that Jewish lawyers themselves drew up the paperwork to change their own names and that they easily and sometimes cheaply performed the same services for Jewish relatives, friends, neighbors, and community members.[28]

While the name-change petitions deposited at the City Court hint subtly at the antisemitism that affected Jews' economic lives during the interwar years, they indicate much more clearly and unequivocally that Jews responded to that antisemitism collectively, in family units, with women and children as well as men changing their names in significant numbers.

In the late 19th and early 20th centuries, name changing in City Court had been an activity dominated by men. The records for official name changes at the court begin in 1887, and for the first 30 years of those records, adult men represented 85 to 95 percent of all petitioners to City Court. As the individuals most likely to be interacting either with the government or with employers, men were more likely to worry that clients or tax collectors might find their unofficial nicknames or changed names suspicious. Men sometimes submitted petitions with members of their families, but before the 1920s, the majority of men were single petitioners seeking success in the American marketplace.

By the 1920s, the percentage of female petitioners had substantially increased from the decades before, and by the 1930s, the percentage of petitioners filing with family members was rapidly rising. By 1932, 30 percent of all name-change petitioners were either girls or women, and roughly 50 percent of petitioners filed their petitions with other members of their families. By 1942, moreover, the numbers of children filing petitions had also increased: roughly one in five petitioners was a child.

The petitions indicate clearly that name changing had become a family strategy for many New Yorkers. In 1917, only 17 percent of name-change petitions were filed by multiple family members, but by the 1930s, 40 to 60 percent of all petitions featured more than one petitioner—parents filing for underage children, spouses filing with each other, adult siblings filing together, or entire family units with adult parents and minor children filing petitions collectively. Even when a man was the sole petitioner, his wife frequently filed an affidavit of consent allowing the change.[29] In 1932, 10 percent of petitions were single petitions filed by one man but accompanied by consenting affidavits from their wives. And when men were sole petitioners to change their names, their reasons for changing their names frequently involved family members who had already done so or who were encouraging them to do it. An additional 13 percent of single male petitioners in 1932 referred to family members as the reason for their name change. The writer and actor Lester Cohn, for example, who sought to change his last name to Cole, explained that not only had he used this name for several years, but his mother and sister had already adopted the name Cole in 1927.[30] Name changing became a family strategy for Jewish families during this era. In tight economic times, with rising antisemitism, family members viewed themselves as one economic unit, and they filed name-change petitions together to allow the unit to thrive.[31]

Indeed, name changing was so significant for families' advancement that petitioners frequently reported that family members—usually older siblings—who had already changed their names were embarrassed by the lingering reminders of their former identities. Thirty-three-year-old David Pelowitz, for example, noted that all of his brothers had already changed their names legally and that "the fact that your petitioner has not changed his name to Pellow has frequently caused embarrassment to his brothers and the other members of the family."[32] Conversely, Nathan Ginsburg reported that it was he who was embarrassed to be the last member of his family with an unchanged name: "It is a source of much embarrassment to your petitioner to be called GINSBURG by people who know that your petitioner's brothers are called GAYNES, and petitioner is the subject of embarrassing questions."[33] Simply changing one's name did not eliminate the embarrassment of being Jewish. Name changers had to manage the stigma of Jewishness continually by encouraging their families to follow suit and by carefully managing interactions between private and public personas.[34]

The significance of families is also visible in the timing of formal name changes. Petitioners explained that they chose to change their names at significant moments in their families' lives: children entering a new school or matriculating at or graduating from college; husbands and wives who were expecting or had just given birth to children; and men and women planning to get married all appeared in the name-change petitions. Rupert Kaplowitz, for example, wanted to change his name to Kapon because he was engaged and wanted to be married under his new name.[35] The composer Abraham Elstein had used the name Elston for two years with friends and family, and when he was about to receive his doctor of music, wanted to do so under his changed name.[36] In 1951, the author Morris Freedman noted in Commentary that "name-changing was common shortly before graduation" for Jewish college students of the 1920s and 1930s.[37]

Children were consistently key subjects in name-change petitions. It was not unusual for parents to change their children's names while keeping their own. Some petitioners, such as Max Greenberger, specifically addressed their children's chances of finding jobs, attracting customers as future businessmen, or succeeding in college or professional school.[38] Others noted that their children had faced (or feared they would face) social ridicule and embarrassment because of their names. "The name of Tomshinsky is difficult to remember and properly spell and because of this, petitioners and their children have been subjected to embarrassment and your petitioners believe that it would be to the best interests of their children as they mature, to have their family name changed to the proposed name of Thomas," Hyman and Dora Tomshinsky testified in their 1932 petition.[39] Still other petitioners, such as the grocer Samuel Lipshitz, explained that they themselves used different names for business purposes and wanted to correct the discrepancy between their own changed names and their children's birth names "to avoid the embarrassment on the part of the children in later years."[40]

It is unclear how much control children had in submitting family name-change petitions, but a good number of petitions suggest that children may have been the driving forces behind the decision to change the family name or at least were important participants in the decision-making process. For example, the petitioner Max Hymawitz explained that his son, Emmanuel, found his name "cumbersome" and "an annoyance" and that Emmanuel's name change to Hayes would "substantiate and promote his son's comfort and interests, socially, educationally, economically and patriotically."[41] Harold Steven Lynton filed a petition for his younger brother, 16-year-old Julian Levine, to change his last name to Lynton, reporting that the two of them wished to go into business together with a shared surname.[42] And petition after petition reported that it was a son, daughter, or older sister or brother who had initially changed his or her name, pushing the rest of the family to follow suit.[43]

American Jewish authors casually described this family pattern. In Jo Sinclair's 1946 novel *Wasteland*, the central character, Jake Brown, changed his name to John. Throughout the novel, he struggles with the implications of this name change for his identity, noting his family name change only once: "if Sig [Brown's older brother] could change our name from Braunowitz to Brown, he argued savagely for a split second, then I can change Jake to John."[44] For Sinclair, the individual change from Jake to John was life changing and traumatic, but the family change from

Braunowitz to Brown, orchestrated by the oldest brother, was incidental and normal, barely worth discussion.

The increase in family petitions in the interwar years corresponded with an increase in the number of women and girls in the name-change petitions. Although females had represented only 13 percent of petitions in 1917, by the 1920s, they represented roughly 20 percent of petitioners, and by the 1930s, they were 30 percent of all petitioners to the City Court of the City of New York.

Although the majority of women submitted petitions with family members—as wives, mothers, or sisters—throughout the first half of the 20th century, an increasing number of individual petitions were filed by women who clearly hoped to find or keep their jobs. From 1892 through 1912, the percentage of individual petitioners who were female was never more than 7 percent. Between 1917 and 1932, the percentage of female individual petitioners was never below 7 percent, and it typically hovered between 10 and 14 percent; in 1937 and 1942, the percentage of female individual petitioners was over 25 percent.[45] For example, the secretary Beatrix R. Salomon filed a single petition to change her name to Salmon, explaining that she "had endeavored to change her occupation to find a new position which promises advances in salary and position, but has found difficulty in procuring a position commensurate with her ability by reason of the name she now has."[46] Pauline Golding explained that she worked both selling and writing copy in radio advertising but that her "foreign sounding name [had] hindered her in her work, in obtaining employment and in her social life." Currently unemployed, she sought to change her name to Pauline Bennett Gould.[47] Single women seeking employment (or already employed) in office work, sales, advertising, journalism, and entertainment petitioned to change their names in the hopes of finding jobs in a market restricted by both gender and ethnic discrimination.

Indeed, even on petitions submitted by families, many women were actually daughters or sometimes even wives either seeking or already engaged in white-collar work. Helen, Lillian, and Edna Sicherman all lived with their parents and worked as private secretaries. In the family petition to change the parents' and seven siblings' name to Sherman, the three women each testified that they had "been known by this proposed name among all [their] business associates and acquaintances for the past 15 years and [had] done business and received a large amount of correspondence under the said name."[48] In 1937, the entire Lefkowitz family petitioned to change their name to Lynford, including 21-year-old daughter Selma Ruth Lefkowitz, who explained that she was assistant manager of an apartment building and had already assumed the name Lynford for business purposes.[49]

With growing numbers of women during this era able to find white-collar work as saleswomen, stenographers, and typists—and even more creative jobs such as writing, acting, and photography—it is unsurprising that women seeking these positions believed a name change would benefit their search.[50] Native-born Jewish women were actually seeking this white-collar work in much larger numbers than were other second-generation ethnic women, such as Italian Americans. These large numbers help to explain the increasing percentages of both single women and Jews in the name-change petitions.[51]

Indeed, some evidence suggests that Jewish women, even more than Jewish men, may have faced economic discrimination as they sought office work. The sociologist Alfred Luverne Severson found that the antisemitic employment advertisements in the *Chicago Tribune* in the 1920s and 1930s were specifically geared toward Jewish women entering white-collar secretarial work. Advertisements for female workers—and particularly for stenographers and typists—discriminated against Jews at much higher rates than did advertisements for male workers. Severson's conversations with "men in thirty-seven employment agencies" highlighted the antisemitism directed particularly toward second-generation Jewish women, noting that all the employment agents offered anecdotes about the inappropriate behavior and appearance of Jewish women in the workplace, while ignoring the subject of Jewish men entirely.[52] In a study of the American Jewish press during this era, the anthropologist Riv-Ellen Prell has found that it was the unsuitable bodies and voices of Jewish women, much more than those of men, that were lampooned, lamented, and policed as they sought jobs in the US marketplace: "While there are thousands of splendid Jewish girls who are ladies in every sense of the word, yet there are others who . . . help bring severe criticism upon all Jewish girls. Her voice is either loud and harsh or shrill. She does not realize that this stamps her as uncultured and vulgar," wrote Julia Weber in the English-language Jewish press in 1918.[53]

Literature of the early to mid-20th century highlighted these stereo-types of Jewish women as unsuitable office workers, with flashy makeup and jewelry, oversexualized clothes, and loud, heavily accented voices. In literary representations, name changing was portrayed as one of the ways that Jewish women managed their appearances and tried to se-cure employment. In the 1918 short story "The Girl Who Went Right," Edna Ferber told the story of Rachel Wiletsky's transformation into Ray Willets in order to acquire her dream job: a lingerie saleswoman in an elegant department store. Rachel's rosy cheeks, delicate hands, and con-servative clothes made her seem like a perfect candidate in the eyes of her superiors, but her "ghetto voice" gave her away and almost lost her the job. It was her "cunning and determination and shrewdness" that led her to change her name to Ray Willets in the personnel office and get the job.[54] In Arthur Miller's 1945 novel *Focus*, the central character, Lawrence Newman, was the personnel director in charge of ferreting out "unsuitable" job candidates, most of them Jewish women. He closely examines the makeup, clothing, and voice of every candidate, as well as their names, but his mistaken decision to hire one unsuitable candi-date infuriates his boss: "Miss Kapp is obviously not our kind of person, Newman. I mean she's obvious. Her name must be Kapinsky or some-thing."[55] Names were an important manifestation of the broader racial stigma that marked Jewish women, both physically and linguistically, as inappropriate office workers.

The fact that many of the single female petitioners were young, mostly in their 20s, offers additional evidence of the stigma that Jew-ish names possessed during these interwar years. After all, women were expected to change their last names after marriage, and just about all of them did so in this era. Many of the women changing their names in the City Court of the City of New York—such as 24-year-old Pauline Golding and 25-year-old Beatrix Salomon—thus might have calculated that they would only use these changed names for another seven years at most, and yet they still pursued their expensive petitions, anxious for the increased economic and social opportunities their new names would provide.

It was not just the petitions of young single women seeking jobs that increased, however. As the 1920s and 1930s went on, the number of mar-ried women and mothers in family petitions also increased, and they may have had at least some control over their changed names as well. In 1937, the Weiss family changed their name to Danner so that their family would match the name of their mother, Gertrude Danner, an amateur tennis player who used her maiden name in professional and private settings.[56] Goldie Lipshitz testified why she had asked her husband, Samuel, to make an application to change her entire family's name to Lipton: "by reason of the fact that I feel confusion of names particularly with respect to the three children. I have been asked by their teachers in school to please finally settle the confusion in names, and it is my desire to see the three children known by the name LIPTON, as they always are known by that name."[57] Divorced and widowed mothers frequently changed their children's names along with their own—either when they remarried or when they needed to find employment as single mothers: Lucille Sternau Frackman, for example, changed her own name, calling herself Lucille S. Whitehead, and then petitioned to change her son's name, Edwin C. Weiskoff, to Edwin C. Whitehead.[58]

Indeed, one anecdote of name changing during this era suggested that it was wives and mothers, not husbands or fathers, who instigated the family decision. In 1941, the *Common Ground* editor Louis Adamic told the story of a New England man named Cabot, who, along with his wife and daughters, had changed the family name from Kobotchnik in 1904.[59] Kobotchnik later successfully petitioned to get his old name back after the death of his wife and the marriage of his daughters. In Adamic's telling, Kobotchnik placed the responsibility for the name change on his wife and daughters: "[My wife] was foreign-born too, but come over as a child. When she grew up, she got ashamed of being a 'foreigner' and wanted to be 'American.' She wanted the girls to be 'American.' She thought nobody who amounted to anything would marry 'em if their name was Kobotchnik; so *I* had to become Cabot." In Adamic's telling, Kobotchnik recounted a parallel story of a dog named Nurmi that the family had adopted. His wife and daughters, unhappy with the dog's unusual name (the name of a Finnish runner), called the dog Buster and yelled at him when he refused to respond: "They liked the dog, all right, but they was dumb. Women!"[60]

Adamic's tale of insensitive, social-climbing women changing their names to achieve upward mobility offers a strikingly gendered twist on the classic story of male immigrants seeking to shed their Jewish pasts.

This portrait was a common one used to attack and label Jewish women in Europe and the United States throughout the 19th and 20th centuries, so it must be taken with a good deal of skepticism.[61] Yet it is worth noting that both married men and women show up with regularity in name-change petitions. Because the names of married women were less frequently interrogated by future employers, these women had less economic need to change their names legally than did single, divorced, or widowed women. For the same reason, wives certainly had less economic need to change their names than did their husbands, yet married women did change their names along with their husbands with some regularity. If women were not typically the shallow social climbers of Adamic's story, neither were they passive witnesses to their husbands' and children's social and economic ambitions. The fact that so many married women actively chose to change their names along with their husbands suggests that women exercised a degree of agency in name changing and that they frequently made a conscious decision that a legally changed family name would benefit their children and their families, as well as themselves.

When married women did not actively decide to change their names legally but instead simply consented to their husbands' name changes, many may have believed that the petition would also legally change their own names. After all, women's names were always immediately changed upon marriage without official documentation. These assumptions were erroneous; a man's name change did not legally change the name of either his wife or his children. A few petitions from married women indicate that their husbands had changed their names earlier, and only later did they realize that they needed to return to the courthouse to change their own names. "It was the belief of your petitioner and her husband that the change of name of her husband automatically resulted in the change of name of your petitioner and petitioner's children," Mary Yankelowitz testified in 1942, explaining that her husband, William, had changed his surname to Young in 1932 and that her entire family had used that name for ten years. "Only the other day it was discovered that your petitioner and her children have no right to use any other name but the name, Yankelowitz," she explained, seeking a name change for herself, as well as her children, Frieda, Ann, and Rubin, and Rubin's wife, Sally.[62]

The familial nature of Jewish name changing offers some interesting parallels with the African American strategy of "passing" for white. Despite the predominant literary image of individual African Americans crossing the color line and refashioning their personal racial identities, the history of African American passing has important familial and communal meanings. Many African Americans who passed, like Jews who changed their names, brought family members with them as they redefined themselves racially and worked with their families to manage the stigma of their racial histories.[63] Yet there is a crucial difference between African Americans and Jews: US law allowed Jews to officially abandon their stigmatized racial markers in large numbers, while prohibiting the legal possibilities for African Americans to pass as white.[64] The strategy of African American passing was thus almost always an unofficial one, forcing black people to cross the color line in secret and making the process of historical recovery and remembrance for both families and historians that much more difficult.

If name changing was a group activity entered into by Jewish families, it was not necessarily a universally embraced Jewish group activity. A few petitioners specifically affirmed their Jewish identity, suggesting that they were concerned about what the Jewish readers of the petition might think of their decision. Lawrence Lipschitz, for example, insisted that he "does not intend or desire to deny his faith but is perfectly willing and in fact is known and it is petitioner's intention to be known as a Hebrew."[65]

These petitioners' fears of Jewish audiences were well grounded. There were several Jewish judges who did indeed reject the petitions of Jewish name changers or who at least soundly scolded them for what the judges perceived as betrayal. Judge Aaron J. Levy of the New York Supreme Court, for example, granted Everett Levy's petition to change his name to Leroy but chastised him angrily for his pursuit of economic gain: "He is wholly ignorant of the fact that the Bible tells us that the Tribe of Levy never worshipped the Golden Calf. Let the application be granted so that his people might well be rid of him."[66] And another judge, Louis Goldstein, outright rejected the Brooklyn salesman Louis Goldstein's petition to change his name to Golding: the judge's own success, he stated, disproved the petitioner's claim that the name Goldstein was "un-American, not euphonious, and an economic handicap."[67] Indeed, one scholar has argued that Jewish name-change petitioners attempted to avoid having their petition heard by Jewish judges.[68]

The small minority of name-change petitioners who wanted to return to their old, ethnically marked names offers us additional, very suggestive evidence that some members of the Jewish community disapproved of the practice and that they ridiculed and even shunned those who had changed their names. Ann Boyd, for example, submitted a petition to change her name back to Anna Kleinman in 1932, explaining that she had changed her name two years earlier while living with friends because she was known by her new name at work. After moving back in with her family, however, Boyd found that her new name had "become an inconvenience and at times an embarrassment," and she sought to change it back to Anna Kleinman.[69] Even more poignantly, the architect Joseph Matthews reported that he had changed his name from Schusheim in 1940, but one year later, he married an Orthodox Jewish woman who "feels deeply" that he had changed his name. "In fact both she and her family felt so strongly about it, that they refused to have the marriage take place under the name of Matthews." Moreover, Matthews reported, his change of name had actually hurt his livelihood: "My change of name has done me severe damage because several people who learned of my change of name . . . have completely severed business relationships with me."[70] Although few individuals actually sought to return to their Jewish names, these petitions suggest communal unease with name changing, as well as a desire within the Jewish community to use Jewish names as markers of belonging.[71]

Popular images of name changing in the interwar years reflected this communal ambivalence, but they did not tell the full story. While Jewish family members changed their names together, newspapers, fiction, and film portrayed name changers almost entirely as second-generation ethnics seeking to "become American" to the dismay of their parents, rather than with their support. Indeed, representations of this "Americanization" tended to portray it as an inevitable step in the lives of immigrants' children, rather than a difficult decision made by families seeking to improve their lives. Moreover, name-change petitioners frequently noted their difficulties in finding jobs or their experiences of humiliation in the workplace or at school, but cultural representations of name changing typically said little about economic or social discrimination.

When ethnic newspapers and journals—Jewish and non-Jewish—looked at name changing, they typically focused on the tension between the need to become American and the loss of ethnic pride. In 1926, for example, the English pages of the *Jewish Daily Forward* excoriated name changers with a piece titled "Why Should Levy Become Lee and Rabinowitz Robins?" In the midst of articles on Americanization geared toward the English-speaking, American-born children of Jewish immigrants, the columnist Nathaniel Zalowitz attacked name changing as a shameful and ultimately fruitless act. Although he acknowledged that Jews faced "calumny, misunderstanding, discrimination," he insisted that "denying one's nationality is hardly the way of a self-respecting man." Moreover, he warned, "you're not fooling anybody," and he nervously noted that Jewish name changers were "needlessly antagonizing Gentiles," who were bound to change their own names to avoid association with Jews.[72] Several weeks later, Jacob C. Rich passionately defended his own decision to change his name from Zaritsky, likening "offensive" surnames to physical handicaps: "Aren't boys and girls congenitally crippled if they are born to such names? And oughtn't they change them as soon as ever they can?" Rich enthusiastically championed a name that he had chosen, rather than inherited, and he sympathized with "the young girl of flapper age and proclivities whose father's name happens to be Chachulowich. . . . You can't flap with an anchor like that around your neck."[73] Name changing as an expression of youthful American identity was obvious here. Speaking to a young, English-speaking Jewish audience, these writers addressed antisemitism as a motivating factor for name changing, but they focused much more on the desires of young, second-generation ethnic citizens to "become American" culturally, socially, and emotionally.

The debate in the *Forward* was not unique to Jews or to Jewish communal newspapers in the years before and during the war. Louis Adamic cited similar debates over name changing in Armenian, Greek, Polish, Slavic, and Hungarian newspapers.[74] The *Armenian Spectator*, for example, acknowledged that "the average immigrant Armenian is torn between loyalty to his forebears and the necessity of having a fairly pronounceable name" but warned, "unless one has reasons to hide [his] background, he has little excuse to bedeck himself with feathers belonging to other birds."[75] Jews and non Jews acknowledged discrimination in the safety of their own ethnic newspapers, but they primarily lamented the loss of identity that young American-born ethnics seemed to display by changing their names.

In the mainstream press, interwar portraits of name changing were similarly broad and generic, focusing on the struggles of all southern and eastern European immigrants to assimilate. These portraits rarely indicted discriminatory practices against any immigrant group, including Jews; instead they subtly encouraged native-born Americans to embrace different ethnic names as part of the nation's heritage. For example, in 1930, the journalist Elias Tobenkin explained to the readers of *American Legion Monthly* that he would not change his name not only because it "would be an insult to the country which gave [him] birth" but also because it would insult his adoptive home, the United States, "if it were said of her with truth that . . . an entrance card, in the shape of a changed name and an obliterated past, is required in order freely to enjoy the blessings of citizenship under her skies."[76] In this patriotic magazine, Tobenkin did not address his Jewish background at all, nor antisemitism; instead, he pled for tolerance for all "immigrants from Eastern and Southern Europe."[77] Similarly, Louis Adamic, in his 1942 monograph *What's Your Name?*, highlighted name changing as a problem for all young southern and eastern European Americans as they struggled with love for their parents and communities, while simultaneously battling discrimination and seeking to identify themselves as American. Adamic called for "organic" name changing that did not result from discriminatory pressure, and he also urged "old-stock Americans" to "curb their impatience with unfamiliar names." "Integration with this country is not determined by an Anglo-Saxon name," he insisted.[78] Adamic thus subtly condemned discrimination but focused on name changing as a struggle that affected all southern and eastern European immigrants and their children as they Americanized.

Interestingly, in Adamic's research, he received several letters from Jews indicating that antisemitism was more intense than discrimination against other ethnic Americans (he did not receive such letters from Italians or Poles claiming the same thing). Adamic's book, however, did not reflect those opinions. He did suggest that Jews changed their names more readily than non-Jews did, but he attributed that to the fact that Jews have "no strong cognominal tradition."[79] Jewish struggles with antisemitism thus played a small role in Adamic's book on name changing. To be sure, there were a few mainstream publications on anti-semitism and Jews during the interwar years that specifically addressed name changing, but for the most part, mainstream nonfiction reports on name changing during the interwar years were broad and universalistic, with an emphasis on the Americanization of all southern and eastern European immigrants.[80]

Name changing in fiction, film, and theater during the interwar years mirrored this broad, universalistic perspective, with portraits of name changers as second-generation ethnic Americans hoping to reinvent themselves. Sometimes filmmakers and writers depicted name chang-ing as an inevitable, and sometimes even positive, step on the way to Americanization. Al Jolson's famous portrayal of Jake Rabinowitz, the cantor's son, becoming Jack Robin ultimately ended in fame, fortune, and a reconciliation of the generations in *The Jazz Singer*.[81] Far darker, however, was Frank Capra's *The Younger Generation*, a film adaptation of the Fannie Hurst play *It Is to Laugh* and short story "The Gold in Fish."[82] After achieving financial success as an auctioneer, the Jewish businessman Morris Goldfish and his wife changed the family name to Fish. But when he moved his parents and his sister, Lena, into his Park Avenue apartment, he made clear his contempt for them and his shame for his upbringing and ultimately brought disaster on the entire family. Although the families in these interwar stories were clearly Jewish, the artists' focus was not on antisemitism or discrimination but instead on the classic struggle of the second generation to Americanize, for good or for ill. Rather than the struggles of Jewish family members to find jobs, housing, or education in an era of rising antisemitism, the stories em-phasized generational conflict, a conflict that many other ethnic groups were experiencing during this era. In this way, popular representations of name changing in the interwar years only partly reflected the reality of name changing among New York Jews.

That reality, unfolding daily in the petitions submitted to the City Court, reflected Jews' economic comfort in the American middle class, as well as their painful struggle to remain or advance in that class in the face of substantial antisemitism. Name changing also reflected the importance of women and children in Jews' pursuit of middle-class success in the United States. And the controversies surrounding name changing indicate that the process of integrating into American life was more complicated for Jewish individuals and more divisive for the Jewish community as a whole than either artists or historians have fully explored.

Those controversies, however, were somewhat masked during World War II, as name changing exploded in the New York Jewish community. The war brought both expanded economic opportunities and intensified anti-Jewish rhetoric, impelling many more Jewish New Yorkers to embrace the familial strategy of name changing that had succeeded among their friends and family members during the previous two decades.

"What's Uncle Sam's Last Name?"

The Impact of World War II on Jews and Name Changing

In 1942, the law student Eugene Martin Greenberg petitioned the City Court of New York City, asking to change his surname to Grant. "While in the U.S. military forces," Greenberg explained, "petitioner believes that his career will be more successful and he may ultimately secure merited advancement on legal assumption of said proposed surname." Greenberg assured the judge that he did not intend "to forsake the Hebrew religion of his family."[1]

Greenberg's name change petition was one of thousands submitted to the City Court in Manhattan during the World War II era. The court records make it clear that World War II catalyzed official name changing in New York City more than any other event in the century. The City Court typically recorded slightly fewer than 100 name-change petitions a year throughout the late 19th and early 20th centuries. From World War I through the 1930s, those petitions increased to 250–300 per year. But in the 1940s, name-change petitions submitted to the City Court rose to an average of over 800 per year; in 1946 alone, 1,127 petitions were submitted. Indeed, the court actually changed its record-keeping to accommodate the massive swell of name-change petitions during this time. The number dropped after 1948 and did not reach such heights again in the 20th century (see figure 2.1). Name changing in New York City during the war era was a phenomenon.[2]

And as we might expect, that phenomenon took on a profoundly Jewish cast. In 1942, roughly 66 percent of those who petitioned the City Court to shed an ethnically marked name were seeking to abandon a Jewish-sounding name. Slavic-sounding names, the next highest category, represented about 11 percent of 1942 petitions, and Italian-sounding names represented about 8 percent. In 1940, Jews represented roughly 24 percent of the entire city population and roughly 14 percent

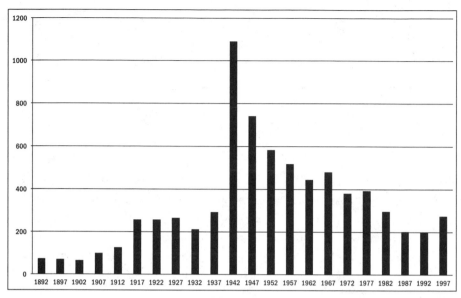

Figure 2.1. New York City Civil Court name-change petitions, 1892–1997. This chart illustrates the boom in name changing in New York City during the era of World War II. The bars represent the total number of petitions submitted to the City and Civil Courts every fifth year from 1892 through 1997. Source: Name Change Petitions Collection, New York City Civil Court, New York, NY; chart produced by Amanda Hession, Center for Statistical Training and Consulting, Michigan State University.

of the population of Manhattan, where the majority of City Court petitioners lived.[3] Thus, even accounting for the city's large Jewish population, Jewish-sounding names were still disproportionately represented among the thousands of petitioners seeking to change their names throughout the war years. Of course, the lopsided nature of Jewish name changing was not new. As we saw in chapter 1, from the early 20th century through the 1930s, Jews were represented disproportionately in City Court name-change petitions. But World War II—marked by growing antisemitism and an expanding state—turned this earlier pattern into a major movement, one that left a powerful impact on the New York Jewish community.

World War II is a crucial moment in the history of New York Jewish name changing. As antisemitism grew to its greatest heights in American history, and the state expanded deeper into ordinary people's daily existence, thousands of Jews came to believe that officially reshaping their personal, familial, and racial identities would provide them with safety, security, and opportunity.

An upsurge in antisemitic rhetoric and violence toward Jews in the United States in the late 1930s, as well as the tortured debate over America's entry into the war, intensified perceptions of Jews as a dangerous race. Father Charles Coughlin used Nazi propaganda in his popular radio speeches to blame Jews for the Depression and the New Deal. Hate groups such as Coughlin's Christian Front picketed Jewish-owned stores, vandalized synagogues, and attacked Jews on city streets in Boston and New York City. Members of the isolationist America First Committee, founded in June 1940, consistently suggested that Jews were pushing the United States to enter the war on the side of the Allies and blamed Jews for the war once the United States became a combatant. And images of desperate Jewish refugees from Europe seeking haven in the United States unleashed a groundswell of xenophobic and antisemitic rhetoric from members of Congress and their constituents.[4]

Jewish names frequently grounded this antisemitic rhetoric. Isolationists insisted that Franklin Roosevelt's name indicated Jewish ancestry and decried the Jewish names of his appointees. "At different times in the history of [FDR's] ancestors, such family names as Rosenblum, Rosenberg, and Rosenvelt have been used," Gerald B. Winrod explained in one pamphlet, while another flyer published the "amazing roster of persons with strange names" who had joined the New Deal, urging readers to "Keep America Christian!" on the front page.[5] And the song "Refu-Jews Go Back," published by the Nationalist Press Association, urged its audience to "slam the door now in the faces / Of Abie and Ikey and Moe."[6]

This intensification of antisemitic rhetoric, intimidation, and violence, and the frequent brandishing of Jewish names as badges of difference, normalized many Americans' beliefs that Jews were a race apart. At the same time, growing antisemitism inspired anxiety among many American Jews, who were sensitive to local acts of intimidation as part of a broader upsurge of violent European antisemitism.

During World War II, these pressures and anxieties exploded. Young Jewish men's and women's efforts to find jobs associated with the war, to serve honorably in the military, and to scale the military hierarchy sometimes met with exclusion and humiliation, and their distinctive names were frequently at the heart of these experiences.

The new economic opportunities and pressures of the war led many Jews to continue the strategy of name changing that the community had begun to develop in the years prior. They submitted name-change petitions that suggested social and economic discrimination, while remaining silent about their Jewish identity. Many petitioners, for example, described their names as hindrances to their efforts to work, especially in civil service, defense industries, or newly relevant professions such as engineering. In the engineer Melvin Applebaum's 1942 petition to change his name to Edmund Bertram Cronin, he explained that he had been using that name since 1933: "In Chicago deponent tried to find work and found it was a handicap to have a name such as Applebaum. It was then petitioner decided to seek another name which was easier to pronounce and shorter, and adopted the name of Cronin. Immediately thereafter petitioner did obtain a position." Petitioners who were not so explicit nonetheless suggested that their current names hurt them economically and that their changed names would be (or already had been) "advantageous" and would "further . . . possibilities for success.[7]

Fears about success were particularly pronounced as men prepared to register for the draft or to apply for officer training and feared that they would face discrimination in the military. Many Jews believed that they were automatically disqualified for certain branches or for officer candidacy because of their background: "I've spoken with many Jewish boys at the camp who told me that the reason they never got appointments to [officer candidate school] was because their name or nose was not Aryan," wrote one Jewish soldier after the war. Although there is no evidence that any Jews were actually denied promotion because of their ethnic background, there is evidence that many officers in the US Army subscribed to classic antisemitic beliefs.[8]

Name-change petitions reflected Jews' fears. Alvin Schneiderman, who submitted his petition with his wife, Rita, explained that his name "distinguishes its bearer to some as a member of a nation or race with which the United States is at war. In view of the fact that applicant is entering the United States Army as an officer, this may be a cause of considerable embarrassment in the future as well as in the past." Similarly, when applying for a commission in the army, Louis A. Friedman petitioned to change his own surname, as well as that of his son David Donn, to Freeman because he did "not want a surname of foreign origin and sound."[9]

Some individuals reported being specifically counseled by senior military officers to change their names officially to avoid trouble. That trouble was usually bureaucratic, when individuals had changed names informally years earlier. For example, in Abraham Elias Lubarski's petition to change his name to Robert Lubar, a name that he had used for several years, he described his effort to enlist in the US Naval Reserve's Midshipman's School, reporting that his interviewer, a lieutenant commander, had advised him "to change his name legally so as to avoid any possibility of [his] application for enlistment being ruled out by the United Sates Navy." More controversially, in 1939, authorities at Annapolis reportedly advised a Jewish family named Einstein to change their name to Easton so that their sons would be able to advance in the military. The Einstein case was a rare one, publicized because it seemed to suggest that the navy actively discriminated against Jews. In the vast majority of these cases, officers were simply asking petitioners to clarify their names, not warning them that their applications might be jeopardized because they had Jewish names. Nonetheless, individuals' fears of antisemitism were magnified by the behaviors of military authorities.[10]

Although only a minority of the petitions of the 1940s were submitted by men and women in the military, the association between name changing and military service was nonetheless significant. About 11 percent of petitions in 1942 were submitted by individuals preparing for, or already in, military service, but by 1946, 30 percent of name-change petitioners were veterans (and another 10 percent were veterans' wives). Impressionistic accounts after the war suggest that individuals' experience in the military had a significant impact on their decision to change their names. One anonymous writer remembered that his brother in the air force had been the instigator in changing their family name: he sent home V-mail "scrawled all over with odd pseudonyms" and explained that the military had given him a "taste for travel" that a new name would facilitate.[11]

Name changing during the war was not grounded only in economic and social aspiration. Anxieties about humiliation, exclusion, and social isolation while serving in the military ran deeply in some Jews' perceptions of their names. When the United States entered the war, classic antisemitic stereotypes about Jews' inability or unwillingness to fight and profiting from war industries emerged in public discourse. Jewish soldiers reported hearing their fellow infantrymen, as well as their officers, complain about the number of Jews who avoided combat. In Pennsylvania and New Jersey, rumors spread that Jewish doctors were labeling Jews 4-F to allow them to avoid service, and in North Dakota, marine paratroopers on leave told their friends that "they had never seen a Jew in the combat zones or the names of Jewish boys on any casualty lists."[12]

Perhaps the most prevalent examples of antisemitism during the war years were found in pamphlets and poems that circulated throughout the country. Much of this ephemera relied on Jewish names as a source of both political message and humor. The most famous and best documented example of an antisemitic jingle was the poem "The First American," which was circulated in military publications and defense-plant journals all over the country:

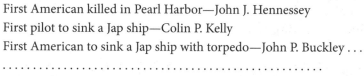

First American killed in Pearl Harbor—John J. Hennessey
First pilot to sink a Jap ship—Colin P. Kelly
First American to sink a Jap ship with torpedo—John P. Buckley . . .
. . . .
First American to get 4 new tires—Abraham Lipschitz.

Although the names varied in different versions, as did the accomplishments, the last line invariably described someone avoiding military service and profiteering during the war, and it always labeled them with a Jewish name. Other widely circulated poems similarly used Jewish names as the foundation for their humor while drawing on images of Jews as instigators and profiteers of war who avoided service. Jews in the military responded with anger and feelings of isolation. The naval officer Tracy Sugarman described for his wife his confrontation with a soldier who had sent home a letter containing "The First American": "I was so angry I came back to my room and sat down. . . . I think I was shaking like a guy with palsy." Although he had previously written of his admiration for his soldiers, he now felt dismay and estrangement from their bigotry: "They revolt and shock me."[13]

In memoirs and oral histories, Jews also described isolation and ridicule in their units, and Jewish names continually played an important role. One Jewish soldier noted that he, like many others, had encountered "Army officers who have been so ignorant as to make derisive remarks about a Jewish-sounding name. . . . No matter what the name, if it smacks of Jewishness, then it's funny." Another noted that antisemitism in the army might typically take the form of "a sergeant pronouncing a Jewish name with an exaggerated accent on a syllable and a smile on his face." Jewish names identified Jews as a distinct group subject to discrimination, but Jewish names were also, in and of themselves, ridiculous. They were badges of inferiority, like the hook noses that Jews supposedly wore on their bodies.[14]

One Jewish veteran described in a memoir the targeting of a Jewish comrade, "Harold U.," who tried to deny his Jewish identity. Members of the unit cruelly transposed his name to "Uffelduffel" and baited him as a Jew until he suffered a nervous breakdown and was transferred out of the outfit. In 1942, Elias Biegelman, a Latvian Jew raised in Brooklyn, submitted a name-change petition along with his wife, Leona, that described his exclusion by fellow soldiers. Noting that his name sounded "Germanic or Teutonic," he explained that "there is a tendency to shun, avoid or perhaps not to fraternize or mingle with anybody suspected of German origin. This of course had a depressing feeling upon [Biegelman] since the most important influence in keeping up the morale of the soldier is to make friends and to be intimate with his buddies." Although many American Jewish soldiers were able to face down antisemitism among their peers, their distinctive names were continual reminders of their difference: for at least some miserable Jewish soldiers, name changes seemed to promise escape and normal life in the troops.[15]

Biegelman's insistence that his name was German was not unusual. Many individuals who possessed Jewish-sounding names claimed in their petitions to fear anti-German, rather than antisemitic, sentiment. It is certainly possible that individuals such as Biegelman did experience anti-German discrimination. Many Jewish names did have German origins, and of course, the United States was at war with Germany. One reporter in 1947 suggested that both Germans and Jews changed their names in large numbers during the war, and at least two German American soldiers' memoirs have described their own name changes, prompted by fears that they would be shot as traitors if captured.[16]

Despite these accounts, very few of the names that individuals petitioned to abandon in 1942 were stereotypical German names or even Germanic-sounding names that could suggest either German or Jewish identity. By contrast, a full 30 percent of names being changed during the war were distinctive Jewish names such as Goldberg, which had been historically associated with Jews in both Europe and the United States. Moreover, the reluctance of virtually all petitioners to identify their names as Jewish or their experiences as antisemitic suggests that they were uncomfortable talking about themselves as Jews. Indeed, at least one petitioner, the immigrant Saly Levy, identified his distinctive Jewish name with obvious religious origins as being "definitely of German origin." Describing oneself as a victim of anti-German sentiment in the midst of a war against Nazi Germany may have been an easier and safer claim within the historical moment.[17]

Some petitioners, like Biegelman, may have experienced both anti-German and antisemitic sentiment. Recent Jewish refugees of Nazi Germany attracted both antisemitism and anti-German prejudice; despite their experiences with vicious antisemitism from the Nazi regime in Germany, they sometimes found themselves in the United States identified as Germans, and thus enemy aliens, and denied jobs and labeled security threats as a result.[18] It would not be surprising if individuals with Jewish names based in Germanic roots indeed attracted hatred for a variety of reasons. Nonetheless, it was distinctive Jewish names, not vaguely Germanic names, that were being changed in large numbers in New York in the 1940s.

It is ironic that so many Jewish petitioners labeled their names Germanic during the war, given the Holocaust that engulfed the European continent. The increasingly desperate circumstance of European Jews in Germany and throughout Nazi-occupied Europe went mostly unmentioned in Jewish New Yorkers' name-change petitions. Yet there are hints that the Holocaust formed a political subtext of the petitions, as petitioners called their names "handicaps" and suggested that current political conditions shaped their fears. For example, Solomon Goldfarb, in his petition to change his name to Saul Robert Gilford, explained that his name was a handicap in his current profession of engineering, that he was engaged to be married, and that he desired that any offspring of his marriage "shall not labor under the handicap of going through life with the name such as Goldfarb": "This is an unfortunate situation in the world we live in, but it is a situation not of my making, and I feel that we must face reality." Similarly, Victor Aguschewitsch called his name an "unnecessary handicap in his business career." Explaining that he had used the name Alin for over a year, he testified that "in view of the unsettling political conditions," he was anxious to formalize the change. Although few petitioners openly discussed Nazi persecution of European Jews, their petitions suggested that they feared that their Jewish-sounding names set them apart for ridicule or discrimination and that the political circumstances of the war exacerbated these concerns. Significantly, these claims of Jewish names as "handicaps" or causing "embarrassment" persisted even in the years immediately after the war, although their political urgency and anxiety was much less evident. Fears about the Holocaust ran mostly beneath the surface of Jews' New York City name-change petitions in the 1940s, but the specter of Nazi racial segregation, humiliation, and violence could not have been completely absent from individuals' consciousness as they fashioned their ethnic identities in City Court.[19]

Jewish defense groups, like individual people, also strategically used names to counter antisemitism. The most striking example of this strategy is found in the records of the National Jewish Welfare Board (JWB), the organization that oversaw Jewish chaplains and represented Jewish soldiers in the US military. In several different projects, the JWB relied on Jewish names to defend the Jewish community—while at the same time grappling with name changing in the Jewish community.

One of the signature programs of the JWB was its establishment of Jewish war records. Twenty-five years earlier, to counter antisemitic rumors that Jews did not fight in World War I, the American Jewish Committee, working with the JWB, conducted an ad hoc survey of Jewish participation in the immediate aftermath of the war, visiting cemeteries and war hospitals to do research. During World War II, however, the JWB developed a more extensive and elaborate defense of the Jewish war effort—in part because of criticisms of the World War I effort and in part because of increased concern about Jewish racial status during that era. In October 1941, the JWB established a separate Bureau of War Records to "record the participation of American Jewry in the second world war." The bureau ultimately launched a massive census of Jews in World War II, tasking volunteers throughout the country with visiting individual homes to ascertain the Jewish identity of soldiers who fought in the war.[20]

On the one hand, this massive counting project made clear to JWB officials that names were not reliable indicators of Jewish identity. Volunteers were urged in their census activities, "Please do not depend on hearsay or the 'sound' of the name for authentication." The Jewish Welfare Board vice president Milton Weill consistently touted the organization's dedication to accuracy by listing the unlikely names of Jewish soldiers: "Every record of a citation . . . is checked and authenticated by the Bureau of War Records before the public relations department uses it, and if you think that's an easy job, let me read some names to you." He then read a list that included names such as S. M. Berkley, Emmet F. Blakemore, and M. M. Coleman—names that did not "sound" like Jewish names (although the list actually included names not infrequently selected by name changers, including Berkley and Coleman). The JWB emphasized in its materials encouraging volunteers to become census takers that 50 to 60 percent of military men who had voluntarily returned questionnaires on Jewish identity bore common American names such as Smith or Brown. The Jewish Welfare Board was thus clearly aware of the significance of name changing in American Jewish life.[21]

Ironically, however, at the same time that Weill touted the JWB's emphasis on fact-finding, rather than listening to the "sound" of the name, the JWB also utilized a new social scientific sampling technique that relied entirely on the sound of the name. In addition to door-to-door interviews, the board also used the "distinctive Jewish names" (DJN) method, a new technique developed by the psychologist Samuel Calmin Kohs, the director of the JWB Bureau of War Records. This method involved creating a list of 106 "distinctive Jewish names," agreed on by a panel of 20 social scientists, divided evenly between Jews and non-Jews (see figure 2.2). "For practical purposes," Kohs wrote, "the group defined a distinctive Jewish name as . . . 'a name which is rarely associated with any person other than a Jew.'" The names on this list were then matched to names listed on the rolls of Jewish welfare organizations and city directories in a given community. Researchers used the percentage of distinctive Jewish names found in each city as a multiplier to ascertain the number of Jews in that community. Although social scientists have not always agreed on how to use the DJN method, it has continued to serve as one way for Jewish scholars, as well as Jewish communal leaders, to track the Jewish population in a given community.[22]

1. Abraham	27. Feingold	56. Katzman	85. Rothstein
2. Abrahams	28. Feinstein	57. Kohn	86. Ruben
3. Abrahamson	29. Feldman*	58. Lefkowitz	87. Rubenstein
4. Abramovitz	30. Finkelstein	59. Lerner	88. Rubin*
5. Abrams	31. Freedman	60. Levi	89. Samuels*
6. Abramson	32. Friedman*	61. Levin*	90. Schulman
7. Adelman	33. Ginsberg*	62. Levine*	91. Segal
8. Aronson	34. Ginsburg	63. Levinson*	92. Shapiro*
9. Bercovitz	35. Gold*	64. Levitt	93. Shulman
10. Berkowitz	36. Goldberg*	65. Margolin	94. Siegel*
11. Berman*	37. Goldfarb	66. Margolis	95. Silverman*
12. Bernstein*	38. Goldman*	67. Markowitz	96. Silverstein
13. Birnbaum	39. Goldstein*	68. Moskowitz	97. Straus
14. Blumberg	40. Gottlieb	69. Nathan	98. Strauss
15. Blumenthal	41. Greenbaum	70. Nathanson	99. Sugarman
16. Bornstein	42. Greenberg*	71. Perlman	100. Weinberg*
17. Brodsky	43. Greenwald	72. Pincus	101. Weiner*
18. Brody	44. Grossman*	73. Rabinowitz	102. Weinstein*
19. Cahn	45. Halperin	74. Rappaport	103. Weintraub
20. Caplan*	46. Halpern	75. Rosen*	104. Wexler
21. Cohen*	47. Halprin	76. Rosenbaum*	105. Zeitlin
22. Cohn*	48. Horowitz*	77. Rosenberg	106. Zuckerman
23. Eisenberg	49. Horwitz	78. Rosenblatt	TOTAL
24. Eisner	50. Hurwitz	79. Rosenbloom*	Total Most Frequent
25. Epstein*	51. Hyman	80. Rosenblum	
26. Feinberg	52. Isenberg	81. Rosenstein	
	53. Kahn*	82. Rosenthal*	
	54. Kaplan*	83. Rothman*	
	55. Katz*	84. Rothschild	

Figure 2.2. The psychologist Samuel Calmin Kohs developed this list of 106 "Distinctive Jewish Names" in 1942 as part of a new social scientific methodology to count Jews. In 1943, the Jewish Welfare Board hired Kohs to conduct a census of Jews in the armed forces, in part by using this list. "Distinctive Jewish Names," in *Handbook of Instructions for Survey Consultants*, by Samuel Calmin Kohs, 56, folder 3, box 3, Records of the National Jewish Welfare Board—Bureau of War Records, 1940–1969, RG-152, American Jewish Historical Society (AJHS), Boston, MA, and New York, NY.

The DJN method offers different but equally important insights for historians. First, it allows us to determine a large number of names that people in the 1940s—both Jews and non-Jews—perceived as distinctively Jewish. Given the problematic nature and historical contingency of the term "Jewish names," the 106 names listed by this method are a valuable historical source. The fact that roughly 30 percent of all names changed in New York City in 1942 can be found on this list illustrates the highly stigmatized nature of distinctive Jewish names at this time; according to Kohs's calculations, those names reflected about 15 percent of the entire Jewish population's names in New York City and only about 3.75 percent of the entire city population. People with distinctive Jewish names thus eliminated them at eight times their rate in the population. Perhaps just as important, however, the DJN method allows us insight into the significance of Jewish names for Jewish community leaders in the 1940s. Antisemitic attacks pushed JWB leaders to treat names as official markers of Jewish identity.[23]

In addition to the official census using the DJN method, the JWB's publicity arm found itself using distinctive Jewish names as a means of countering antisemitic propaganda. Working through a nonsectarian intermediary organization, the Institute for American Democracy, the JWB placed one national advertisement that asked "What's Uncle Sam's Last Name? It's Everybody's Name!" and another that listed, "Smith? Kelly? Cohen? Swoboda? They Died Together—So That We May Live Together" (see figures 2.3 and 2.4). JWB vice president Milton Weill similarly highlighted distinctive Jewish names by encouraging the Jewish singer Eddie Cantor to perform a song that championed "the Smiths and the Jones / And the Kellys and Coh'ns / They're all America's sons." Antisemitic propaganda forced the JWB to rely on distinctive Jewish names in its publicity, as well as in its census taking, thus drawing attention to names that had become badges of inferiority for many Jewish Americans.[24]

Antisemitic propaganda also, however, forced the leadership of the JWB to contend with the Jewish identities of individuals and families who might have changed their names. Communications with volunteers throughout the country illustrated how the JWB grappled with the "American" names that so many Jews had adopted. Rather than expressing anger with Jews who had changed their names, the JWB—a major

Figures 2.3 and 2.4. Working through a nonsectarian intermediary organization, the Institute for American Democracy, the Jewish Welfare Board (JWB) created these Bulova watch advertisements to counter antisemitic propaganda. Bulova Watch Company, publicity materials, enclosure attached in letter, Stanley Musicant to Frank L. Weill, October 10, 1946, folder 11, box 1, Milton Weill Papers, RG P-34, American Jewish Historical Society, Boston, MA, and New York, NY.

Jewish communal organization—publicly included Jewish individuals who sported new non-Jewish names.

To be sure, official inclusion by the JWB does not indicate that all Jewish community leaders or members embraced name changing. Eugene Greenberg's insistence that "he [did] not intend to forsake the Hebrew religion of his family" suggests anxiety that a Jewish audience might condemn him for changing his name. By the end of the war, the innovator of the DJN methodology, Samuel Kohs, privately noted that "change of name" was one of the key elements of "self-depreciation" that plagued the American Jewish population. Nonetheless, in the context of rising antisemitism during the war years, name changing became one way of mediating hatred, and Jewish community leaders in the JWB during the war treated it as such.[25]

If name changing was not simply an individual decision but one that engaged the larger Jewish community, it was also shaped and facilitated by the state. Local, state, and federal government played a role in making name changing a viable and attractive activity for the thousands of individuals who chose to submit petitions in the 1940s. To be sure, the government never asked that citizens change their names. Nonetheless, name changing was a behavior that relied on state mechanisms and responded to state pressures.

One way in which the federal government encouraged name changing was through the expansion of state power into ordinary daily activity. Of course, name changing itself was not a new phenomenon in the 1940s. Immigrants of many different backgrounds had been unofficially changing their names for generations in the United States.[26] What was new during World War II was an upsurge in official name-change petitions, filed primarily by second-generation Americans, not immigrants: 75 percent of the name-change petitions in New York City in 1942 were submitted by native-born Americans.[27] That upsurge reflected the changing historical moment, as the state penetrated individuals' daily lives with the buildup and entry into war.

During World War II, the federal government expanded its reach far beyond levels reached previously. The Selective Training and Service Act of 1940, which instituted a military draft, and the Servicemen's Readjustment Act (the GI Bill) in 1944, which helped to pay for the education and home ownership of returning veterans, were only a couple of the most significant ways that the government affected ordinary individuals' lives immediately before and during World War II. Yet another, less visible way was through the defense industry: throughout the 1930s, aircraft companies had been required by US law to validate workers' names through their birth certificates, a legal requirement that became far more significant as war approached.[28]

The growth of the state during World War II came on the heels of significant state expansion into personal identity during World War I. World War I marked the beginning of the international passport system, defining the national citizenship—and thereby the personal identities—of citizens throughout the world, who thereafter found their movement constrained or enabled by personal names appearing on government documents. Perhaps even more relevant for the subject of name changing, World War I witnessed tremendous ethnic violence directed at German American individuals, as well as zealous efforts to purge German language and culture from Americans' midst. History texts are filled with descriptions of German name changing of all kinds, as sauerkraut became "liberty cabbage" and German street names were Anglicized, indicating the interrelationship between language, identity, and state power during World War I.[29]

The name-change petitions submitted at City Court suggest that the expansion of the state into personal identity during World War II must also be considered. Perhaps surprisingly, given the significance of foreign language to persecution during World War I, the numbers of name-change petitions submitted during World War I did not equal the total numbers or the rate of increase during World War II. Between 1913 and 1916, roughly 122 petitions were submitted each year. In 1917, name-change petitions in City Court doubled to 259, and in 1918, they almost tripled to 343. In 1942, however, petitions rose to over 1,000—a number quadruple the average of the previous decade. If World War I had introduced pressures to conform and techniques of bureaucracy that would shape citizens' relationships with the state in years to come, World War II fine-tuned those techniques and directed them more energetically toward the personal name itself, as documents such as the birth certificate rose to significance, equaling and perhaps exceeding that of the passport.[30]

Men and women who petitioned to change their names regularly pointed to the expansion of the federal government as a crucial factor in their decisions. Individuals applying to work in defense industries during the war, as well as individuals enlisting in the military, were among the most numerous petitioners. Many of these people were concerned with name discrepancies on their vital documents, particularly birth certificates. These men and women explained that they wished to change their names officially, as they had inconsistent names on a variety of documents, and court approval of their change of name would ease their way through government bureaucracy, allow them to find jobs, and silence any disturbing questions about their identity. "In view of the fact that I intend to register . . . for Selective Service, I do not wish there to be any confusion with respect to my identity," stated Saul Jack Kaufman in his 1942 petition to change his name legally to Jack Kay, a name he had used for over 20 years. Laura Ginsberg petitioned to change her surname to Gale, a name that she had used while working as a secretary for the past seven years, because she was "about to apply for employment by the United States Government and said application has to be accompanied by a birth certificate." Indeed, roughly 70 percent of petitioners in 1942 testified that they had informally changed their names years earlier. Virtually the same statistic held true in 1946, after the war had ended, although by 1946 and 1947, petitioners much less frequently mentioned the military or government bureaucracy. To a great extent, then, the explosion of official name changing during the war years was a codification of informal name changes that individuals had adopted in private settings before the war began.[31]

Popular literature of the era emphasized the impact of the wartime bureaucracy on individuals' names. One magazine editorial counseled parents to name their children wisely because names on birth certificates showed the "appellation by which you will be known in all your official relationships," including those with the government and particularly the army. In 1942, the writer Louis Adamic wrote *What's Your Name?*, a book on name changing, noting in his preface that the wartime era of bureaucracy had inspired his text. Since Pearl Harbor, he explained, "we are filling out all sorts of forms—applications, questionnaires, statements, depositions. We are required to show birth certificates. . . . Right and left, we are being asked, 'What's your name?'" The federal bureaucracy of World War II thus directed individuals' attention to names more intensely than ever before, leading many to legalize name changes that they had previously considered casual matters of personal choice.[32]

This bureaucratization did not just affect Jews; many other individuals of Slavic, Italian, German, and Greek heritage similarly found themselves during the war needing to make official previously informal name changes. But the expanding bureaucracy of World War II affected Jews disproportionately because of ethnic patterns developed in the interwar years. The bureaucratic explosion of the 1940s catapulted the small but significant Jewish interwar pattern into a major movement, as friends, neighbors, and kin of earlier name changers took advantage of the same state mechanisms under the far greater pressures of World War II.[33]

The growth of wartime nationalism, promoted by the federal government, also led large numbers of New Yorkers to change their names. Worries about "foreign" names ran consistently throughout name-change petitions, as petitioners testified to their American origins and identities. The designation of identities from southern and eastern Europe as "foreign," rather than "American," had existed before World War II, but the war clearly exacerbated the dangers of "foreignness" and the desirability of being "American."[34]

Foreign names were understandably worrisome if the names reflected Axis nationality, and a number of individuals with Italian-, German-, and Japanese-sounding names applied to change them. Christine Bianco, for example, asked to change her name to Christine Banks, finding "it difficult to gain the employment which would otherwise be available to her in view of her last name," while Joseph Randazzo petitioned to change his name to Randall, stating "that your petitioner is a true American in each and every respect. . . . That his name being a foreign name, is a handicap and detriment to him, particularly in these strenuous times." Florence Wikawa, an American woman who had been married to a Japanese man, applied to change her daughter's surname to Bridges after her divorce, because her "foreign-sounding name belies her American citizenship and tradition."[35]

But even individuals whose names reflected the nationality of allies, rather than enemies, sought to change their "foreign-sounding" names to more "American" ones. The five members of the Russian-sounding Bolotovsky family testified that their "present name is of foreign extraction and connotation" and that they were "very desirous of having a more American surname," Bolten. And Herbert Sakowitz, whose name seems to have reflected Polish roots, requested permission to change his name because it was "foreign." That names such as Bolotovsky and Sakowitz also sounded Jewish—and that Jews were among the staunchest supporters of the war in the United States—only highlights the ways that American identity was being narrowly configured during the war. That petitioners with Jewish-sounding names continued to identify them as "alien" and "foreign-sounding" even after hostilities had ended, suggests that that narrow definition of American identity lasted beyond the immediate years of the war.[36]

At the same time that the federal government encouraged name changing with its bureaucratic and nationalistic turn in the 1940s, it also made conscious public efforts to embrace a policy of tolerance officially, particularly regarding antisemitism. In its military, employment, and public relations policies, the federal government attempted to battle antisemitism and even to embrace distinctive Jewish names as American ones.

In the military, for example, top leaders cracked down on jokes that maligned Jews. When the American Jewish Committee (AJC) protested the publication of "The First American" in military journals to top brass, the navy issued a formal directive to avoid publishing the poem, while the army punished individuals who used military equipment to type or mimeograph it. "When the attention of Public Relations officials in Washington was called to these instances, immediate action was taken," the AJC noted approvingly. Top military leaders did not condone the bigotry of "The First American," and they took very public steps to root it out of military publications.[37]

In employment policy, the federal government included Jews in its discussions of racial inequality in the defense industries. After Franklin Delano Roosevelt established the Fair Employment Practices Committee (FEPC) in 1941 as a response to A. Philip Randolph's planned March on Washington protesting discrimination against black workers in defense industries, some Jewish leaders formed the Coordinating Committee of Jewish Organizations on Employment Discrimination in Defense Industries (CCJO) and surveyed Jewish groups throughout the nation about economic antisemitism. Although FEPC's discussions focused on discrimination against African Americans, the CCJO testified to anti-Jewish discrimination at FEPC's public hearings. The federal government thus recognized antisemitism as a problem of racial inequality, even if it made insufficient efforts to address that problem for members of any racial group.[38]

Finally, the federal government's efforts to sell the war through the Office of War Information (OWI) consistently trumpeted the nation's opposition to antisemitism by using Jewish and other ethnic names as symbols of the nation's commitment to tolerance. For example, in 1942,

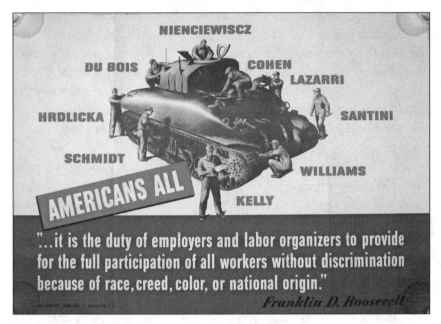

Figure 2.5. This poster for the War Manpower Commission, "Americans All," used ethnic names such as Cohen to signify the US government's battle against discrimination during World War II through the creation of the Fair Employment Practices Committee (FEPC). War Manpower Commission, "Americans All," 1942, poster, Prints and Photographs Division, Library of Congress, Washington, DC, www.loc.gov.

the OWI released the *Government Information Manual for the Motion Picture Association*, a document designed to help filmmakers create films that meshed with the administration's vision of the war's purposes. That vision emphasized the American commitment to tolerance, democracy, and the "Common Man," and it specifically called for filmmakers to create multiethnic platoons "using names of foreign extraction." Responding to OWI encouragement, Hollywood film after Hollywood film featured the cliché of the multiethnic platoon, reliably including Jewish characters who bore names such as Feinstein and Rosenthal.[39]

It was not only films that embraced Jewish names. A 1942 war poster embraced names such as Cohen, Santini, and Schmidt as "Americans All," workers united together and protected from discrimination by FEPC (see figure 2.5). And a handbook distributed to leaders working with the troops insisted that "men of all races, men of all religions call themselves Americans; men with names like Richards and with names like Schultz, Isaacs, Ryan, Alvarado, Kovacs, and Piazza." Ironically, the fact that these materials drew attention to "Jewish" names, using them as symbols of tolerance, may actually have increased some service members' anxieties about their names. Nonetheless, the federal government's intention was to discourage antisemitism and other forms of ethnic prejudice and to incorporate white immigrants such as Jews into the body politic.[40]

This propaganda emphasis on white ethnic names had emerged in World War I. Both Howard Chandler Christy's famous poster "Americans All" (see figure 2.6) and Theodore Roosevelt's dramatic prowar speeches hailed long lists of the distinctive ethnic names—including Levy and Cohen—of men who fought together as Americans. These stirring roll calls were designed to "nationalize" European immigrants, to make them American through military service. In World War II, however, the message shifted from one designed to turn immigrants into Americans to one designed to justify the war to ethnic American citizens.[41]

Federal policy during World War II ultimately had contradictory effects on name changing. On the one hand, the federal government opposed antisemitism at high levels, making sustained efforts to eliminate poems that ridiculed Jewish names and trumpeting an American identity that embraced stigmatized Jewish names. On the other hand, however, the nationalism and bureaucracy engendered by the war (as well as the unintended consequences of the war's publicity campaign) encouraged many American Jews to change their names officially to escape their stigma despite the stated goals of the federal government.

Name changing, moreover, was not merely a product of top-down policies instituted by the federal government. Even as the top officials in the military forbade "The First American" from being reproduced with US military equipment, many local post commanders disagreed with AJC representatives that the poem was bigoted at all. Individual military recruiters and private defense contractors pressured young men and women to change their names officially, while some officers turned Jewish names into jokes, humiliating and isolating Jewish soldiers. The decisions made by leaders at the top levels of federal government were not always reproduced by representatives of the state at lower levels.[42]

Figure 2.6. This poster for Victory Liberty Loans, "Americans All," used ethnic names such as Levy to signify the Americanization of immigrants in the war effort during World War I. Howard Chandler Christy, "Americans All! Victory Liberty Loan," 1919, poster, Prints and Photographs Division, Library of Congress, Washington, DC, www.loc.gov.

Citizens' name changing was a process that the US government had always delegated to state governments and to local courts. All of the name-change petitions researched for this book, for example, were submitted to a local city court, under laws promulgated by New York State. The only active interventions of the federal government in this process were affidavits attached to each eligible man's petition swearing that he had registered for the draft. Official name changing was a state behavior, but it was not a federal behavior. Before World War II, the decentralized federal system shaped ordinary lives through a wide variety of well-established mechanisms, such as name-change law and civil court procedures. The circumstances of the war invested these long-standing procedures with new vitality and meaning for ordinary people. It was not simply federal legislation, agency directives, or military policy that affected Americans' racial identity and self-perception.

Finally, it is worth noting that the social conformity that the government had helped to engender during the war may have been responsible for the high number of name changes after the war. It was not until 1948 that the extremely high levels of name changing during the war fell somewhat and not until the 1980s that name-change petitions resumed their pre–World War II numbers.[43]

The name-changing phenomenon of New York City Jews during the war years illustrates the complicated relationship between the state, race, and personal identity. Increased numbers of name-change petitions in New York City offer poignant evidence of the heightened racialization of American Jews during the era of the Holocaust, intensified by the expansion of the federal government into individuals' personal identities during the war. At the same time, however, name changing decreased the racialization of Jews and hastened their integration into the white mainstream, as flexible name-changing law allowed their distinctive linguistic badges to vanish overnight.

Amid the pressures of the war, these complicated racial maneuvers were accepted as normal by established Jewish organizations such as the JWB. As Jewish leaders battled heightened anti-Jewish sentiment in the United States, they sought to present a unified and dignified presence on the national stage. But, as we will see, in the years after the war, name changing became a subject for communal alarm, public debate, and sociological study.

PART II

Responses to Jewish Name Changing after World War II

3

"I Changed My Name"

Cultural Debates over Name Changing, Passing, and Jewish
Identity in the Postwar Era

In February 1948, *Atlantic Monthly* published an article titled "I Changed My Name." Written by a New Yorker who ironically chose to remain anonymous, the article described his decision—along with his brother—to abandon his "forthrightly Jewish" name in favor of something more "neutral." He attacked the antisemitism that had contributed to his name change, the "hypocritical universities, polluted employment agencies, churchgoers ignorant of Christianity, canting business leaders, haters of people they haven't met," while also describing his own joyful elation "at having joined the human race" and at escaping the "parochialism" of the Jewish world. "I like best to describe myself simply as a human being," he insisted. Perhaps most striking and surprising for Anonymous was the anger and bitterness with which his friends responded to his decision, calling him "a coward and deserter." The piece was clearly written in an effort to defend his decision to them and to others.[1]

The article deeply affected readers. *Atlantic Monthly* published a rebuttal in April by the Mississippi writer David L. Cohn, and in June, it published numerous letters from readers responding to the debate. Meanwhile, the liberal *Congress Weekly* published an angry rejoinder to Anonymous from the managing editor, Shlomo Katz. As further evidence of the provocative nature of the debate, both the Anonymous and Cohn pieces were reprinted in *Reader's Digest* in 1948 and in an anthology of Jewish writing called *Mid-Century* in 1955. This debate—and indeed the subject of name changing more generally—clearly struck a nerve among readers in the immediate postwar era, particularly as it linked name changing to the hot-button issue of antisemitism.

Cohn belittled the anonymous author's charges of antisemitism and championed his own connections to both Jewish and American history and identity. He insisted that the United States was the "kindliest of countries" for Jews: "being a Jew has been no deterrent either to my happiness or to my career." To be sure, Cohn noted, there were probably clubs or hotels that did not "take" Jews, and he was surely excluded from them. Those institutions, he assured his readers, were peopled by socially insecure snobs, predominantly middle-class women, with whom he would not want to associate anyway: "Do you blame me if I reject them?" More fundamentally, it was his pride that prevented him from changing his name: "it would not be wholly admirable if I should, by changing my name, reject the fifty centuries' history and tradition of my people in order to gain a hotel room at Newport."[2] Cohn thus painted Anonymous's name change as a cowardly and foolish betrayal of the Jewish people, while simultaneously arguing that American antisemitism was simply snobbishness that had no impact on ordinary individuals' lives.

This anguished and very public debate over name changing and antisemitism allows us to see both change and continuity in the years after World War II. First, the debate made clear that antisemitism was still an ugly presence in American Jews' daily lives after the conclusion of World War II. Research has tended to focus on the decline of antisemitism and the extraordinary levels of integration attained by Jews in the years after the war, especially in comparison with the growing antisemitism of the prewar years. Indeed, at least one historian of Jewish life in the post–World War II years has labeled those years a "golden decade," looking at growing rates of Jewish suburbanization, economic success, and social comfort. While scholars acknowledge that antisemitism declined only gradually in the years after World War II and that it was a presence in American life until at least the early 1960s, the ways that Jews continued to contend with antisemitism as a relevant part of their lives has been given little attention.[3]

Jews continued to change their names in disproportionate numbers in the years after World War II. Indeed, 1946 saw the highest number of name-change petitions throughout the entire 20th century, and Jewish petitions accounted for more than 50 percent of those petitions—far and away more than any other ethnicity. Name changing declined somewhat after 1948, but the numbers still remained far higher than they had been before the war, and Jews were still disproportionately represented throughout the 1950s and 1960s. Indeed, it was not until the 1980s that Jews' distinctive ethnic familial strategy of name changing really disappeared from the petitions of the New York City Civil Court. Despite the image of the "golden years" then, good numbers of New York Jews still believed that their distinctive names held them back from success.

The *Atlantic Monthly* debate also illustrates how antisemitism became entwined with mainstream Americans' perception of name changing in the postwar years. During the 1920s and 1930s, most discussion of Jewish name changing took place in communal newspapers and venues, such as the *Daily Forward*. As we have seen, when name changing emerged in mainstream literature or film, such as *The Jazz Singer*, it was typically portrayed as a universal problem for second-generation southern and eastern Europeans (including but not limited to Jews) who were trying to become American. But in the years after World War II, conversations about generational struggles over Americanization were transformed into agonized discussions about antisemitism. Indeed, in the three years immediately following the war, when Jewish name changing was at an all-time high and antisemitism dominated public discourse, the uncertainty of Jewish racial identity, symbolized by either an ambiguous name or a name change, became an important metaphor in American film and fiction. The *Atlantic Monthly* debate indicates the degree to which name changing had become publicly identified in the postwar years as both a Jewish strategy to evade hatred and as a symbol of Jews' uncertain racial identity.

The *Atlantic Monthly* debate also gives us insight into the angst that name changers created in the American Jewish community after the war. Name changing in American life seemed to many Jews a signal that Jews were actively trying to "pass," to escape the Jewish community and assimilate completely into the non-Jewish world. In the press, name changers were pilloried, caricatured either as foolish or as selfish self-haters, dangers to themselves and the Jewish community. As Cohn's and Katz's pieces illustrate, name changing inspired scorn and anger among many.

Unpublished responses to the *Atlantic Monthly* debate, along with name-change petitions and other fictional and journalistic pieces, suggest, however, that fears of Jews "passing" as non-Jews when they took on new names were misplaced. While Jewish writers worried that name changers were trying to escape the Jewish world, the social reality of name changing did not typically merit those concerns. As we will see, a few Jews did convert to Christianity or deny their Jewish identity and embrace secular universalism, but many more used their new names to engage a changing, uncertain world, both Jewish and non-Jewish. While these Jews frequently protected themselves from antisemitism by retaining Jewish social networks, they found themselves able to develop and maintain new relationships with non-Jews. Jews believed that name changing would help them manage their complicated relationships with both Jews and non-Jews. To be sure, we will see that name changers did not always achieve the desired results. Some experienced humiliation, isolation, or ridicule from both Jews and non-Jews *because* they chose to change their names. Nonetheless, many Jews changed their names because they hoped it would allow them to take advantage of new opportunities, while still remaining part of the Jewish community.

World War II had tremendous social impact in the United States and in the lives of American Jews, but it did not put a halt to domestic antisemitism, despite many popular and scholarly assumptions to the contrary. The historian Leonard Dinnerstein has actually called the first few years after World War II, from 1945 to 1947, the peak of antisemitism in the United States. Moreover, even after 1947 and, indeed, all the way through at least the early 1960s, antisemitic restrictions in employment, education, and social accommodations continued to limit the lives of ordinary Jews, although decreasing in intensity as the years went on.[4]

In the years immediately following the war, Jewish agencies reported a significant continuation and even an increase in employment discrimination, especially in the arenas in which Jews most sought work: employment agencies seeking white-collar skilled and semiskilled labor and in the professions. In a 1946 survey, the National Community Relations Advisory Council (NCRAC), an umbrella organization for Jewish self-defense and civil rights groups, found that "employment discrimination against Jews had increased markedly in the months following the war."[5] Between 1945 and 1946, the number of discriminatory help-wanted ads increased 195 percent, according to the NCRAC.[6] In 1948, the B'nai B'rith Anti-Defamation League (ADL) interviewed faculty and administrators in three professions—engineering, accounting, and law—and found substantial restrictions on Jewish employment: "As far as Jewish students are concerned, it is an almost impossible task for them to get a job in a public accounting firm," one informant reported, while his counterparts in law and engineering similarly reported that "discrimination against Jews is pretty bad" and described "a great many firms" that specifically asked that Jewish and other minority students not be sent for interviews.[7]

Moreover, although these high levels of discrimination declined after the 1940s, significant employment discrimination against Jews continued in the 1950s. In 1952, the ADL interviewed employment-agency employees, who reported that Jews were by far the hardest religious group to place in jobs. Forty-six percent of agency employees labeled Jews "hard to place" or "never placed, even if qualified"; these categories were never used to label Catholics or Protestants. And in 1956, the Bureau on Jewish Employment Problems of Chicago reported that of 20,000 job orders placed with commercial employment agencies in the city, about 18 percent restricted Jews, using specific statements such as "This is a Gentile firm, a Jewish girl wouldn't be comfortable here." One large Chicago agency placed only nine out of 100 Jews seeking jobs, while it placed 20 out of 100 Protestants and 17 out of 100 Catholics.[8] These numbers were far better than they had been in the 1930s and 1940s, when as many as 95 percent of agencies reported an almost total ban on Jewish applicants, but they still reflected significant limitations on Jewish employment opportunities.[9]

By the early 1960s, employment discrimination had clearly waned. Jewish self-defense agencies reported fewer concerns with antisemitism both in employment agencies and in the professions. Yet studies of the insurance and banking industries still found Jews significantly underrepresented, particularly in the ranks of executives, and Jews still had trouble being placed as engineers and accountants.[10] Employment agencies, moreover, still used codes for Jews and other minorities, such as "No Sabbath Observers Wanted," to screen potentially undesirable candidates for discriminatory employers.[11] Reports of discrimination against Jewish white-collar workers continued to feed Jewish fears of antisemitism. For example, a 1961 sociological study reported that 17 percent of young Jewish men in one midwestern city felt that their religious identity "had either restricted their occupational choice, limiting them to fewer and less desirable occupations, or impeded their opportunities for advancement within their chosen fields."[12] This number was surely far lower than what it would have been 30 years earlier, but it indicates that lingering fears of antisemitism still shaped Jewish perceptions of employment throughout the 1950s, as antidiscrimination laws took effect in different states, at different times, with different levels of enforcement.

Discrimination against Jews in education also persisted. A 1946 study of New York State schools found that some elite colleges in New York accepted one Jewish student for every four non-Jewish students. The extent of discrimination was particularly severe when considering differences in academic preparation; at these colleges, more non-Jewish students in the bottom half of their class were accepted than Jewish students in the first quarter of their class.[13] In 1948, the American Council on Education found that an application for admission to college submitted by a Protestant had a 77 percent chance of being accepted, while a Jew had only a 56 percent chance.[14] Surveys conducted by the ADL found that 9 percent of liberal arts institutions failed to send application forms or catalogues or to give correct information about application deadlines to inquiring Jewish high school students.[15] In New York and throughout the nation, colleges and universities gathered information allowing them to determine racial and ethnic background, and they used that information to limit the applications of Jews.

Rather than encouraging an embarrassed retreat from discrimination, then, the end of the war saw the most prestigious schools continuing the antisemitic admissions policies they had adopted in the prewar years. Not all were as open in their prejudices as the outgoing president of Dartmouth, Ernest M. Hopkins, who told the *New York Post* one week before V-J Day, "Dartmouth is a Christian college founded for the Christianization of its students." However, not one prestigious school quickly and voluntarily began accepting significant numbers of Jewish applicants in the years right after the war.[16] Well into the late 1950s, Ivy League schools such as Princeton and Yale continued to maintain unofficial quotas of Jewish students by emphasizing admissions standards of "character and personality" and deemphasizing—sometimes even treating as liabilities—strong academic records.[17]

To be sure, the years immediately after World War II saw some legislative success, including the passage of Fair Educational Practices (FEP) acts in New York, New Jersey, and Massachusetts[18] (see the discussion of Jewish civil rights efforts for FEP laws in chapter 4). Those laws forced schools such as Columbia, Princeton, and Harvard, as well as other less prestigious schools, to relax their emphasis on athletic ability, social skills, and "character and personal promise."[19] The number of Jews at many elite institutions, and their percentages in the incoming classes, thus rose throughout the postwar years, but they did so slowly and at steady annual rates that resembled fixed quotas: 12 to 15 percent at Princeton and Yale, respectively, for example.[20] And it was not only elite schools that continued to maintain these quotas, either officially or unofficially; in 1956, at least one Jewish student received a letter from a Massachusetts junior college informing her that its "quota from New York and New Jersey" had already been filled.[21] For the most part, however, undergraduate discrimination during the postwar years went underground. As discriminatory practices became socially unacceptable, school administrators still clung to their discretion over admissions as a means of shaping college classes to fit their racial and religious stereotypes and desires.

Professional schools, including medical, law, and dental schools, similarly discriminated against Jews throughout the postwar years, at least until the mid-1950s and sometimes beyond. In 1948, an ADL survey found that 98 percent of application forms for five types of professional schools—accountancy, dentistry, law, medicine, and optometry—featured discriminatory questions, including open inquiries into applicants' race, nationality, and religion.[22] In 1950 and 1952, two independent New York State reports found that the state's medical colleges had systematically restricted the admission of Jewish students. One report disclosed that five out of 29 Jewish applicants to Cornell University Medical School had been admitted, as compared with 15 of 35 non-Jews (with an average of 10 percent lower grades).[23] And at schools with no quotas, professional associations lobbied for them. In 1945, for example, the Council on Dental Education of the American Dental Association released a confidential report to the dental schools at New York and Columbia universities to urge them to adopt a quota based on racial origins, targeted at Jews: "It must be noted that the student body is made up overwhelmingly of one racial strain and is not even a cross-section of the various racial groups to be found in Greater New York."[24] If antisemitism at the undergraduate level required Jewish students to apply to more schools and earn higher grades than non-Jews, antisemitism at the professional level could dissuade students from pursuing certain careers, thus shaping their economic lives for years to come.

In the late 1940s and early 1950s, as Fair Educational Practices laws took effect in some states, discrimination in American higher education was definitely reduced, but by no means did it disappear. It was not until the 1960s that most American universities and colleges (including the most elite) formally investigated their admissions practices, eliminated Jewish quotas, and called for academic standards rather than personality or religious background to govern admissions.[25] Until then, however, antisemitism in higher education was a well-known phenomenon in the postwar era, something that Jews were aware of and that shaped their understanding of the limitations they faced.

The discrimination with perhaps the most staying power throughout the postwar years involved antisemitic restrictions in hotels, resorts, and clubs. As public accommodations with private functions, many remained restricted through the 1960s and even 1970s.

Complaints of antisemitism in hotels and resorts actually increased in the years immediately after World War II. In 1947, for example, the ADL noted that complaints against hotels restricting Jewish patrons had increased 50 percent between 1946 and 1947.[26] In 1947, the New England branch of the ADL found that 46 percent of surveyed hotels restricted their clientele to Gentiles, in contrast with the 36 percent identified in 1946.[27] To be sure, hotels in the postwar era increasingly refrained from open or "vulgar" antisemitism; advertisements that read, "We do not seek Hebrew patronage" or "No consumptives! No dogs! No Jews!" were no longer fashionable after 1945, and indeed they were illegal in many northern states by that date.[28] More circumspect and coded language, however, that spoke of "selected clientele," "congenial atmosphere," or "churches nearby" continued to appear in the pages of newspapers and in promotional brochures. A study conducted by the ADL in 1947 found that, of the hotels that advertised with this language, roughly 30–40 percent would not even respond to a Jewish patron's request for information. Moreover, travel agencies, state tourist agencies, and even the American Automobile Association (AAA) generally participated in this discrimination, maintaining separate lists of restricted and unrestricted accommodations and either ignoring Jewish patrons' requests altogether or explaining hotel policies to them and suggesting they make reservations at unrestricted resorts.[29]

It was not until 1954 that the prestigious Camelback Inn in Phoenix, Arizona, faced public controversy and angry boycotts over its policy to restrict Jews.[30] A 1956 ADL survey of hotels and motels found that roughly 22 percent of participating institutions openly discriminated against Jews. Even more damning, the fact that a large number of hotels—many of which had already been cited for antisemitic discrimination—refused to participate in the survey suggests that 22 percent is probably an understatement of the extent to which antisemitism pervaded public accommodations in the 1950s.[31] The Camelback Inn, even with the embarrassing public scrutiny in the early 1950s, refused to relax its restrictions on Jews until 1961. The emergence of democratic Holiday Inns throughout the nation's highway system in 1952 put pressure on older hotels and resorts to accommodate Jews when they traveled.[32] Nonetheless, the restrictions that still existed in so many hotels and resorts throughout the nation circumscribed Jews' understandings of their ability to travel and pursue leisure throughout the postwar era.

Change was even slower for social clubs. Since the beginning of the century, elite clubs had systematically discriminated against Jews. By the postwar era, their policies were rigid and inflexible and seemingly impervious to criticism. From the 1940s through the 1960s, numerous exposés attacked these restrictive policies, criticizing the exclusion of Jews from the "power structure" that dominated economic and political life in big cities and small towns throughout the country. Noting that Jews were almost universally excluded from every "prestige" club in every American city, Carey McWilliams angrily charged in his 1948 A Mask for Privilege that this exclusion was "not so much a prejudice against Jews as a desire to augment power by excluding the Jewish group."[33] Ten years later, little had changed: in Vance Packard's popular attack on the class stratification and artificiality of new suburbanites, The Status Seekers, he cited a Cornell study finding that Jews were excluded from all three major avenues of social acceptability—the club, the exclusive neighborhood, and the Junior League—in 49 of 50 cities throughout the country, and he argued that Jewish exclusion was economically and socially harmful for the nation.[34] And even by 1964, when antisemitic restrictions in employment and education had mostly dissipated, the sociologist E. Digby Baltzell argued that continuing barriers to Jews in prestigious social clubs threatened American democracy. The nation's traditional standards, he argued, were "in danger of losing authority" because the upper class of "White-Anglo-Saxon-Protestants" had become too exclusive, demanding "the dishonorable treatment of far too many distinguished Americans" for it "to fill its traditional function of moral leadership."[35]

How did American Jews, caught between openness and restriction, respond to these very gradual and unclear processes of economic and social change? How did they understand their social status and their possibilities in life?

Name changing is one way that Jews in New York City managed the contradictions of the postwar era. During the three years between 1946 and 1948, when antisemitism was arguably at its peak, at least 1,000 New York Jews abandoned their Jewish names in City Court.[36] Even after 1948, Jewish name changing continued at rates higher than before the war. Name-change petitions averaged about 550 per year in the 1950s and about 450 per year in the 1960s, and Jews erasing their ethnically marked names filed between 50 to 65 percent of all the petitions in all of those years. No other ethnic group even came close to those numbers. In 1947, for example, the total number of petitions submitted by people erasing Slavic-, German-, Italian-, and Greek-sounding names all together equaled only one-half of the petitions submitted by people eliminating Jewish-sounding names. Roughly the same statistic was true ten years later.

Lingering fears and experiences with antisemitism even in the 1950s and 1960s played a role in these petitions. As before and during the war, most petitioners did not speak openly about antisemitism, but they did state that new names would help them both in work and in social situations. In 1946, Robert H. Goldberger, along with his wife, Gloria Diane, petitioned the court to allow them to change their surname to Gilder because it would "assist [Robert] materially in his business relations and his social intercourse."[37] That same year, Roy B. Levine and his wife, Blossom, explained that before the war, "[Roy] could not find employment in the advertising industry and after adopting his mother's maiden name, Mitchell, he found that he had more luck. Now that he has re-entered the workforce he would like to legally adopt Mitchell."[38] And in 1952, Edward Sokolowsky requested that he be allowed to change his surname to Trent because he feared that Sokolowsky "would be an impediment to [his] progress in the field of banking."[39] Antisemitism was rarely addressed openly, but the petitioners frequently described their original names as a "hindrance," "embarrassment," or "impediment."[40]

It is worth noting that after the war, fewer petitioners were worried about job hunting with their Jewish names. Instead, they discussed the difficulties they faced when dealing with coworkers and clients or a desire to better present themselves in business. The dental student Jerry Harold Linchitz asked to change his surname to Lynn, describing his current name as "cumbersome" and explaining that it would cause "confusion and embarrassment" after he became a dentist, when "it will be necessary that [he] continually make new contacts and acquaintances."[41] Ernest Aronowitz was a medical student who wanted to change his name to Arons because he found that "nurses, patients, and others are unable to pronounce, spell, or easily remember [his] present name," and he worried that would lead to "much difficulty and confusion" when he ultimately received his medical degree.[42] Particularly as male Jews entered the professions in larger numbers, their concern was less with discriminatory employment agencies and more with their own ability to attract patients or clients and command respect from both peers and subordinates.

Long after World War II made German (and Jewish) names suspect, and in the midst of a Cold War that made Russian (and Jewish) names suspect, American-born petitioners continued to describe their names as "foreign sounding" and to request "American" names. Leonard and Mildred Furstenberg asked to change their surname to Forrest in 1957, describing their current surname as "typically foreign and lengthy and, therefore, objectionable to them. They wish to Americanize their names for simplicity and for the purpose of having their names easily understandable in the business world."[43] Rita and Hyman Bershinsky explained they wanted "to assume a name which is more consonant with that of this country in preference to one of foreign origin," by changing Bershinsky to Bershan.[44] And in 1957, Joseph and Renee Shapiro asked to change their name to Sands because it would connote "American identity" as Joseph began a new career in international business.[45]

While these concerns about foreignness were particularly notable among American-born citizens, there were a number of European refugees who similarly wanted to Americanize their names and avoid the perception of a foreign—and Jewish—name. In 1952, Victor and Olga Sternberg explained that they wanted to change their names to Sternby, "for the reason that their present names are typically German and, therefore, objectionable to them. Your petitioners expect to remain in the United States permanently and to bring up any children born to them in the American manner. They believe it to be in the best interests of themselves that their names be more Americanized."[46] And the refugees Peter and Hedwig Oppenheimer petitioned to change their family's surname to Oliver, citing "confusion and embarrassment" over their "cumbersome" name in 1957, four years after the American Jewish physicist J. Robert Oppenheimer's loyalty became a matter of national debate.[47] Worries about nationality, ethnicity, identity, and loyalty persisted in American Jewish life throughout the "golden years" of the 1950s and 1960s.

Just as before and during the war, large numbers of Jewish families continued to change their names together. Petitions that involved family members outnumbered those filed by lone individuals two to one in the postwar years. And women were still a sizable proportion of name changers in the postwar era—between one-third and one-half of all petitioners. One unpublished letter to David L. Cohn in 1948 illustrates the ways that women and children, working together as members of a family unit, perceived name changing as a practical strategy necessary to escape antisemitism. Mrs. Harry Snyderman described in detail the discrimination that she had faced as a secretary in Chicago before the war and that Jewish boys in her current Arizona community had recently experienced while applying to Ivy League colleges. She insisted adamantly, "If my daughter . . . goes out of the state to work someday, I would definitely have her shorten her name."[48] Although antisemitism was declining, the strategy of Jewish familial name changing persisted throughout the postwar years, as Jewish husbands and wives, parents and children, continued to perceive their Jewish names as distinctive badges that could limit their economic and social advancement and obtrude into their daily lives in uncomfortable and restrictive ways.

The family decision to change a name was not always cohesive and communal. Name changing could be divisive, painful, and even gut wrenching for family members. The physician Sherwin Nuland has described in detail the painful journey he and his brother Harvey undertook to change their surnames from Nudelman in 1947. As "infants" under the age of 21, they could not petition the court themselves and thus had to bring their father, Meier, along as the petitioner. When Meier asked, in broken Yiddish-inflected English, "Vy not I shoot beink Nulant, too?" both Harvey and Sherwin quickly and guiltily worked to convince him that the new name was inappropriate "for a guy like you."[49] Name changing was not always an inclusive experience—but it was an important familial decision for husbands, wives, mothers, fathers, children, and siblings to contemplate, consider, and ultimately act on together, particularly in the midst of the baby boom in the wake of World War II. As veterans and their families worked to reestablish their lives and take advantage of the new opportunities in the postwar service economy, unracially-marked names seemed to many to be a valuable economic and social asset that might help them capitalize on the skills they learned in the military and on the home front during the war, especially since the shadowy antisemitic limitations that had dogged Jews for years continued to linger in the American workplace and educational system.

Were name changers attempting to escape their Jewish backgrounds? Was name changing an effort to enter the Gentile world and never look back? A closer look at New York's name-change petitions and at contemporary sociological descriptions of name changers suggests that while some Jews may have been attempting to escape the Jewish community, many more were incorporating their name changes into their communal lives as Jews.

There were dire warnings and communal anxieties about the efforts of Jews to "pass" in the postwar era. Those anxieties centered around the image of the "self-hating Jew," a concept developed in an influential 1941 article by the psychologist Kurt Lewin, inspired by Jews' marginal status. Jewish elites, Lewin argued, were frustrated by their exclusion from Gentile circles, but, rather than express anger toward Gentiles, they directed it to other Jews or to themselves. Following the publication of Lewin's article, Jewish psychologists, sociologists, intellectuals, and communal leaders made combating self-hatred one of their chief ideological and practical goals. Pages and pages of the Jewish press and of Jewish psychological and educational research were devoted to understanding and identifying self-hatred among other Jews.[50]

Name changing was a potent image within this discourse, a classic symbol of self-hatred, and a poignant example of Jews' fears about survival in an assimilated world. For example, in *Commentary*, David Bernstein noted that most American Jews considered changing one's name a key component of assimilation and a "hypocritical flight from Jewishness." Equating name changing with conversion to Christianity, he noted that both behaviors, for most American Jews, reflected similar (and despicable) ways of "denying or at least hiding the fact that one is Jewish."[51] In a 1945 book developed for the Hillel organization, which operated on college campuses throughout the country, Rabbi Milton Steinberg explained that elite Jews who traveled close to Gentile circles wanted "nothing more than to cease to be Jews and be accepted as Gentiles." When this desire became great enough, "Jews change their names, dissociate themselves from their fellows, calculatingly conceal their origin and try to 'pass,'" Steinberg warned.[52] For many American Jewish leaders in the 1940s and 1950s, name changing represented a form of self-hatred and a signpost on the way to passing.

The Jewish community's fears of passing may have been influenced by prevalent cultural portraits of African Americans passing. For African Americans, without legal permission to erase their racial designation and with far harsher racism a daily presence in their lives, passing typically included secrecy and lies, an erasure of racial identity, and an escape from racial community. Some African Americans who passed maintained ties with family and friends, but their performance frequently relied on others in the black community maintaining their pretense. As portraits of African American passing became increasingly negative in American mainstream media in the postwar era, so too did images of Jewish name changers as passers and self-haters.[53]

Portraits of name changers as self-hating Jews seeking to pass flourished in the fiction, film, and theater of the postwar years, and those portraits were quite different from those of earlier eras. Fictional portraits after 1945 consistently portrayed name changers as confused, desperate, or even caddish Jews who hated their backgrounds and longed to escape them. In *Wasteland* (1946), Jo Sinclair portrayed John Brown agonizing over the name he changed from Jake Braunowitz out of shame over his lower-class, dysfunctional Jewish family. In *Whisper My Name* (1949), Burke Davis fictionalized the true story of a wealthy Jewish businessman who had lied to his adopted southern city for years about his background. And in Herman Wouk's *Marjorie Morningstar* (1955), the heroine's feckless love interest, Noel Airman, changed his name from Saul Ehrmann, disgusted by the bourgeois sentimentality of his middle-class Jewish roots. Marjorie too had changed her name, hoping for a career on the stage, but she sensibly changed it back to a Jewish one after marrying the solid, middle-class Milton Schwartz. Story after story in the postwar era described Jews who changed their names and, in some cases, even converted to Christianity to escape or at least hide their backgrounds; by the end, however, most fictional name changers were shamefully exposed and frequently convinced to return to the Jewish community.[54] Through these didactic messages about the dangers of name changing, Jewish authors indicated the power that the concept of "self-hatred" had on American Jewish artists, as well as the threat that passing seemed to pose to the Jewish community.

But did these portraits reflect reality? A few sociological descriptions of Jews in the 1950s and 1960s do suggest that some elite Jews tried to pass by converting to Christianity. For example, E. Digby Baltzell, in his description of elite antisemitism, described discrimination against several Jews who had converted to Christianity and moved out of the Jewish community. In 1961, one country club in Scarsdale, New York, made national headlines after it banned a young man with one Jewish parent from the annual club ball. The man had been baptized in an Episcopalian church.[55] Moreover, many of the recent antisemitic incidents in fraternities, Baltzell explained, "arise over boys who have no Jewish convictions or ethnic characteristics and who, moreover, are often converts to Christianity."[56] Certainly some elite Jews attempted to leave the Jewish community during this era.

Several New York City Civil Court petitions (most filed by people with less elite status than those described by Baltzell) involve individuals who changed their names because they had converted and/or sought to raise their children as Christians and wanted no lingering questions about their own or their family's religious identity. Aaron and Olga Cohen petitioned in 1957 to change their family's surname to Curtis because their children, Robert Alan and Patricia Diane, "are being raised in the Catholic faith and the surname of Cohen is not an appropriate one."[57] The graduate student Edward Goldstein too explained that he was a practicing Catholic, had been raised by his mother in the Catholic faith, and wanted to take on her maiden name, Russell. Moreover, the petition added, as a university instructor, he believed that "the name he intends to use will be easier for his associates and students to pronounce and remember, and further it will materially aid him in so far as his relationships with his associates and superiors."[58] And in 1967, Martin Goldberg asked to be allowed to assume the name Martin Grayson: "I have converted to Catholicism with the intention of marrying a Catholic girl," he explained. "Our children will be raised as Catholics and, in all likelihood, will be sent to Catholic schools. A change of name is therefore extremely important."[59] Only one or two such petitions were submitted each year, but they did reflect a small subset of Jews who used name changing to escape the Jewish community.

Another, somewhat larger subset of Jews probably chose not to convert but to "assimilate" into the surrounding world, disavowing the Jewish community and living a wholly secular life. In this decision too, name changing was a practical aid. Jews affiliated with universities, particularly elite ones, were famous for this choice. The 1946 appointment of the Jewish philosopher Paul Weiss to the Yale faculty, for example, made him "Yale's Jew" for years because all the other Jewish faculty members, a number of whom had changed their names to get their jobs, refused to be identified publicly as Jews.[60] It was not just Yale, either. By the early 1960s, throughout the country, in a number of different disciplines, prominent Jewish academics proclaimed their intellectual commitment to a secular life of the mind that privileged universal knowledge over parochial ties. For some of them, that commitment included a change of name and a formal distance from the Jewish world.[61]

One of the most significant sociological studies of name changers during the postwar years suggested that name changing was a step for elites on the road to secular assimilation and withdrawal from the Jewish community. In 1955, the sociologists Leonard Broom (who made no secret of the fact that his own name had been changed from Bloom), Helen P. Beem, and Virginia Harris studied name-change petitions in Los Angeles from 1946 to 1947 and found that Jews who lived in high-status neighborhoods were most numerous in the name-change petitions. The authors hypothesized that "assimilation, high social rank, . . . and disassociation from prior familial units" were the key factors that distinguished Jewish name changers from other Jews.[62]

There is no discussion of this type of secular detachment from the Jewish community in the New York City petitions, but testimony from a few name changers in the postwar era does suggest that a vision of secular "assimilation" and abandonment of Jewishness appealed to some name changers. In the *Atlantic* essay, for example, Anonymous deliberately separated himself from Jewish communal, religious, and intellectual life, noting that his "education was entirely secular," that he found Jewish tradition uninspiring and irrelevant—"I feel well-rounded despite ignorance of both Sanskrit and Hebrew"—and perhaps most provocatively, that he felt no special connection to the survivors of the Holocaust: "I generally feel as bad about a dying Hindu as about a dying Jew." Although he explained that he chose not to join a church and called himself and his brother Jews, his claim that "I like best to describe myself simply as a human being" made clear that he linked his name change to a broader secular assimilation into the Gentile mainstream.[63] Interestingly, the most riveting letter to the editor published by the *Atlantic* in response to "I Changed My Name" came from a New York man named George N. Caylor, who described in detail the daily antisemitism he and his family had experienced until he and his wife changed their names. He made clear, however, not only that his name change eliminated discrimination from his life but also that it reflected his own alienation from the Jewish community: "I am not a believer in or follower of the Jewish (or any) religion, and I am not influenced by 'the fifty centuries history and tradition of my people.' My only kinship with the Jews is that of kinship with oppressed peoples, and if I feel closer to the Jews than to other oppressed peoples, it is only because they have suffered more for a longer time than the others."[64] For both Caylor and Anonymous, as well as for some other elite Jews, the secular intellectual trend of universalism, popular after World War II, made assimilation a powerful intellectual credo. Name changing and distance from the Jewish community fit well within that credo—while also enabling them to escape significant social and economic discrimination.

Although some Jews may have chosen to change their names as a signal of alienation or as part of a substantial separation from the Jewish community, evidence suggests that the numbers of name changers seeking to abandon the Jewish community altogether were actually quite small. For the large majority of Jews who sought new names, name changing did not entail flight from the Jewish community at all. It was instead an open secret within the community, a way of hiding in plain sight.

Perhaps the most astute contemporary commentator on name changing as a complex part of Jewish identity, rather than an abandonment of Jewish community, was the sociologist Erving Goffman. Goffman was a Canadian Jew whose personal experiences with the criminal underworld, the acting profession, and mental illness, as well as anti-Jewish discrimination, shaped his influential work on the public performance of identity.[65] In 1963, Goffman published *Stigma*, a meditation on "the management of spoiled identity." Amid a sprawling host of stigmas that needed to be managed, including mental illness, prostitution, and homosexuality, Goffman included Jewishness. The management of Jewish identity, Goffman noted, might be an overt declaration of Jewish identity, as in the wearing of Star of David necklaces or dressing in Hasidic clothing, to preempt social disapproval or embarrassment.[66] But Goffman also noted, more circumspectly, that the "change in name and change in nose shape" exhibited by "ethnic minority groups" allowed the members of those groups "to restrict the way in which a known-about attribute obtrudes itself into the center of attention."[67]

With this guarded but undeniable reference to Jewish name changes and nose jobs, Goffman observed far more complexity in the act of name changing than many in the Jewish community acknowledged. He suggested that name changing was an example of "covering," an effort to hide a stigma that may not be visible to everyone (such as homosexuality or Jewishness) but that would be unpleasantly obtrusive if it were visible to all. By covering, Goffman explained, name changers could ensure that their stigmatized names did not become the center of attention. This would allow them control over how, or whether, to make their stigmatized identities known.[68] Their intention, he made clear, was not to pass and hide their stigma permanently. Although he defined "covering" as a practice distinct from the more familiar "passing," Goffman did acknowledge that the two practices were closely interrelated and that they might operate in tandem. The effort to make a stigma less discomfiting for coworkers or neighbors who knew about it (to cover the stigma) might hide the stigma entirely from someone who knew nothing (thereby allowing the individual to temporarily pass).[69]

Goffman's insight is borne out by hundreds of the petitions in New York City Civil Court. These petitioners, to a great extent, did not say anything at all about abandoning their Judaism, and indeed, at times, they insisted on the reverse. They did, however, say much about the obtrusiveness of Jewish names in their ordinary daily lives. Petitioners complained about the inability (or unwillingness) of employers, coworkers, and subordinates to spell and/or pronounce their names correctly. Many petitioners, such as the Liebowitz family in 1952, explained that their names were "difficult . . . to spell, pronounce, and understand."[70] Sometimes petitioners focused on the troubles of mail delivery; others talked about misunderstandings over the phone.[71] Harold and Florence Katzenson complained in 1947 that their name "caus[ed] confusion in mail and with telephone conversations. To avoid confusion, embarrassment, annoyance and inconvenience," they petitioned to change their name to Kenson.[72] And the Katzensons were not alone; many petitioners complained that they faced "annoyance" and "embarrassment" because of their names.[73] To be sure, some of this language about spelling and pronunciation, and even embarrassment, was formulaic legal language. Nonetheless, it did speak to the daily ways that names obtruded into Jews' daily lives and the ways that Jews hoped they could manage those obtrusions effectively. A name change allowed petitioners to go about their daily business without having their stigmatized names present troubles in every social and work interaction. Jewish names were conspicuous and drew attention to their possessors; they required individuals to think about those names daily as they managed complicated relationships with both Jews and non-Jews.

While a small minority of petitions do indicate a desire to pass socially and religiously, and another unknown subset of petitioners may have silently envisioned themselves as secular assimilators erasing their parochial ties, the petitions far more frequently suggested that Jews were covering: simply managing their stigmatized identities so they would cause less damage. Although Goffman does not address it, many of these Jews covered while maintaining their Jewish relationships and identities.

Unpublished letters to David Cohn offer insight into Jews' perception of name changing as a way to manage a complicated marketplace, rather than an abandonment of community. "I don't consider my new name a camouflage or an evasion," Beverly Winston wrote (after changing her name from Weinstein years earlier). She explained that she viewed her new name simply as a piece of acceptable clothing, like "a corset, shoulder pads, or a 'sincere' tie." "The process of presenting ourselves in the most attractive light possible," Winston insisted, "is as old as the world itself." "We really like Winston much better than Weinstein!" she exclaimed in her cover letter.[74] Other writers insisted that their former "Jewish" names were not actually Jewish but were instead Polish, German, or Russian and thus did not reflect their true Jewish identities. Mrs. Harry Snyderman emphasized the ways that Jews had borrowed and adapted their music, food, and names from the European cultures in which they had lived and suggested that it was foolish to withstand the discrimination she and her family and friends had experienced in applying for jobs and schooling solely to protect foreign names that had nothing to do with Jewish life.[75] These writers did not indicate alienation from the Jewish community but instead identified themselves wholeheartedly as Jews.

Contemporary sociological, journalistic, and literary descriptions of name changing in Jewish life in the postwar era echoed these testimonies. In a 1961 study of Jews in Minneapolis, *Children of the Gilded Ghetto*, the sociologists Judith R. Kramer and Seymour Leventman noted that at least one-quarter of upper- and middle-class second-generation Jews who belonged to the prestigious country club in town changed their surnames and gave their children Anglo-Saxon names in the hopes of avoiding the "negative evaluation . . . attached to names with a minority group background." The authors noted, however, that these naming patterns did not reflect wealthy Jews' passage out of the Jewish community.[76] Instead, they hoped to provide their children "a better future . . . with a potentially non-Jewish identity. This new identity may not be needed, but it is at least available for participating in non-Jewish circles or applying for jobs or club memberships from which Jews are excluded."[77] The goal for these middle- and upper-class Jews, according to Kramer and Leventman, was simply to manage Jewishness so that it did not interfere with mobility.

Other reports on name changing during this era were similar. In 1952, *Commentary* published a widely cited article, "Name Changing and What It Gets You," in which J. Alvin Kugelmass interviewed 25 men (and some of their wives) in the New York metropolitan region who had changed their names. Influenced by the discourse of self-hatred, Kugelmass described these name changers as pathetic souls, reporting that they all longed to return to "their old, comfortable names."[78] To his seeming surprise, however, Kugelmass's interviewees did not seem to have "passed" in any significant way: "in no case could I sense even the remotest inkling of a wish to abandon their Jewishness," Kugelmass reported, illustrating the cultural assumptions of the moment, even as he upended them. Indeed, the interviewees were eager to talk to Kugelmass and to prove that they were "still Jews," actively involved in their local synagogues and engaged in the Jewish community.[79] Kugelmass did note, however, that there had been "some impulse towards concealment of Jewishness," as all the men believed they had faced discrimination and hoped to overcome it: "it was obvious that they were seeking not so much to escape Jewishness completely as to live a dual existence in which their private lives would be Jewish but their exterior lives would be as smooth and even as they fancied the Gentiles."[80] Kugelmass's account illustrates Goffman's theory of covering at work among name-changing New York Jews in the postwar era.

And even popular fiction, with its didactic messages about self-hatred, nonetheless reflected the ways that name changing worked for many people as a cover for Jewish stigma, rather than an outright effort to pass into the Christian world. In *Home Is the Hunted*, a 1948 novel about a name changer who is exposed and learns to mend his ways, the author, Abraham Bernstein, draws a sharp distinction between the efforts of some Jews to pass altogether and the efforts of others simply to cover. The antihero of the story, Ted Cannaday, not only has legally changed his name from Cohen but also has made "careful preparations . . . to keep him[self] away from Jews, to train his facial expressions, his gestures, his diction, to meet and cultivate Christians."[81] He changes his name on all his school records and his birth certificate and then transfers to Columbia University: "Deliberately, he divested himself of all the friends he had known, and . . . gained Christians to substitute."[82] His efforts to pass are, however, foiled by newspaper casualty reports during the war that listed his mother's name as "Mrs. Rose Cohen, Sherman Ave., Bronx." Bernstein's negative portrait of Cannaday clearly fit the stereotype of the

Jew who was alienated from Jewishness and sought to escape the degradation of its racial markings.

But Bernstein's novel went on to portray a different kind of Jew engaged in a different kind of name changing. After Cannaday loses his job at a bigoted advertising agency, he gets a job at a Jewish firm, with Jewish clients and an owner whose name change did not reflect a desire to escape: "Why had Joe Goldberg changed his name to Joe Gould, if not for good and sufficient business reasons?" Cannaday muses to himself. "Nevertheless, they were shortchanged by a continuing loyalty to their background. They limited apostasy to a matter of nomenclature." The Goulds had not worked to obliterate their Jewish ties. They simply covered them to aid their business: "Everybody knew your identity but it was the accepted convention to pretend ignorance."[83] In the end, Cannaday is able to succeed by covering rather than passing: he uses his Jewish contacts to make his bigoted former employer hire him, and thus he triumphs within the non-Jewish world but still remains part of the Jewish world.

Other artists in the postwar era similarly noted the ways that new names were an open secret in the Jewish community, indeed inviting audiences to consider the contrast between a very public Jewish identity and a changed name. In 1964, for example, the comedian Lenny Bruce highlighted the artificiality of Jews' changed names, including his own. In his routine on the 1964 presidential candidate Barry Goldwater, Bruce lampooned Goldwater's Jewish name, outing him as a Jew not because of his last but because of his first name: "Forget 'Goldwater.' 'Barry?' 'Barry!' Are you kidding with that? Mogen David. Barry! Where is there one goy [non-Jew] with the name of Barry?"[84] The joke actually mirrored one that the comedian Rodney Dangerfield (born Jacob Cohen) had made at Bruce's own expense years earlier: "All you guys who try to get away from being Jewish by changing your last name always give the secret away by forgetting to change your *first* name. What kinda *goy* has a first name Lenny?"[85] And indeed, many Jews in the New York City name-change petitions, not simply famous ones, similarly changed their distinctive Jewish last names and kept their Jewish-sounding first names. Rather than seeing this as a mistake, as Dangerfield's joke suggests, it seems more likely that this practice reflects the complex realities of name changing as a form of covering, not passing. The first names might seem Jewish, but they did not necessarily obtrude into daily life the way a last name such as Goldstein might (they would not automatically disqualify you for a job, for example), and thus they did not need to be changed.

The rest of Bruce's routine on Goldwater offers more insight into the openness of name changing in Jewish life: "Not many Jews feel hostility towards Goldwater cause he is Jewish and changed his religion. See, *all* Jews did that. I'm Leonard Alfred Schneider, not Lenny Bruce. I'm Lenny Bruce legally, but it was a pain in the ass, man. A lot of dues. So dig. Goldwater lives in Arizona. He did a switch, man. He says, 'Frig it. I'll keep my name and I'll change my religion.' That was his bit."[86] Bruce here addresses the complex realities of name changing in a number of ways. On the most basic level, he acknowledges his own name change, making it clear that name changing did not always entail passing or hiding. More significantly, he acknowledges the prevalence and acceptability of name changing in the Jewish community—and the hypocrisy of that stance. All Jews, of course, did not change their religion and keep their names; the joke lies in the fact that it was precisely the other way around. Jews perceived conversion to Christianity as the ultimate apostasy, while high rates of name changing were an open secret in the Jewish community. Far from offering escape, artists such as Bruce pointed out, name changing frequently enmeshed Jews further into the Jewish world.

Name changing became such an open and explicit part of postwar American Jewish life that large numbers of non-name-changers were affected in some way by the phenomenon: if they did not change their names themselves, they frequently knew someone who had or faced questions from friends or relatives asking why they had not. The editors of *Commentary* introduced Kugelmass's piece on "name changing—and what it gets you" with a knowing nod to the practice's widespread nature: "We all know someone who has grown tired of his 'outlandish' and 'Jewish' surname and tried to make life easier by shortening or 'Americanizing' it." They noted too that Kugelmass's article was "stimulated ʰʸ questions suffered by him as to why he did not do something about ₌is own 'cumbersome handle.'"[87] The same communal pressure was recounted in 1985 by Charles Silberman, who recalled, "as if it were yesterday, a well-to-do aunt taking my brother and me aside without our parents' knowledge to urge us to abandon the name Silberman for one more likely to assist our rise out of genteel poverty. She was enraged when we demurred."[88] Indeed, in 1950, the psychologists Gerhart Saenger and Norma Gordon found that virtually all of their 181 Jewish survey respondents from the Bronx knew someone who had changed their name.

Name changing may have been an open part of New York Jewish communal life, but that does not mean that all Jews approved of this behavior. Indeed, many thought name changing was deeply shameful. In the Saenger-Gordon study, for example, about half of the Jews surveyed said they believed name changers had acted out of economic necessity, while the other half called name changing "a shame" and a reflection of "a lack of pride."[89] The articles by Alvin Kugelmass and Anonymous similarly reflected this communal tension. Anonymous, as already noted, described the anger and disappointment among his friends and family members when he and his brother changed their names, while Kugelmass reported that his 25 name-changing subjects experienced "frosty and curious stares by many of the tribe who bear the old name."[90] The historian Daniel Horowitz remembered how much his father resented people who changed their names in the 1940s and 1950s: "My dentist was William Lawrence, nee Levine. Then the haberdasher Fenn-Feinstein. . . . They lived two doors down. Or our backyard neighbor—Gant . . . formerly Gantmacher."[91] And Sherwin Nuland remembered a gym teacher, Julius Beckenstein, who proudly retained his own Jewish name and "gleefully poke[d] fun" of Nuland's new name, calling him "Narvell" and pretending he could not remember the new "goyish"-sounding name.[92] Many Jews may have disapproved of name changing, choosing to isolate or humiliate name changers, but it is important to see how open this conversation was. Jews debated name changing on the very public stage of mainstream media but also in very personal, intimate arenas: in schools, in neighborhoods, and at work in the postwar era.

Petitions, sociological reports, unpublished and published correspondence, and fiction of the postwar era all suggest that name changing, for the most part, was an open secret in New York Jewish life. Jews were not forced to hide when they changed their names, as were light-skinned African Americans who sought to pass as white. Instead, Jewish name changing was an openly acknowledged popular activity with which almost all Jews had at least some familiarity. Although a minority of Jews did seek to convert or assimilate into a secular intellectual world, the majority of New York Jews sought to change their names together with family members and frequently remained an integral part of the Jewish community.

If the New York Jewish community was deeply affected by the name changing taking place within its midst, so were American Jews throughout the country who responded to the increasing and changing representations of name changing in mainstream American fiction and film. Before the war, mainstream magazines and books portrayed name changing as the normal striving of all second-generation southern and eastern Europeans to become American. Even when characters were obviously Jewish, their name changing was portrayed as a generational struggle with fathers and mothers, not a political battle with antisemitic discrimination. After the war, however, that image changed: the dominant mainstream image became that of the victimized Jew seeking to escape antisemitism. During the immediate postwar era, roughly between 1945 and 1949, in particular, portraits of desperate, confused, and self-loathing Jewish men and women in their 20s and 30s facing social exclusion and economic discrimination were everywhere. At the height of the name-changing phenomenon in New York City, stigmatized Jewish names, indeterminate Jewish names, and Jewish name changers were at the heart of a national conversation about American antisemitism and fluid Jewish identity.

The Anonymous–David Cohn debate in *Atlantic Monthly* offers us evidence of the charged portrait of name changing that appeared in mainstream culture in the postwar years. Anonymous, of course, described in detail the antisemitism that legitimated his decision to change his name, while Cohn scoffed at the notion of antisemitism, suggesting that only shallow social climbers—most of them women—cared about discrimination in country clubs.

In June 1947, *Atlantic Monthly* published four letters on the Anonymous-Cohn debate, indicating the public fascination with this subject matter. Perhaps unsurprisingly, three of the four letters supported Cohn over Anonymous, endorsing the southern writer's courage, pride, and respect for his religion and heritage, while painting Anonymous as a self-hating Jew and implicitly questioning the antisemitism he had detailed. Paula Freedman of Los Angeles made clear that she had abandoned an Irish name for her present Jewish-sounding name when she married: "And I must say that I am unaware of a single disadvantage it has caused me," she wrote proudly, calling name changers "immature." Martha Murphy Stine of North Vernon, Indiana, offered "sympathy" for Anonymous but regretted his "resentment of his ancestry" and "elementary psychology." And Theresa S. Fitzpatrick of Newport, Rhode Island, called Cohn's essay "admirable" but took him to task for having used her city, Newport, as an example of snobbish antisemitism; she ignored entirely the real problem of antisemitic discrimination in public accommodations, in Newport or elsewhere.[93] None of these writers acknowledged the existence of American antisemitism or Anonymous's strategic response to discrimination.

The most powerful letter to the editor, however, came from New Yorker George N. Caylor, who described in detail the antisemitism he and his family had experienced in school, in employment agencies, and at hotel reservation desks, until he and his wife changed their names. "Changing my name has somewhat helped to lessen the practice of antisemitism. Just the mention of my previous name was sufficient to bring it to the surface. Now I live the life of the average undiscriminated-against mortal, and that's all I ask of life."[94] Caylor's personal, pained account made clear not only how deeply some Jews felt themselves limited and hampered by hatred in the years after the war but also how these Jews understood name changing as a strategic response to hatred. Moreover, *Atlantic Monthly*, a mainstream magazine read by upper-middle-class Americans of many different ethnic backgrounds, chose to publicize linkages between name changing and antisemitism.

In 1948, when *Reader's Digest* republished the debate between Anonymous and David Cohn, the magazine further validated the connections between name changing and antisemitism and placed them before an even broader readership. Although it might seem surprising that Jewish name changing would hold any interest for the traditionally conservative, white, midwestern readers of the *Digest*, in fact, it was probably the focus on antisemitism that attracted the magazine. For several years, the founders of the *Digest*, DeWitt and Lila Acheson Wallace, had faced considerable criticism for antisemitism from other media institutions. In 1945, the *New Yorker* published a five-part series that attacked the *Digest* for its simplistic discussion of complicated material and its willingness to present antisemitism (and antiblack racism) as a reasonable and defensible position.[95] The Anonymous-Cohn debate offered the Wallaces a chance to publish a piece on American antisemitism, allowing one Jew to voice his frustrations with hatred and exclusion, thus defusing arguments that the magazine itself was a voice for racism. At the same time, however, the debate offered the soothing voice of another Jew who insisted that it was only social climbers who might care about discrimination and, ultimately, that America was a bountiful and fair land: a message that the *Digest*'s readers surely would have wanted to hear. The fact that *Reader's Digest* may have republished this debate over Jewish name changing as a way both to salvage its reputation and to soothe its readers further suggests that name changing and antisemitism had become linked for the general American public after World War II.

In mainstream fiction during this era, both Jewish and non-Jewish writers consistently put Jewish name changing motivated by antisemitism at the heart of their stories. In 1948, *Jewish Book Annual* commented that it had become a "gimmick" for novelists to describe non-Jews passing for Jews, as in Arthur Miller's *Focus* and Laura Z. Hobson's *Gentleman's Agreement*, and then highlighted several books that turned the gimmick on its head by describing Jewish efforts to pass as non-Jewish by changing their names, such as Abraham Bernstein's *Home Is the Hunted* and Merle Miller's *That Winter*.[96] The immediate postwar years saw many other depictions of name changers from writers such as Jo Sinclair, Joseph Wechsberg, Burke Davis, Martha Gellhorn, and Henry Berkowitz; later in the 1950s, literary stars such as Bernard Malamud and Herman Wouk produced their own stories about name changing.[97]

These multiplying fictional representations of name changers typically linked name changing to the problem of self-hating Jews seeking to escape antisemitism and/or the Jewish community. As noted earlier, almost all of these fictional portraits were didactic, reflecting a communal distaste for name changers, as well as communal anxieties that Jews who changed their names were abandoning and betraying the Jewish community. Fictional name changers in the 1940s and 1950s were almost always exposed as pathetic and typically returned to the Jewish fold by the end of the story.

These cautionary tales did reflect, however, the very real social experiences of both the texts' authors and their readers. Some stories offered specific descriptions of legal name-change documents, rather than simply shorthanded descriptions of a new name, suggesting authors' and readers' acquaintance with the legal process itself. In *That Winter*, for example, Lewis Colinsky, who has changed his name to Cole because of the significant antisemitism he faces, is visited by his mother, who takes a "small square of paper" from her purse and hands it to the narrator, Lew's friend: "It was the legal notice of Lew's change of name."[98] In Abraham Bernstein's *Home Is the Hunted*, the name changer Ted Cannaday parodies the vague legal language on name-change petitions: "the euphemism for fear and terror had been denominated business reasons, or it's easier to get a job, or it's more American, but never fear of the *pogromchiks*, or terror of relapsing to the ghetto again. The reasons were sunny and optimistic and easily conveyed to the magistrate who made the change legal."[99] Even Lenny Bruce's Goldwater bit highlighted for audiences the money and trouble that his legal name change had cost him: "It was a pain in the ass, man. A lot of dues."[100]

If these texts offered literal descriptions of the complicated social reality of Jewish name changing in the postwar era, they also offered figurative portraits of liminal, uncertain, and constantly changing Jewish identity. These images reflected the anxieties that the phenomenon of name changing provoked for Jews in the years after World War II, especially the years between 1945 and 1949.

Perhaps the most famous of these unstable fictional representations was Laura Z. Hobson's best-selling 1947 novel *Gentleman's Agreement* and the Oscar-winning film version produced in 1948. The story of a Gentile reporter, Philip Schuyler Green, who poses as a Jew for six months to expose antisemitism, *Gentleman's Agreement* broke taboos by detailing the many varieties of genteel antisemitism, including employment and housing discrimination, exclusion from social accommodations, and social ridicule and isolation. Yet both the novel and the film offer a curious and ambivalent portrait of names and name changing—one that is scornful of name changing, to be sure, but one that also uses names and name changing to symbolize the possibility that boundaries between Jew and non-Jew could be transgressed and to question the meaning of those boundaries.

On the one hand, Phil Green's secretary, Elaine Wales, a self-hating Jew who changed her name from Estelle Walovsky to get her job, is clearly framed as a negative character. She fears that any change to her firm's discriminatory policy will harm her own privileged position, and she uses antisemitic slurs to get her points across: "If they just get one wrong one in, it'll come out of *us*," she confides in Phil. "Don't you hate being the fall guy for the kikey ones?"[101] Her inauthentic self-hatred is juxtaposed with the virile, authentic pride of Phil's friend Dave Goldman, a Jew who does not back down from a fight and who bears a distinctive Jewish name (and is played by the Jewish actor John Garfield in the film version). Yet, at the same time that the novel and film clearly condemn Miss Wales and champion Dave, Phil Green's own ease in becoming a Jew symbolizes the liminal status and problematic nature of Jewishness, with his name at the heart of the problem. Phil Green could transcend the boundaries of Jewishness not just because he could "look Jewish," as some scholars have noted, but also because his name could "sound Jewish": "his name wasn't Jewish—well, Phil Green might be anything; he'd skip the Schuyler and not have to bother with assumed names."[102] The book and film play with the possibilities of Phil's indeterminate name, something that could easily have been changed from a distinctive Jewish name. In the film, Phil sends job inquiries to the same employers as both "Green" and "Greenberg" to see what the response will be, and he encounters hostility from his janitor when he writes both Green and Greenberg on his mailbox. In the novel, Phil sends inquiries to Miami Beach hotels, identifying himself as Green but sometimes also mentioning his cousin "Capt. Joseph Greenberg"—a clear suggestion that Green might be a changed name. And when Elaine Wales finds out that he is Jewish, she asks him if he changed his name, highlighting the commonality of the practice, as well as the flexible, nondistinctive, and indeterminate nature of his name: "If your name was Irving Green or Saul, it wouldn't have worked this way."[103] Green's indeterminate name marks *both* his ability to be a Jew *and* his acceptance in the Gentile world.

The specter of name changing, from Schuyler to Phil or from Greenberg to Green, confuses the categories of *Gentleman's Agreement* at the same time that it helps to construct them by setting up a contrast between Elaine Wales and Dave Goldman. In the film, a name changer could be a Gentile masquerading only partially as a Jew (Green lets some people in on his secret, and he is done in six weeks) or a Jew whose masquerade as a Gentile is only partial and incomplete (like Miss Wales, who lets another Jew, Green, in on her secret). If Hobson indicts name changers as transgressors of Jewish boundaries, she also portrays name changing as a very common, very complicated act that did not necessarily entail permanent transition from Jew to Gentile.

The fact that some of the most prominent figures associated with the film and the book, including Hobson herself, as well as the actors John Garfield and June Havoc, had changed their own names magnified the questions about Jewish identity that the film posed. For example, although June Havoc was not Jewish, her original name, Hovick, became part of a national conversation about Jewish changed names in 1947, right after the release of *Gentleman's Agreement*. After Havoc signed a petition opposing the House Un-American Activities Committee, Senator John Rankin targeted her in a famously antisemitic, anticommunist speech that highlighted the changed names of Jewish actors, such as Danny Kaye and Edward G. Robinson.

> They sent this petition to Congress and I want to read you some of the names. One of the names is June Havoc. We found that her real name is June Hovick. Another is Danny Kaye, and we found that his real name was David Daniel Kaminsky. . . . There is one who calls himself Edward Robinson. His real name is Emmanuel Goldenberg. . . . There are others too numerous to mention. They are attacking the Committee for doing its duty to protect this country and save the American people from the horrible fate the Communists have meted out to the unfortunate Christian people of Europe.

Rankin thus used changed names to equate Havoc (and other movie stars) with both the stigma of Jewishness and radicalism, indeed implying that the two were one and the same.[104]

Laura Z. Hobson's career was filled with ambivalence over her own Jewish name and identity. The child of a prominent Jewish socialist, Michael Zametkin, Hobson used her mother's maiden name, Keane, when searching for jobs as a young woman and then used her ex-husband's name when she wrote *Gentleman's Agreement*. At the same time, however, in her memoirs, Hobson writes that she always told potential employers that her middle name was Russian and Jewish before she got the job: "The Z is for Zametkin, my maiden name, and I have clung to it through all my years because it held my identity intact before that Anglo-Saxon married name of Hobson," she began her 1983 memoir, *Laura Z: A Life*.[105] Hobson's ambivalence over her own name, and indeed over Jewish names in general, runs as a theme throughout her memoirs and her earlier works.[106] In the second volume of *Laura Z*, Hobson offers a compelling description of an incident at the *Gentleman's Agreement* premiere, when her friend Dorothy Massey persistently called John Garfield by his original name, "Julie Garfinkle." "You might as well call him Julie Jewboy," Hobson angrily charged, ending their years-long friendship.[107] In Hobson's perception, Jewish names were antisemitic slurs, social and economic burdens, markers of Jewish pride, and flexible identities that could be adopted or shorn—all at the same time.

Given Hobson's preoccupations with Jewish names and changed names, and indeed given larger cultural anxiety and scrutiny regarding Jewish changed names, as in the Rankin speech, it is not surprising that *Gentleman's Agreement* highlighted names as symbols of Jewish difference, while at the same time emptying those symbols of content and playing with them as possibilities for transgression as well. In the end, to be sure, both the book and the film clearly insisted that Jewishness was a fixed category—you could "look Jewish" and have a "Jewish name." At the same time, however, both threw doubt on the meaning of that category, by highlighting men and women who slipped between the boundaries of Jew and non-Jew (as creators, characters, and performers), aided to a good extent by indeterminate linguistic markers. The anxieties surrounding name changing thus helped to shape cultural questions surrounding Jews' problematic racial and ethnic status in years after World War II.

Jewish name changing did not end with World War II. Indeed, it reached some of its greatest heights in the years right after the war, as Jews faced continuing antisemitic restrictions in employment and education that declined but still lingered throughout the 1950s and even through the early 1960s. Although Jewish communal leaders reacted fearfully and angrily to name changing, seeing it as self-hatred and abandonment of the Jewish people, their anxieties were probably misplaced. Jews who changed their names did not, for the most part, disappear from the Jewish community but instead used their new names to manage a complicated new economic and social world. And even as American Jewish artists created unrealistic portraits of pathetic name changers that mirrored larger communal anxieties over self-hatred, they also illustrated the very real antisemitism Jews faced, the legal steps Jews took to overcome that antisemitism, and the unclear racial status that Jews inhabited during this era.

Clearly name changing had a profound cultural and social impact on the Jewish community in New York (and throughout the nation) in the two decades after World War II. In chapter 4, we will see the legal and political impact of name changing on New York and the nation during the same time period. During these two decades, the cultural image of a liminal Jew with an indeterminate racial status, facing antisemitism and struggling to achieve upward mobility, also became a legal and political problem that American Jewish organizations sought to address through legislative, judicial, and administrative remedies.

4

"Have You Been Known by Another Name?"

Name Changing and the Politics of Postwar Civil Rights Legislation

In February 1948, *Congress Weekly*, the newsletter of the American Jewish Congress, featured a scathing piece ridiculing the anonymous *Atlantic Monthly* testimonial "I Changed My Name," which had created so much controversy months earlier. In the *Congress Weekly* piece, the managing editor, Shlomo Katz, derided Anonymous—the New Yorker who had proudly defended his decision to evade antisemitism with a new name—for his unwillingness to publish that name. "Why didn't you use it? . . . Were you ashamed of it?" Katz asked caustically.[1] Throughout his piece, Katz, a member of the most liberal and powerful Jewish civil rights organization of the era, sharply criticized the limitations of Anonymous's struggle against American antisemitism.

While David Cohn, a southern Jew, had criticized Anonymous by insisting that the United States was the "kindliest of countries" for Jews, as evidenced by his own friendship with, and membership in, the liberal white elite in Greenville, Mississippi, Katz validated the existence of antisemitism but insisted that it was closely associated with racism against American blacks.[2] The civil rights activist lashed out at Anonymous's complacent insistence that he had joined "the human race" and his willingness to abandon both oppressed blacks and Jews in the hopes of self-advancement. When confronted with bigots who admitted their hatred of "Jews, Negroes, Italians, etc.," Katz pointed out, Anonymous could not protest, for fear of giving himself away: "Willy-nilly you have to grin and approve their fascist obscenities. You are not confusing the enemy, as you claim; you have joined him."[3]

Katz's angry rebuttal to "I Changed My Name," published in a major civil rights newsletter, illustrates how name changing affected not only American Jewish culture and social relationships but also the community's legal and political activism. As Jewish communal agencies organized after World War II to battle discrimination in housing, employment, and education, they operated in a community that had been shaped by three decades of name changing. Jewish civil rights activists who were developing legal strategies to battle discrimination against minorities were acutely aware of the prevalence of name changing among their friends, family members, neighbors, and community members. Questions about name changing came to pervade the push for early civil rights legislation in New York, as well as the legislation itself. Name changing even became central to civil rights jurisprudence in the 1940s and 1950s.

Legal efforts to ban discrimination in states such as New York and New Jersey between 1945 and 1964 focused on the bureaucratic machinery of middle-class life: the employment agency and university applications that had been instituted in the 1910s and 1920s, to a large extent, in order to ferret out and eliminate Jewish candidates. The three most prominent Jewish civil rights organizations in the country—the American Jewish Committee (AJC), the American Jewish Congress (AJCong), and the B'nai B'rith Anti-Defamation League (ADL)—attacked questions about names and name changing in job and college application forms and worked to eliminate them during this early civil rights era. By the 1950s, name changing emerged as a central element in civil rights legislation and administration and in judicial decisions regarding discrimination.

At the same time, civil rights activists' strategies ironically mirrored those of name changers themselves. Layers of bureaucracy over the preceding five decades—including application questions about names—had racialized Jews; and thus the Jewish struggle for civil rights made one of its central goals removing those bureaucratic racial markers and making Jews racially unmarked to the dominant society. To be sure, civil rights activists such as Shlomo Katz might have viewed name changers as traitors or as passive victims, but AJCong lawyers ultimately defended name changers' right to evade detection as Jews when seeking jobs or education. Civil rights lawyers and activists pursued legislation that mirrored name changers' goals and even strategies. If Jewish name changers erased their racial markers privately, as individuals and as families, Jewish civil rights activists sought to erase racial markers for all Jews in public, political, and legal settings.

In the end, civil rights activism contributed to the decline of Jewish name changing as a phenomenon. By successfully making illegal any questions about religion, nationality, or names on employment and college applications, organizations such as the American Jewish Congress unintentionally helped to make Jews more unproblematic members of the white middle class, able to proceed through life unmarked by racial stigma, deploying their ethnicity only as they chose. As civil rights legislation made it easier for the entire Jewish community to move through the world unmarked by their racial background, Jewish name changing became less necessary as an individual or family strategy. Jews thus innovated new means of using the state during the postwar era; while ordinary Jews had previously transformed their individual and familial racial identities through the legal mechanisms of name-change petitions, Jewish activists in the 1940s and 1950s used state legislative, executive, and judicial systems to effect civil rights reform and, by doing so, inadvertently reshaped the Jewish community's racial identity as a whole.

In chapter 1, we noted that schools and employers imposed antisemitic limitations on Jews' rise in the middle class during the interwar years. Here we will take a closer look at the origins and structure of those limitations. In the early years of the 20th century, schools, businesses, and professions innovated bureaucratic procedures and mechanisms that made Jews a race apart. One of the central mechanisms was the college application form. In 1917, Columbia University established the modern college application form. Before that, the college, like other institutions of higher education, admitted students primarily on the basis of their ability to pass the preparatory curriculum offered by feeder secondary schools. There was no elaborate application process. Students who met the academic requirements were admitted on the basis of a brief form asking them to list their name, birthdate and place, and previous schooling (see figure 4.1).[4] Indeed, Columbia, hoping to identify the most qualified students for admission to its undergraduate schools and thus for preparation for its graduate schools, had actually made it easier for graduates of public secondary schools to be admitted in 1909 by standardizing examinations and admissions requirements. These standards encouraged Jewish immigrants and their children in the New York City public schools to enter Columbia in large numbers, an unexpected and unwelcome prospect for the school's president, Nicholas Murray Butler. By 1915, a large proportion of Columbia undergraduates, roughly 40 percent, were either Jewish immigrants or their children. Concerned

APPLICATION FOR ADMISSION   **Columbia University**   COLUMBIA COLLEGE
ADVANCED STANDING

Name _____   (Last Name)   (First Name)   (Middle Name)   Date _____

N. Y. City (or local) address _____

Permanent residence (Street, town, state) _____

Name and address of nearest relative (parent or guardian if applicant is a minor) _____

Candidate for the degree of _____   Date of birth _____   Place of birth _____

Previous training:

Name of Institution	Location	Dates of Attendance	Degree or Diploma and Year received
Secondary Schools			
Colleges			
Graduate and Professional Schools			

Have you been a student of Columbia University previously? _____ If so, indicate below under which Faculty or School you were then registered, and give dates of attendance: (e.g. Journalism 1912-13, 1913-14. Summer Session 1911, 1912.)

Remarks _____

FILL OUT AND FORWARD TO DIRECTOR OF ADMISSIONS, COLUMBIA UNIVERSITY.

Figure 4.1. Applicants who sought to enter Columbia College with advanced standing before 1917 only had to fill out a brief application form, which requested little biographical or personal data beyond their name, address, previous schooling, and grades. Application for Admission, Columbia College, Advanced Standing, n.d., folder 3, box 330, "Historical Subject Files Collection," University Archives, Rare Book & Manuscript Library, Columbia University in the City of New York.

administrators, such as the undergraduate Columbia College dean Frederick Keppel, then began to consider how they might stem this influx to solve their Jewish "problem."[5]

Keppel and other university administrators contemplated geographic quotas, residential requirements, and limited scholarship programs to limit the numbers of New York Jews entering the college, but in the end, they settled on detailed application forms (commonly called "application blanks" at the time) with exacting criteria as the most promising instrument for limiting Jewish enrollment.[6] The new 1917 forms included multiple questions that might be grouped into one of two categories. Some questions clearly sought to determine candidates' "character," a purposely nebulous word that summed up native-born, elite Americans' discomfort with Jews. Jews were understood to be "greasy grinds," who studied instead of socializing, and the new proliferation of application questions about extracurricular activities, sports interests, or leadership positions were designed to ferret out the lack of "character" that Jews supposedly displayed. The second category of questions was genealogical, including queries into a candidate's religious affiliation, as well as questions about his father's name, place of birth, and occupation. They also asked for a photograph, three letters of recommendation, and a personal interview.[7] The discriminatory nature of these new, invasive questions was immediately apparent to students at Columbia, and they gathered petitions to oppose them—unsuccessfully.[8]

Several years later, Harvard began publicly and controversially debating the need to impose a formal quota against Jews. Although the faculty ultimately voted against a formal quota, the Harvard administration quietly imposed an informal one and used extensive applications, much like the one pioneered by Columbia, to help them administer it. This initiative substantially limited the number of Jews admitted to Harvard, keeping the percentage of Jews in the undergraduate college at roughly 10–16 percent by the late 1920s, down from over 21 percent at the beginning of the decade.[9]

Significantly, names were one of the key means of identifying and weeding out Jewish applicants on both Columbia's and Harvard's application forms. By 1931, the application form at Columbia had grown to eight pages, and it requested not only a candidate's father's name but also the candidate's mother's maiden name. It also included the question, "Have you been known by another name or used any variations of your name?"[10] In the fall of 1922, when Harvard quietly began debating quotas on Jewish students, its application form began asking, "Maiden Name of Mother?" and "What change, if any, has been made since birth in your own name or that of your father? (Explain fully)"[11] (see figure 4.2). Both institutions were clearly familiar with the practice of Jewish name changing and sought to use these questions to identify and eliminate Jewish candidates. Indeed in 1922, Harvard had commissioned a statistical study on Jews at Harvard that specifically addressed the significant numbers of changed names among Jewish students and the need to use mothers' maiden names to identify them as Jews.[12] At both Columbia and Harvard, these new extensive application forms allowed administrators to cut their Jewish populations substantially; at Columbia, Jews dipped from 40 percent of the entering class before World War I to 21 percent in 1921.[13] By the 1940s, discriminatory application blanks had spread to colleges throughout the country.

It is worth looking more closely at the questions designed to ferret out Jews. Questions about religious affiliation could be blatant ("What denomination are you?"), but they could also be indirect ("Of what clubs, social or church organizations are you a member?") The same was true of questions about nationality: candidates could be asked whether they were American citizens, but they could also be asked for parents' birthplace or occupation. A birthplace in Russia, Romania, or Poland could be a telling sign of Jewishness, as could a father who worked in the garment industry or in a small family grocery store. Photographs were used to examine potential visible racial markings, such as noses and hair, while personal interviews would expose not just these visual markings but accents, manners of speech, and styles of dress that were similarly seen as essential in identifying Jews. (Photographs and interviews could also, of course, be used to discriminate against African Americans and other people of color.) Questions about names and name changing were just as telling: a Jewish name itself would automatically expose candidates' Jewish identity, administrators assumed, so they designed questions that would sniff out the name changing they assumed candidates had already undergone. They asked whether candidates had changed their own names, whether fathers had changed their names; they asked what mothers' and wives' maiden names were; and they sometimes

HARVARD COLLEGE

Received by
COMMITTEE ON ADMISSION APPLICATION FOR ADMISSION
MAY 8 1935 — *To be filled out in the candidate's own handwriting (not typewritten)*
AND MAILED TO THE COMMITTEE ON ADMISSION

17 University Hall, Cambridge, Massachusetts, *before May 1*

1. Legal name in full *Kennedy* *John* *Fitzgerald*
   Last Name · First Name · Middle Name

2. Home address in full *294 Pondfield Rd., Bronxville, New York*

3. Place of birth *Brookline, Mass.* Date of birth *May 29, 1917*

4. (a) Father's name in full *Joseph Patrick Kennedy* Living or Deceased? *Living*

   (b) Where and when was your father born? *Winthrop*

   (c) If father was not born in America, has he been naturalized? _____

   (d) Father's occupation? *Chairman Securities and Exchange Comission*

   (e) If father graduated from college, state where and when *Harvard 1912*

   (f) Mother's maiden name in full *Rose Fitzgerald* Living or Deceased? *Living*

   (g) If mother graduated from college, state where and when _____

5. What schools or colleges have you attended during the past four years? Give dates of entering and leaving each school and name of principal or headmaster in each case.
   The Choate School for the last four years
   Mr. George St. John

6. If you have left school, state exactly how you have been occupied since leaving. If you have been working, give names and addresses of all employers.

7. Have you ever been dismissed or excluded from any school or college? If so, give full particulars.
   No

8. If you have already taken examinations for admission, give the date or dates of these examinations and subjects taken. (September examinations cannot be counted.) If you have not already sent your Board certificates to the Harvard Committee on Admission, you should enclose them with this application.
   I took examinations in 1933 in French Cor
   Latin Cor, Algebra — Passed them and have six credits but
   am now going new plan

Figure 4.2. This is the first page of John F. Kennedy's three-page application to Harvard College in 1935. The application form asks numerous biographical and personal questions, including the maiden name of his mother. Pre-enrollment material, 1935–1936, Harvard Records, Harvard, Personal Papers, Papers of John F. Kennedy, accessed February 26, 2018, https://www.jfklibrary.org/.

asked for grandparents' names as well—any of those names might expose a Jewish background. All of these questions—both those designed to ascertain "character" and those focused on genealogy—were unnecessary for any reason other than to determine the racial background of candidates, particularly Jews.

Discriminatory applications emerged in blue- and white-collar industries at roughly the same time they emerged in education. Using the contemporary scientific literature on race, experts in scientific management began elaborating racial hierarchies for employers to embrace and use in their hiring practices at the turn of the 20th century. Industrial magazines featured lengthy rationales for racial discrimination, as well as guides to hiring founded on firm beliefs in racial difference.[14] Discriminatory application forms with questions about race and religion began appearing as stock features in the industrial world. Employers might go to a magazine or stationery store to find a standard application form that featured discriminatory questions, such as "Maiden Name?" or "Church Affiliation?"[15] More overtly, help-wanted advertisements that specified "Christians only" and directions to employment agencies insisting that no Jews be sent for positions added further layers to the bureaucratic gauntlet Jews faced in finding jobs. And the interviewing process itself further weeded out any undesirable applicants, as memorably described in Arthur Miller's 1945 novel *Focus*: "Did you give this Miss Kapp a personal interview?" Lawrence Newman's boss, Mr. Gargan, asked him. Newman, the personnel manager who prided himself on his ability to identify Jews with intangible markers such as clothing, hair, and demeanor, insisted, "I always give everybody a personal interview," "Then you can't be seeing me clearly now," Gargan replied angrily, insisting on Miss Kapp's "obvious" unsuitability for the position.[16]

The same discriminatory application process emerged in the middle-class professional world at roughly the same time. The legal profession was particularly notorious in this regard. White, native-born, Anglo-Saxon, Protestant lawyers reeled at the demographic changes in their profession as Jewish and Italian immigrants pursued the study of law to aid their communities and boost their social status in the late 19th and early 20th centuries. In New York City, for example, Jewish lawyers represented fully 80 percent of new admissions to the bar between 1930 and 1934.[17] Responding to these enormous demographic changes, the legal establishment worked to establish a discriminatory two-tiered legal system that separated immigrant "ambulance chasers" from native-born elite corporate lawyers. The new system also wielded the ideal of "character" as a weapon against struggling immigrant lawyers who needed to advertise their services and charge contingent fees.[18]

Names were a prominent feature of the legal profession's genealogical application questions, as well as the profession's concern for "character." Beginning in the 1910s, questions about social background became standard on applications to practice law in states such as New York, Illinois, and Pennsylvania.[19] In the 1920s, the New York State Department of Education began to look into name changing among students at the NYU School of Law, suggesting that political officials identified name changing as an undesirable practice of immigrant, particularly Jewish, students.[20] By the 1940s, over 50 percent of state applications to practice law throughout the nation asked if applicants had changed their names.[21] As more immigrant, and Jewish, candidates entered law school, elite, native-born lawyers sought to use the bureaucracy of the application process to limit the demographic change to the profession.

It is important to note that these questions in the academy, the workforce, and the professions did not simply function by excluding Jews from employment or education. They actually helped to *make* Jews an undesirable racial group. To be sure, Jews were treated as white men and women in the political and civic life of the country during this era; their right to naturalize as citizens or vote in elections, for example, was never questioned. However, the layers of questions that schools and employers asked applicants in the first half of the 20th century formed a bureaucratic gauntlet that limited Jews' lives and shaped their identities. Those questions became racialized markers that Jews bore every time they applied for education or employment from the 1920s through the 1950s. Whether the questions were about religion ("What is your pastor's name?") or national origins ("Where was your father born?") or name ("Have you ever changed your surname?"), they ultimately made Jewishness into an unavoidable racial category. The specter of the racially undesirable Jewish applicant—the greasy grind, the flashy secretary, and the ambulance chaser—formed the subtext of all the questions, and that specter haunted all Jews seeking employment, education, and middle-class mobility throughout this era. Certainly, these bureaucratic questions were not the sole factors that racialized Jews in midcentury America; they were, however, crucial elements of the American middle-class world that structured American Jewish racial identity and economic opportunity.[22]

Since names and name changing formed an important part of the bureaucracy that racialized Jews, it is not surprising that name changing played a role in Jewish organizations' efforts to dismantle that bureaucracy. Discriminatory applications infuriated and energized Jewish civil rights activists in the post–World War II era, encouraging them to focus on bureaucracy as a major source of racism and even to highlight questions about names and name changing as a particularly oppressive element of that bureaucracy. The impact of name changing on Jews was evident in the 1940s and 1950s: first, in the push for civil rights legislation, then in the administration of civil rights laws, and later in the judicial decisions that interpreted those laws.

Liberal groups pushed immediately after the war for comprehensive civil rights laws on both the federal and state levels, after having achieved domestic successes during World War II with the Fair Employment Practices Committee (FEPC), designed to stop discrimination in the defense industry in 1941. New York was the first state to be targeted in the waning years of the war and the first state to successfully pass effective antidiscrimination bills: first the 1945 Law Against Discrimination, which outlawed discrimination in employment, and then the 1948 Fair Educational Practices Law, which outlawed discrimination in higher education. Both became models for other states that passed antidiscrimination laws in the 20 years leading up to the federal passage of the Civil Rights Act of 1964.[23]

Jewish groups were active, and indeed crucial, members in these battles for civil rights legislation. At the end of World War II, the AJ-Cong established a Commission on Law and Social Action (CLSA) to pursue a strategy of legal activism against discrimination. Led by the lawyers Will Maslow and Joseph B. Robison and directed by the chief consultant Alexander Pekelis, the CLSA wrote model antidiscrimination bills, lobbied legislatures and organized public support for civil rights bills, and brought complaints of discrimination to civil rights commissioners.[24] The AJC and ADL, meanwhile, pursued different strategies that focused on research into the dynamics of prejudice and tolerance

Figure 4.3. This 1946 graphic illustrates the American Jewish Congress's concern with discriminatory application blanks as it lobbied for civil rights legislation in New York. J. X. Cohen, *Who Discriminates and How?* (New York: American Jewish Congress, 1946), 24.

education. Researchers at both the AJC and ADL compiled data on discrimination in schools, employment agencies, social clubs, hotels, and real estate agencies that were fundamental to making the public case for civil rights legislation in the 1940s and 1950s. All three organizations made the battle against discrimination their primary objective in the years after World War II, joining together with a host of activist groups that included the National Association for the Advancement of Colored People (NAACP), the Japanese American Citizens League (JACL), and the League of United Latin American Citizens (LULAC).[25] And in all of the work that Jewish organizations did in these coalitions, they put discriminatory application blanks—the instruments that schools and employers used to segregate and discriminate against Jews for years—at the front and center of their efforts.

During the public hearings for the New York Law Against Discrimination in employment in 1944, for example, Rabbi Jacob X. Cohen from the AJCong highlighted the offensiveness of discriminatory applications: "A legislative act such as we are now considering would ban questions on race and religion, thereby outlawing one of the most potent devices for cutting off a man's right to a job, to a living, to fulfilling his obligations as a citizen of this state and nation." He pointed to an AJCong study finding that 18 percent of discrimination claims centered on application forms (see figure 4.3).[26]

That study was only one of many; after the war, civil rights organizations conducted multiple studies that showed bias against minorities in application forms.[27] In 1949, for example, the ADL reported that discriminatory questions, including questions about surnames and maiden names, appeared in almost 93 percent of the 450 application forms surveyed throughout the nation.[28] Civil rights activists continually highlighted the importance of questions about race, nationality, and religion on application blanks in their writings and correspondence as they pushed for antidiscrimination legislation. "It seems to me to stand things on their head to say that the application forms requiring this information lead to discriminatory practice," CLSA lawyer Will Maslow wrote in one letter. "Obviously, they do not merely facilitate discrimination. They demonstrate its very existence."[29] And activists particularly excoriated questions about names as discriminatory as they pushed for new legislation. "Anyone may change his name from Yeshillian to Young; but the mother's maiden name probably carries the true racial or national stamp," New School founder Alvin Johnson argued in defense of civil rights law.[30] Jews' struggle for civil rights legislation was clearly shaped by their community's painful experiences with name changing and the bureaucratic regime that it sought to evade.

Jews' concerns about bureaucracy ultimately affected legislation. New York's law against employment discrimination—written in part by the American Jewish Congress—specifically prohibited employers from using discriminatory application forms. It became illegal "for any employer or employment agency to print or circulate . . . any statement, advertisement, or publication, or to use any form of application for employment. . . . which expresses, directly or indirectly, any limitation, specification, or discrimination as to race, creed, color, or national origin."[31] Discriminatory application forms were at the heart of Jewish organizations' struggles for fair employment from the very beginning, and understandably, they remained significant as antidiscrimination principles were inscribed in law.

Jews' concerns about application forms similarly affected the administration of the law. The commission established to investigate complaints and administer the New York Law Against Discrimination, the State Commission Against Discrimination (SCAD), devoted a great deal of time and attention to employers' application forms. Each year,

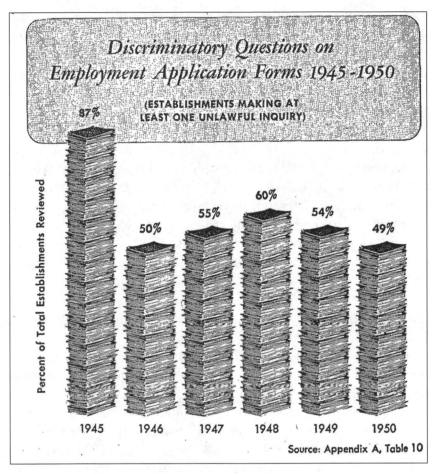

Figure 4.4. New York's State Commission Against Discrimination (SCAD) reported its accomplishments in 1950 with this graphic illustrating a drop in discriminatory questions on employer application blanks between 1945 and 1950. New York State Commission Against Discrimination, *1950 Report of Progress* (Albany: State of New York, 1950), 22.

SCAD gathered hundreds of forms and analyzed them for discriminatory questions.[32] In its 1949 and 1950 annual reports, the commission proudly touted its work thus far in examining thousands of application forms and noted the high percentage that featured discriminatory questions and required revision; in 1950, it printed a graphic illustrating a decline in discriminatory questions since its initial year of work (see figure 4.4).[33]

Pushed by the AJCong, moreover, SCAD continually deliberated during its early years on those discriminatory questions. In November 1945, for example, the AJCong asked SCAD to rule whether employers could ask a host of potential questions, including pastors' names and wives' and mothers' maiden names; SCAD ruled that all of the questions were inadmissible.[34] By 1948, SCAD had ruled illegal not only these questions but also questions about other family members' names and about candidates' changed names: the 1948 SCAD annual report listed "original name of an applicant whose name has been changed by court order or otherwise" as an "unlawful pre-employment inquir[y]."[35] And SCAD members heatedly debated whether employers could ask applicants if they had ever used an alias or nickname; by 1951, the committee ruled that these types of questions were also unlawful.[36] American Jews' concerns with the bureaucracy of application forms—with names and name changing as a crucial part of that bureaucracy—had not only become a part of the Law Against Discrimination in employment but had also shaped the activities of the commission charged with administering the law.

In education, the battle was a bit different. To activists' dismay, the Fair Educational Practices Act of 1948 did *not* explicitly address application blanks as forms of discrimination. Activists used that omission to push state administrative bodies to enforce antidiscrimination with greater vigor. In March 1949, American Jewish Congress president Stephen S. Wise accused the New York Board of Regents of "undermining in its entirety the operation of the Fair Educational Practices Law" by allowing institutions to continue asking questions about race and national origins on their application forms.[37] Yet the Regents still highlighted the "elimination from admission forms of prejudicial questions on race, color, religion, or national origin" as an important result of the law. Indeed, in June 1949, the State Education Department's annual report actually offered images of older discriminatory application forms, which included questions about both maternal and grandparents' names and of new, nondiscriminatory forms to boast about its civil rights victories (see figure 4.5).[38] And in 1952, the department claimed that "all questions relating to color, race, and the nationality of the applicants' parents have disappeared from the application blanks of all the higher education applicants in the state."[39] To be sure, discrimination continued in the wake of these bureaucratic changes. Nonetheless, Jewish activists' focus on application forms had significant impact on the administration of civil rights law in New York.

In the late 1940s and early 1950s, discriminatory applications shaped the administration of civil rights law, in large part because of the efforts of Jewish civil rights activists. These men and women had been raised in an environment where name changing was a commonplace activity, and application forms were the enemy, asking questions that could only mark them as Jewish and disqualify them for jobs. For these activists, lawyers, and scholars, the transformation of application forms—monitored by state bodies such as SCAD or the University of the State of New York—was a victory, even if only a partial one.

Finally, and perhaps most importantly, name changing had a significant impact on judicial interpretations of civil rights law. *Holland v. Edwards* (1954), a name-changing case that challenged New York's Law Against Discrimination, ultimately became an important decision in the history of civil rights legislation. Although I have found no evidence that any Jewish organization was actively involved in this case, *Holland v. Edwards* still reflects the ways that Jewish name changing, a subtle and complex practice of racial reshaping, affected legal understandings of race, racism, and discrimination in the middle of the 20th century.

In 1951, a New York woman named Rue Lehds went to the Holland Vocational Service, an employment agency for clerical workers, to apply for an advertised secretarial position. She was given an application form that asked, among other things, "Family Name or Your Name Ever Changed Legally or Otherwise." Lehds answered that her family name had been Winston. The owner of the agency, Helena Holland, looked over her application and then questioned Lehds "concerning the religion of one of her employers, the maiden name of the latter's wife—'What sort of name is that?'—and the applicant's national origin, as reflected by her name and schooling."[40] Lehds did not receive the job and complained to SCAD.

SCAD ruled in favor of Lehds, deciding that both the application form and the interview violated the Law Against Discrimination and ordering Holland to stop making inquiries regarding race, creed, color, or national origin of applicants, including inquiries into changes of name. Perhaps most striking, SCAD argued that name changing, in itself, was

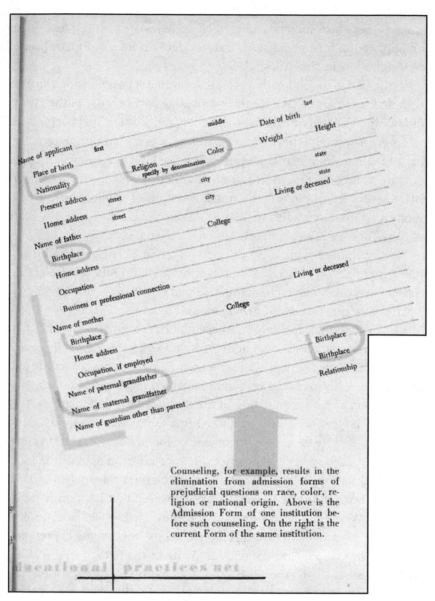

Name of applicant first middle Date of birth last

Place of birth Weight Height

Nationality Color state

Present address street Religion specify by denomination city state

Home address street city Living or deceased

Name of father College

Birthplace

Home address

Occupation Living or deceased

Business or professional connection College

Name of mother

Birthplace Birthplace

Home address Birthplace

Occupation, if employed Relationship

Name of paternal grandfather

Name of maternal grandfather

Name of guardian other than parent

Counseling, for example, results in the elimination from admission forms of prejudicial questions on race, color, religion or national origin. Above is the Admission Form of one institution before such counseling. On the right is the current Form of the same institution.

Figure 4.5. The University of the State of New York lauded the state's civil rights progress in its 1949 annual report by contrasting a new nondiscriminatory application form with a sample discriminatory form that inquired about a candidate's nationality, religion, and grandparents' names and birthplaces. State Education Department, University of the State of New York, *Education in New York State 1949: A Preliminary Annual Report of the Education Department for the School Year Ending June 30, 1949* (Albany: University of the State of New York, 1949).

The 1948 Legislature, in order to assure equality of opportunity in college admissions, enacted the Education Practices Act (Laws of 1948, Chapter 753) requiring that "students, otherwise qualified, be admitted to educational institutions without regard to race, color, religion, creed or national origin." Placed under the administration of the Education Department, the Act became a reality on September 15, 1948, when the Office of Administrator was established. Through the Administrator's counseling with institutions of higher education, institutions are bringing admission procedures and practices into conformity with the Act.

Name of applicant _____

first   middle   last

Place of birth _____ Date of birth _____

Citizenship _____

Present address _____

street   city   state

Home address _____

street   city   state

Name of father _____ Living or deceased _____

Home address _____

Occupation _____ College _____

Business or professional connection _____

Name of mother _____ Living or deceased _____

Home address _____

Occupation, if employed _____ College _____

Name of guardian other than parent _____ Relationship _____

an indication of ethnic or religious background, because it was so common among people "of a particular national origin or a particular religious faith." For this reason, a simple bureaucratic question about name changing would "raise a presumption" for potential employees that they faced "a limitation, specification or discrimination as to creed or national origin."[41] By linking together national origin and religious faith in this way, SCAD strongly suggested that it associated name changing with Jews, illustrating the impact of the Jewish name-changing phenomenon on civil rights law. Operating in New York City in the early 1950s, the members of SCAD were aware that name changing was primarily a Jewish phenomenon and that questions about name changing would primarily disadvantage Jews.

When Holland appealed the SCAD decision, lower courts issued decisions very similar to SCAD's, similarly suggesting that New Yorkers would recognize name changing as a fundamentally Jewish behavior, and thus any question about name changing might signal to Jewish applicants that they faced discrimination. In the words of New York Supreme Court justice Joseph Gavagan, "the application used by the employment agency contains a question, from which an applicant's racial origins or religious belief . . . might be readily established by any person reasonably familiar with the names common to those racial and religious groups, members of which or their descendants comprise the population of this city."[42] Gavagan's finding, like SCAD's, did not specifically name Jews, but his linkage of "racial origins" and "religious belief" and his reference to groups whose "descendants comprise the population of this city" suggest strongly that at this point in time, New York City residents—both Jews and non-Jews—understood name changing as a Jewish behavior. These judicial interpretations of civil rights law—though subtle—reflect decades of Jewish name changing in New York City.

As Holland continued to appeal the SCAD decision, higher courts adopted a slightly different understanding of the case, one that would have a very different impact on civil rights law. Rather than simply suggesting that name changing was a known phenomenon among Jews and that questions about names represented anti-Jewish discrimination, higher courts agreed with lower courts that Lehds had suffered discrimination, because questions about name changing represented one element of a complicated puzzle of racism. Judges such as Francis Bergan of the Appellate Division of the New York Supreme Court argued that "discrimination is quite apt to be a matter of refined and elusive subtlety. Innocent components can add up to a sinister totality."[43] And Judge Stanley Fuld of the New York Court of Appeals, the highest court in the state, insisted that "one intent on violating the Law Against Discrimination cannot be expected to declare or announce his purpose. Far more likely is it that he will pursue his discriminatory practices in ways that are devious, by methods small and elusive."[44] In the higher courts' understanding, name changing was not necessarily Jewish behavior, and asking about name changing was not clearly evidence of discrimination. Instead, racial discrimination was a subtle and complex behavior that reflected the complicated and shifting terrain of race, and the courts were tasked with identifying that complex behavior.

The decision in *Holland v. Edwards* that name changing could be an invisible and problematic, but still meaningful, signal of ethnic and racial identity had significant impact on civil rights legislation. As the first case to reach a hearing in the highest court in New York regarding the administration of the first Fair Employment Practices law in the country, *Holland v. Edwards* set legal precedent on a number of different issues. More than 100 cases, in New York and elsewhere, have cited *Holland* since 1954. In these cases, judges have rarely addressed name changing itself, and they have frequently looked at issues that were very distant from name changing or even discrimination.[45] But there is no question that one of the most important precedents set by *Holland* was Judge Fuld's insistence that ferreting out concealed practices of racism is the job of commissions and courts and, indeed, is sometimes the only way to ensure that antidiscrimination law is followed. Fuld's warning that discriminators will not openly announce their intentions but will instead employ "discriminatory practices in ways that are devious, by methods small and elusive," has been quoted in legal cases for decades, on issues ranging from public accommodations discrimination against African Americans in Seattle in the 1950s to the segregation of Mexican Americans in Texas schools in the 1970s to employment discrimination against Arab Americans in Colorado in the 2000s.[46] Indeed, a number of judges have referred to *Holland v. Edwards* as a historic case, one of the (if not *the*) earliest and most important judicial decisions that affirmed the complexity of demonstrating racial discrimination. They have also viewed *Holland* as an early decision calling for the need to prosecute more subtle forms of discrimination.[47]

To be sure, *Holland v. Edwards* was not universally embraced. For many activists—both Jewish and non-Jewish—the case's emphasis on the "devious" and "elusive" methods of discrimination, rather than more concrete demonstrations of structural inequality, was frustrating and inadequate. By the late 1960s, many African American activists and their allies (many of them Jewish) had turned against *Holland v. Edwards'* focus on the subtlety of racism and the need for civil rights commissions to ferret out employers' intentions to discriminate. This focus on intentionality, they argued, was misguided in its aim to create a "color blind" society.[48] Activists called instead for an approach that examined the "disparate impact" of a business's employment policies, looking closely at the percentages of minorities working in firms to ensure that they did not discriminate and calling for affirmative action as a remedy. Indeed, perhaps unsurprisingly, *Holland v. Edwards* became the hallmark "color-blind" case that these activists criticized and sought to supplant. "It is not too helpful to be told that discrimination can be practiced by 'methods subtle or elusive,' if we are not told of its contours," Alfred W. Blumrosen, a former official at the Equal Employment Opportunity Commission (EEOC), pointedly remarked in a groundbreaking article attacking the assumptions of state commissions such as SCAD and encouraging a "disparate impact" legal strategy.[49] Blumrosen may have been overly critical of *Holland v. Edwards*, since the decision has actually lent itself to citation in a variety of different cases on racial discrimination, even cases that ultimately called for affirmative action. Nonetheless, the "color-blind" strategy that *Holland v. Edwards* typified is still at the center of much legal and political debate over race and racial discrimination.[50]

Thus, a legal case based on Jewish name changing—a practice that subtly transgresses and rewrites racial boundaries—has been at the center of decades of civil rights law that has found racism to be a subtle and unspoken behavior, a behavior that requires an understanding of context and that is rarely announced or proclaimed. It is worth noting that SCAD and lower courts initially found important—though unspoken— links between name changing and Jews and developed an understanding of discrimination that was more clear-cut and obvious, and higher courts could have continued to direct their arguments in this direction. But instead, higher courts moved away from these findings, more interested in the ways that name changing blurred the lines between Jews and non-Jews. These judges interpreted the subtle and complex nature of name changing as a signal of the broader problem of racial discrimination: race itself—as indicated particularly in name changing—was a flexible and mutable concept, and racial discrimination mimicked that instability. The liminal racial identity of Jews, and the very specific experiences of Jewish name changing, in the middle of the 20th century thus helped to shape an influential—if controversial—legal understanding of racism for decades afterward.

Although historians have written in some detail about Jews' active engagement in the early civil rights movement, none have noted the fact that Jews' problematic racial status—and their efforts to grapple with that status through name changing—actually distinctively shaped their activism, as well as civil rights law itself.[51] The hallmarks of "color-blind" legal thought—particularly the focus on the subtlety and intentionality of racism—were shaped by the *Holland v. Edwards* case and indeed by judges' reading of the complicated nature of name changing itself. Civil rights jurisprudence in the 1940s and 1950s was thus clearly shaped in multiple ways by the phenomenon of Jewish name changing in New York City.

Beyond influencing the state's civil rights legislation, Jewish name changing reverberated in surprising ways with civil rights activists themselves. Shlomo Katz's outraged attack on Anonymous's name change might signal to us that civil rights activists were simply offended and angered by name changing, but it is important to note that there were many more connections between name changers and civil rights activists than we might imagine.

For one thing, some Jewish civil rights activists had changed their own names or came from families that had changed their names.[52] Civil rights activists were raised in Jewish neighborhoods, in Jewish families, and had Jewish friends; they were part of a community where name changing was an open part of life. Moreover, many Jewish civil rights activists were trained as lawyers: a profession that both helped to facilitate the process of name changing and encouraged its practitioners to change their own names. Name changing was not an alien strategy for

Jewish civil rights activists—it was a part of their profession, their community, and sometimes their own identity.

Even more importantly, civil rights activists saw name changers as a part of their constituency. In 1950, the American Jewish Congress helped to fund the psychologists Gerhart Saenger and Norma Gordon's study of the impact of the Law Against Discrimination on ordinary New Yorkers. Saenger and Gordon asked 504 white Protestant and Catholic, African American, and Jewish residents of the Bronx a series of questions about discrimination and the law, including what they thought about strategies such as "changing your name" or "passing for white" in order to find jobs. About half of the members of all ethnic groups said that they approved of these behaviors "on the grounds of economic necessity." The psychologists concluded that ordinary African Americans, Jews, and Catholics tended not to fight actively against discrimination and that name changing was a part of their seemingly passive attitude: "we find that minority group members are unlikely to engage in positive action on their own behalf, and prefer to evade discrimination either by disguising their identity, or more commonly, by seeking jobs in fields in which they believe there is little discrimination."[53] Saenger and Gordon concluded that the American Jewish Congress needed to defend ordinary Jews who saw individual strategies such as new jobs or name changing as their only solutions to discrimination.

Importantly, neither Saenger and Gordon nor the American Jewish Congress (Shlomo Katz excepted) sought to attack or belittle name changers. They did not charge name changers with abandoning the Jewish people. Instead, these Jewish civil rights advocates and organizations saw name changers as part of the Jewish community that needed to be protected.

Perhaps most crucially, civil rights activists and name changers had a great deal in common. They shared the same concerns: the discriminatory application forms that isolated, labeled, and segregated Jews. They shared the same enemies: the employers, admissions officers, and bureaucrats who created and used these forms. Their strategies were strikingly similar: they both sought to erase the markers that racialized Jews, limiting them from upward mobility.

Finally, the transformation that both name changers and civil rights activists accomplished was a fundamental redefinition of Jewish racial identity as white. For the first half of the 20th century, although European Jews were politically understood to be white people, most Jews had not experienced the invisibility or ethnic options that members of the white middle class take for granted. Layers of bureaucratic forms in education and employment had identified Jews as a separate race with questions designed to expose their religion and ethnic origin (including questions about their names). Jewish civil rights activists fought to erase those bureaucratic layers, to give Jews the invisibility that would allow them to participate in mainstream economic and social life unmarked, with their Jewishness a matter of religious or ethnic choice, not a racial badge.[54]

In very different, much more individualistic ways, Jewish name changers sought precisely the same invisibility. Name changers generally did not seek to escape Jewish community or religion: what they sought was to shed names that made their religious and national origins inescapable and denied them the opportunity to find jobs and get an education. Both groups pursued invisibility and ethnic options, sometimes working together in tandem and always reflecting the complications of Jewish racial identification in the postwar era.

There are, of course, important differences between name changers and civil rights activists. For one thing, they used the state in very different ways. While name changers before and during the war turned to the state for their personal transformations of identity, civil rights activists employed the state for legal and political transformations of group identity. If name changers responded to the expansion of the state during the Depression and the New Deal to transform their personal identities within private and bureaucratic settings, the civil rights movement emerged as the power of the state in the United States expanded further into the lives of ordinary citizens, regulating even private and bureaucratic spaces and ensuring individual rights to all citizens. Activists harnessed the power of federal and state legislation, executive action, and judicial decisions to erase Jews' racial markers, unintentionally creating a more permanent and widespread transformation in their racial identities.

It is important to say here that these activists did not intend to transform Jews into white Americans. This was a second, and crucial, difference between name changers and civil rights activists. While ordinary name changers *did* simply want personal invisibility and social and economic advancement for themselves and their families, Jewish civil rights activists sought much more. Many, if not most, Jewish civil rights activists at midcentury were passionately concerned with civil rights for all minority groups, and they were not satisfied simply with attaining invisibility for Jews. Like African American activists, Jewish civil rights activists questioned the efficacy of SCAD and its reliance on individual citizen complaints.[55] Jews, like African Americans, did not believe that cleansing discriminatory applications alone was the solution to racism. And groups such as the American Jewish Congress consistently promulgated outspoken public statements in defense of racial equality in the 1940s and 1950s: "America is losing friends and alienating people by our denial of full equality to 15 millions of our citizens because of their color," AJCongress president Israel Goldstein proclaimed in 1958.[56] Indeed, Jewish lawyers and activists helped construct and fight for civil rights legislation, such as the Civil Rights Act of 1964, that led to substantial advancement for many different minority groups in the United States and indeed sometimes worked for equality for people of color rather than advance Jewish interests as whites.[57] Many Jewish civil rights activists were truly committed to a project of nondiscrimination for all, and it would be far too cynical to suggest that they sought primarily to contribute to Jews' advancement in the white middle class.

Nonetheless, despite having practical and ideological commitments to equality, Jewish civil rights lawyers and activists affiliated with the American Jewish Congress, American Jewish Committee, and Anti-Defamation League unintentionally used strategies and pursued state policies that facilitated a white racial identity for Jews—at exactly the same time that individual ordinary Jews and their families employed the state to construct the same white identity. These policies allowed Jews to be understood more easily as white people, unmarked by the racial stigmas found on application forms (including questions about names and name changing) throughout the first half of the 20th century. Decades of antisemitism had ensured that being Jewish was a racial badge of inferiority that limited many Jews' possibilities in the United States, even into the postwar era, despite Jews' economic success and privileges as citizens with white skin. Antisemitic discrimination in the United States had been, in part, historically grounded in markings made visible on paper, and thus the goal for many Jews in the postwar era was to erase those markings—either by making them invisible or by making them illegal. Jews in civil rights organizations did not naively ignore their own whiteness, as conflicts between African American and Jewish activists might suggest.[58] Instead, Jewish civil rights activists unintentionally helped to establish a new, more secure, white identity for the American Jewish community. In the hopes of eliminating racial hierarchy in the United States, Jewish civil rights activists inadvertently facilitated the construction of a new hierarchy in which Jews could move about their daily lives unmarked by their racial and ethnic origins—that is, a hierarchy in which Jews could be unproblematically white.

The early civil rights movement, culminating in the passage of the 1964 federal Civil Rights Act, changed the lives of Jews in the United States in ways that have not been fully acknowledged by American Jewish historians. To be sure, scholars have importantly noted that the activism of American Jews was central to the decline of American antisemitism. Although the horrors of the Holocaust and the establishment of the State of Israel helped to contribute to a sea change in attitudes toward Jews after the war, scholars have rightly noted that Jewish activists themselves were instrumental in fighting American antisemitism in the second half of the 20th century.[59] Scholars have not paid enough attention, however, to the importance of the bureaucratic goals that American Jewish civil rights lawyers sought in their struggles for equality: the goals of eliminating discriminatory questions from employment and education applications. By the 1960s and 1970s, civil rights activism had mostly erased markers of Jewishness from American middle-class bureaucracy and thus alleviated the significant pressure that many young American Jews felt to change their names. As employers were forced to eliminate questions about ancestry, background, and names from their application process, Jews benefited. Jews were newly able to find jobs and matriculate at the colleges of their choosing without feeling the need to change their names. In 1962, the percentage of Jewish applications to change names in New York City Civil Court was cut in half from the rates of the previous decade, and Jewish name changes remained relatively stable at roughly 30 percent of all name-change applications from 1962 through 1982. Jews were still disproportionately represented in name changes during this era but just barely. Jewish name changing was no longer a phenomenon, with thousands of people submitting petitions each year. Instead, many fewer Jews changed their name, seeing less need for it.

The decline of American institutional antisemitism was gradual, to be sure, and not solely defined by civil rights legislation. The passage of civil rights laws did not immediately eliminate discrimination from employment or education application forms. Civil rights commissions were charged with examining application forms and investigating individual claims of discrimination, and that process took years. And other cultural and social changes in American life, such as suburbanization, helped to shape new understandings of American Jews. By the 1960s, the Jewish name-changing phenomenon in New York City was declining, as the impact of civil rights legislation took effect, both because fewer Jews in the city felt the need to change their names for work or school and because more Jews had been accepted in white suburbs. The decline of the name-changing phenomenon correlated with increasing Jewish integration in white, middle-class America.

The different strategies of name changers and civil rights activists overlapped and worked in tandem. As Jewish civil rights organizations pressed the state to erase Jewish markers through legislation, ordinary Jews no longer needed the government to erase those markers or re-shape their personal identities. At the same time, however, for Jews who had already changed their names in the 1930s and 1940s, new civil rights legislation protected their identities: with no lasting Jewish markers on their names or their applications, Jews with changed names could escape detection and discrimination in unprecedented ways, enabling much smoother integration into American middle-class life.

The 1988 memoir of ADL general counsel Arnold Forster, *Square One*, offers us insight into some of the curious connections between name changers and civil rights activists. Forster's name change in many ways typifies the story of name changers in the interwar years. Born to a lower-middle-class Jewish family in the East Bronx in 1912 and raised in a secular Jewish milieu, Forster went to law school in the 1930s and drew up papers to change his name from Fastenberg in order to find clients after he opened up his own law office in 1936. His three brothers changed their names along with him, and although his parents may not have changed their names formally, he refers to them as "the Forsters" after he has changed his own name.[60] Like this familial strategy of name changing, Forster's choice of new names fit interwar Jewish patterns as well. When he worked as an actor in his youth, a director had insisted Forster change his name to "John Arnold," but when he went to change his name legally, that name seemed to him "too artificial, too smooth."[61] Instead, he followed more typical Jewish patterns of name changing: he kept his first name, Arnold, an Anglophilic name typical of second-generation American Jewish boys in this era, and then selected an unremarkable last name with the same initial and a similar sound as his Jewish surname. And Forster's choice of a changed name suggests Jews' tendency to cover rather than pass: Forster was a leader in Jewish organizations and causes his entire life, regardless of his name change.

Even as Forster's story illustrates the typical story of Jewish name changing during the interwar years, his prominent position at the ADL indicates the complicated and curious relationship between name changing and civil rights. Forster describes himself transforming from a passive name changer to an activist in the 1930s after encountering violent antisemites on the streets of Washington Heights. In his telling, he and his friends in law school were "almost detached" from the growing onslaught of violent antisemitism in Europe in the early 1930s, and they were largely accepting of the American antisemitism that barred them from colleges, professional schools, and jobs.[62] "It had not yet occurred to the rapidly organizing Jewish community that we *could* fight," he explains.[63] Forster suggests that his 1936 decision to change his name was a part of this passive social milieu; he describes himself "rationalizing the change" in an environment where it was well known that few law firms hired Jews.[64] Immediately after his description of the name change, the lawyer suggested that he was ashamed of that decision, describing himself actually "becom[ing] a Jew" during an incident a year later, in 1937, when he and his friends fought a violent brawl with a dozen young men who shouted antisemitic chants as they marched down his parents' street.[65] In the aftermath of the battle, Forster began to organize with other Jews to fight violent antisemitism, joining the ADL in 1938 and beginning a lifetime of professional activism. If the lawyer expresses some embarrassment over his name change, he also expresses pride that he ultimately decided to fight his battles for the secular, Americanized, apolitical Jewish community in which he was raised and in which name changing was commonplace: "my lifelong struggle against anti-

Semitism was also a battle for my mother, father and grandfather, as well as for their values," he explains.[66] Indeed, as he describes his youth from the distance of 1988, even as he is frustrated by the antisemitism that he still perceives on the world stage, Forster cannot help but highlight the differences between the world in which he was raised and the world that he helped to create.

Activists such as Forster helped to construct a very different Jewish community by the 1970s and 1980s. After the civil rights gains that Forster helped to bring about in the 1940s and 1950s, later generations of Jews in the 1970s, 1980s, and 1990s grew up in prosperous, white, middle-class communities, only vaguely understanding the bureaucratic restrictions that would have made their privileged lives impossible 30 years earlier. Those later generations of Jews had far fewer reasons to change their names, and indeed, they did so far less frequently; but as we will see, names and name changing still played an important symbolic role in their identity and community.

PART III

The Decline of Jewish Name Changing in the 1960s and Beyond

"My Resentment of Arbitrary Authority"

The Decline and Erasure of Name Changing in American Jewish Society

In the popular 1976 book *What Really Happened to the Class of '65?*, David Wallechinsky—the son of the novelist Irving Wallace—described his decision to reclaim his family's original name. In an interview that primarily described his experiences with drugs, radical politics, and other efforts to drop out of mainstream society in the 1960s, Wallechinsky explained that he had changed his name not to dissociate himself from his famous father, as many people assumed, but instead to express his "resentment of arbitrary authority." "In Russia, my grandfather's name had been Wallechinsky, but when he came to this country it was changed by an immigration clerk who didn't think it was 'American' enough."[1]

Wallechinsky's decision represents a significant departure from the name changing of the first half of the 20th century in a number of ways. First, and most obviously, Wallechinsky did not seek to erase an ethnically marked name, as had so many Jews before him; instead he chose to reclaim an ethnic name, erasing instead the generic American name chosen generations earlier. Second, Wallechinsky made his decision as a child of the comfortable upper-middle-class California suburbs, not the lower-middle-class urban Jewish neighborhoods of New York or even Chicago, where Irving Wallace grew up. Wallechinsky's name change was thus not an agent of social mobility but instead a product of it. Finally, and perhaps most intriguingly, Wallechinsky framed his own name change as an act of agency designed to remedy the passivity of his grandfather's name change, an act perpetrated on the family by the American state. Far from active Jewish engagement with the state, Wallechinsky portrayed name changing as an act committed by the US government on Jews, a portrait that took on important cultural meaning in the 1970s.

Wallechinsky's decision offers us insight into the changing nature and meaning of name changing in the last three decades of the 20th century. The success of Jewish civil rights activism, the decline of antisemitism, the upward mobility of the Jewish middle class, and substantial Jewish migration to the suburbs led to a significant decline in Jewish name-change petitions in New York City by the 1970s and 1980s. By 2001, the practice of name changing had fundamentally disappeared from the experiences of New York Jews. For the most part, the humiliations suffered by Dora Sarietzky, Elias Biegelman, George N. Caylor, and Rue Lehds were distant from—and sometimes forgotten by—Jews living in the last three decades of the 20th century.

On the contrary, many Jews, like David Wallechinsky, experienced a newfound pride in Jewish names and identity. With the emergence of a new political culture that embraced ethnic difference, Jewish parents began to reclaim Jewish first names for their children, while a host of films, books, plays, and stories during this era championed a newfound familial and communal pride invested in Jewish names. Jewish artists such as Barry Levinson and Mel Brooks began to proclaim their ethnic identity loudly, and Jewish names played a prominent role in their works.

This newfound enthusiasm for Jewish names had limits, however. For one thing, despite Wallechinsky's well-publicized decision, few Jews actually chose to reclaim their distinctive names. Despite or perhaps because of Jews' economic success, non-Jewish names were still helpful in middle-class suburban settings.

Perhaps even more significantly, the new enthusiasm for Jewish identity was also accompanied by amnesia in American Jewish culture regarding the circumstances of name changing: amnesia about the daily presence of antisemitism in the lives of American Jews, amnesia about the complicated racial identities that contributed to name changing in the first place, and amnesia about the state processes that had enabled those changes. Nostalgic portraits of authentic Jewish life and identity suffused American Jewish popular culture in the last quarter of the 20th century. In that environment, name changing came to symbolize not merely an abandonment of the Jewish community but the inauthenticity and impoverishment of the United States itself.

Ironically, then, as name changing dropped out of the experiences of New York Jews, it flourished as a symbol in American Jewish culture, signifying decline and decay for audiences unfamiliar with the experiences of name-changing Jews a generation or two before. Name changing had successfully allowed Jews to integrate into the white American middle class, but once they were integrated, the bureaucratic, legal, and state processes that had enabled their very success disappeared from popular consciousness. Instead, American Jewish culture imagined a different relationship with the state, a relationship in which Jews were victimized immigrants who had submitted to an insensitive Ellis Island bureaucracy that demanded name changes as the price of admission to the country.

Jewish name changing in the last four decades of the 20th century declined steeply. From 1962 to 1982, the percentage of name changers who were Jewish (25–33 percent of all name-change petitions in the New York City Civil Court) was half what it had been from 1942 to 1952 (55–60 percent). And from 1987 through 1997, there were no recognizable Jewish names at all in this study's sample of Civil Court name-change petitions.

To be sure, there were petitions that still requested changes for names such as Weinberg, Rosenbaum, Hyman, Cohen, and Kaminstein through the 1960s and 1970s.[2] And their reasons still echoed those of earlier name changers: Dov Moshe and Sandra Norma Fischbaum, for example, petitioned in 1967 to change their names to Dov M. and Sandra N. Fischer because their last name was a "handicap . . . in their business and social relationships," and they did not want to "labor under the handicap of going through life with so long and so foreign sounding name."[3] But these types of petitions declined substantially as time went on.

Moreover, there was no significant countertrend of ordinary New Yorkers reclaiming former Jewish (or indeed any ethnic) names in the last decades of the 20th century. From 1972 to 1992, petitions requesting more ethnic names ranged from 3 to 11 percent and typically hovered around 5 percent. In 1967 and in 1997, not one petitioner in this sampled study requested a more ethnically identified name.

There were, to be sure, a few individuals who sought to reclaim earlier ethnic names (or to acquire new ones) during these years. In 1977, for example, Ann Marie Williams changed her name to Ann Marie de Filipis Guglielmo Magenta because she wished "to bear a name that represents her parental and maternal heritage which genealogy traces back at least two hundred years."[4] There were also a small number of petitioners who sought new names that would identify them more immediately with their religious background, such as the rabbinical student Howard Seth Anolick, who requested that he be called by his Hebrew name, Tzvi Shmuel.[5] But these petitions represented a small percentage of the already shrinking numbers of name changers during these years.

One reason for this substantial decline was demographic. The Jewish population of New York City declined significantly during this era, as suburbanization led hundreds of thousands of Jews to leave the city, cutting Jewish numbers from 2.1 million in the 1950s to 1.23 million in 1970.[6] By the 1980s and 1990s, Jews represented around 15–20 percent of the New York City population, down from roughly 25 percent of the population in the 1940s and 1950s.[7] It is unsurprising that as Jews became less numerous in the city, they would be less numerous in the name-change petitions.

But it was not only the smaller numbers of Jews that drove the smaller numbers in the name-change petitions; after all, Jews still remained a significant proportion of the New York City population, even as they disappeared from the name-change petitions altogether. With the passage of strong civil rights legislation and the disappearance of university quotas and restricted hotels in the 1960s, changed names had far less utility for New York Jews in later decades. By this time, many working-class and lower-middle-class Jews had already moved into a more solidly middle-class status and may have felt less need to shield their background from scrutiny.

Perhaps most significantly, radical movements of the 1960s and the 1970s, including the African American civil rights movement, may have encouraged many Jews to embrace their distinctive names as symbols of authenticity, rather than hindrances to success. The growth of radical ethnic movements among Asian Americans, Latinos, and Native Americans, as well as the emergence of movements for women's and gay liberation, encouraged a new cultural discourse that celebrated minority experiences, cultures, and identities as valuable and desirable. These cultural trends toward celebrating ethnic authenticity strongly shaped Jewish culture at the end of the 20th century, discouraging Jews from participating in practices that smacked of "passing" or "assimilation."

Strikingly, as Jews stopped petitioning for name changes, the nature of official name changing itself changed. The number of petitioners of any background abandoning ethnic names and adopting generic American names declined steadily in the years after the 1960s. Between 1947 and 1957, roughly 60 to 70 percent of name-change petitions were submitted to erase ethnic names. But from 1962 to 1972, those who petitioned to abandon ethnic names dropped to roughly 40 percent, and from 1982 to 1992, those who wanted to erase ethnic names dropped again to roughly 20 percent.

Name changing as a family strategy also declined. In the 1940s and 1950s, more than half of all petitioners changed their names with other family members.[8] But by the 1980s, those numbers reversed, and fewer than half of all petitions were submitted with other family members or mentioned other family members' name changes as motivation.[9] When Jews stopped submitting family petitions to erase ethnic names, their absence had a dramatic impact on name changing in New York City more broadly.

The last three decades of the 20th century saw a very different New York City as the backdrop to declining name-change petitions. As Jews left in the 1950s and 1960s, African Americans and immigrants from Asia, Latin America, and the Middle East gradually moved into the city's apartment buildings and tenements, ultimately changing the city's demographics substantially by 2001. The city's economic structure changed markedly as well. The fiscal crisis of the 1970s shattered New York's working and middle classes. Jobs disappeared, the population declined, and the city's public institutions were decimated as political leaders sought to recover their financial footing.[10] This new context did not encourage name changing; new ethnic groups, such as Latinos, did not employ name changing in large numbers, either because they did not perceive it as a viable strategy for upward mobility or because the cultural trends toward celebrating ethnic identity discouraged them from doing so. Moreover, a fleeing middle class meant that fewer individuals in the city could actually afford to change their names.

New York Jews' name-changing strategy was created during a particular historical moment and was specifically geared toward the anxieties, limitations, and capabilities of the Jewish community in the 1930s, 1940s, and 1950s. As Jews left the city in the 1960s and 1970s, and as they became accepted into the white middle class, their distinct familial practice of name changing gradually disappeared. So too did their enthusiastic embrace of the state to remake their personal identities. Prosperous middle-class Jews after the 1960s no longer needed government intervention to maintain their economic or social status—a luxury that shaped American Jewish culture in the last decades of the 20th century. From their comfortable perch in the middle class, Jews began to reevaluate Jewish names. Since Jewish names were no longer markers of race or lower-class status and, indeed, since ethnic heritage had become a new status symbol in 1970s America, these names became objects of affection and badges of authenticity in American Jewish culture.

This trend is particularly visible in the case of Jewish parents' naming practices. Although the decision to give children Jewish first names may seem unrelated to the decision to erase a Jewish last name, in fact, name changers in the middle of the 20th century were frequently attuned to both last and first names that communicated Jewishness. Jews frequently changed first names along with their last names and occasionally instead of their last names.[11] Thus, a shift in Jewish parents' naming practices can offer us important evidence that Jews were ascribing new value to Jewish names during this era. Beginning in the 1970s and intensifying in the 1980s and 1990s, Jewish parents were increasingly interested in giving their children identifiably Jewish first names. In the 1940s and 1950s, Jews had doggedly chosen popular American names for their children. They avoided English names such as Irving that their immigrant parents had turned into recognizable Jewish names two decades earlier, as well as biblical names such as Joseph or Ruth or Yiddish names such as Yankel or Gittel that had marked Jews as different in earlier generations. "I don't see why people should persist in giving children Jewish names," Rose Heller confided in Manny Kassell in Meyer Levin's 1937 novel *The Old Bunch*, as they scoffed at monikers such as Shulamith and Mordecai. "After all, we're Americans."[12] Selectively avoiding popular names such as Mary, Christopher, and James, which sounded too Christian, Jewish parents in the 1940s and 1950s nonetheless flocked to such popular American names as Susan, Barbara, Robert, and Stephen. Indeed, a 1948 book published to guide American Jews in selecting baby names noted the contemporary trend of parents moving away from names that marked their religious roots. "The tendency today is definitely away from Biblical names."[13]

But by the 1970s and 1980s, comfort and pride in Jewish identity, as well as changing name fashions throughout the country, had reversed this trend. American Jews began searching for Jewish names to give their children, as evinced by the emergence of popular books in the 1980s and 1990s that offered guidance for naming a Jewish baby.[14] In one of these guidebooks, Anita Diamant told prospective parents, "the most recent pattern of Jewish American naming is a return to roots," and explained that biblical names like Sarah, Rebecca, Benjamin and Aaron enjoyed "enormous popularity today."[15] Both in New York and nationally, Anglicized biblical names such as Sarah and Aaron, which had been uncommon in 1940 when compared to names such as Linda or Robert, shot up in popularity during the last 25 years of the 20th century.[16]

To be sure, non-Jews as well as Jews were giving their children biblical names. Sarah was one of the top-ten most popular names given to girls throughout the United States from 1978 through 2002.[17] But there is some evidence that Jewish parents began using those names earlier in the 1970s than non-Jewish parents did, actually setting the trend for biblical names in the last quarter of the 20th century.[18] Moreover, there is also evidence that in the first decade of the 21st century, Jewish parents preferred Anglicized biblical names to a greater extent than did non-Jews, even while both groups liked these names for their children.[19]

It was not just biblical names that Jewish families chose to reflect their ethnic and religious background at the end of the 20th century. Modern Hebrew names imported from Israel, such as Shira, Shoshana, Ari, and Dov, also emerged as popular choices for both secular and religious Jewish families.[20] Although these Hebrew names were not among the top 1,000 baby names in the country during these years, they were in the top 1,000 in New York State in 1980 and 1990.[21] And Orthodox parents in New York increasingly selected Yiddish names such as Chaya and Moshe after the 1970s as well.[22]

Perhaps most intriguingly, parents from the 1970s through the 2000s began to "reclaim" the Anglicized names that the first generation of Jewish immigrants had used as they first entered the country. Names such as Max, Lily, Rose, and Sam were not Jewish names by etymological standards, but popular baby-name books explained that they "felt" Jewish to contemporary parents. After "a resurgence of ethnic identity and pride," as well as significant distance from the immigrant generation, baby-name books explained, Jewish parents felt comfortable reclaiming immigrant names. Indeed, one book called this trend "the kosher curve": "By the 1970s, the Jewish world was ready for a new era of Maxes, Sams, Bens, Jakes, Mollys, Beckys, and Annies."[23] Jewish first names thus made a comeback in the years after the 1960s, as Jewish parents began to choose names for their children associated with the Bible, with Israel, and with earlier generations of Jewish immigrants.

At the same time, novelists, filmmakers, and playwrights increasingly began using Jewish names not merely as a means of identifying their characters as Jewish but also as a way of authenticating their artistic work as Jewish.[24] Jewish names showed up far more regularly as titles for books and as main characters within books, as Jewish artists sought to reclaim stigmatized names and to celebrate their own ethnic identity. Artists also hoped to attract Jewish audiences who were in the midst of celebrating their own Jewish identities. Finally, artists sought to make a connection with an "authentic" experience. In the midst of a revival of ethnic identity and culture, in which connections to the Old World connoted authenticity and meaning, Jewish names conveyed that authenticity and suggested these works would embody the American Jewish experience.

Titles with Jewish names emerged in popular culture with regularity after 1970. To be sure, earlier in the century, particularly in the 1910s and 1920s, the titles of many comic plays and films had featured Jewish names, such as *Abie's Irish Rose*, frequently as extensions of vaudeville routines featuring stereotypical Jewish comedy. In the 1930s and 1940s, however, Jewish names were rarely highlighted in the titles of serious literary or even middlebrow Jewish fiction and theater, perhaps in an effort to avoid being associated with the stereotypical uses of years past. Even in midcentury works of art that centered on Jewish life, Jewish artists and their publishers shunned Jewish names and selected instead universal-sounding titles such as *Awake and Sing*, *Call It Sleep*, and *The Young Lions*.[25] To be sure, this trend probably reflected more general trends in book publishing, eschewing personal names in titles altogether. But it probably also reflected both publishers' and authors' ambivalence about using stigmatized Jewish names to market their books.

By the 1960s and 1970s, however, Jewish artists such as Philip Roth began explicitly using Jewish names to identify their characters, themes, and identities as typically (even stereotypically) Jewish. Roth initially became prominent with short stories such as "Eli the Fanatic" and "Epstein," in 1959, and then made his career in 1969 with the publication of *Portnoy's Complaint*, a text whose Jewish-named title helped Roth situate his characters within several Jewish cultural worlds: psychoanalytic culture; the Jewish enclaves of Newark, New Jersey; and liberal politics in New York City.[26] Roth was ambivalent about seeing himself as a Jewish writer, but he acknowledged that he was writing about Jewish people and Jewish spaces; and by the 1960s, typical Jewish names were an important means of advertising that.[27] Indeed, Roth's early work inspired controversy in the Jewish community in part because of the Jewishness that his titles conveyed. Roth used a title such as "Epstein" because he wanted readers to understand his flawed protagonist as part of a specific Jewish milieu, while his readers expected texts with such titles to provide more flattering stories of Jewish life.[28] Both author and audience, however, believed that the Jewish names at the heart of the story should, and did, signal significant engagement with the Jewish world.

Famous men such as Roth were not the only ones who began to reclaim Jewish names. Popular feminist novels in the 1970s and 1980s advertised their heroines' Jewish names as a means of identifying the lives of Jewish women in particular as worthy of attention. Gail Parent's *Sheila Levine Is Dead and Living in New York*, Louise Blecher Rose's *The Launching of Barbara Fabrikant*, Edith Konecky's *Allegra Maud Goldman*, and Sarah Schulman's *The Sophie Horowitz Story* all used their characters' distinctive Jewish names to locate them in a particular Jewish community (Long Island, the Lower East Side, Brooklyn) or to identify them as outsiders in distinctively non-Jewish settings (a New England women's college).[29] The books all identified particular Jewish concerns, such as antisemitism or religious worship, and described them intersecting with women's feminist concerns, such as economic inequality and sexual exploitation. Sheila Levine—an overweight single woman who tries to commit suicide because she cannot find a husband—was a satiric symbol for an American Jewish culture that valued nothing but marriage for Jewish women: "Why would a nice Jewish girl do something dumb like kill herself? Why? Because I am tired. I have spent ten years of my life trying to find a husband and I'm tired."[30] Sophie Horowitz has sex with a female photographer in the women's gallery of an Orthodox synagogue as an ironic response to the sexism embedded within Jewish religious practice.[31] These feminist Jewish characters were funny and sharp, and they wore their Jewish names as badges of pride, not shame. Making these women's very Jewish names the titles of the books reclaimed them from stigma, proudly claiming dignity and meaning in the lives of previously marginalized Jewish women.

As Jewish names became repositories of Jewish history, culture, and identity in American Jewish fiction, name changing came to be seen as an act of cultural destruction. In some ways, this was not new: as we have seen, in the middle of the 20th century, name changers had been portrayed as self-hating fools or villains in American Jewish culture. But by the 1970s, 1980s, and 1990s, negative images of name changers were wedded to broader criticisms of American life, rather than internal Jewish struggles over loyalty. To eliminate Jewish names was not merely to betray other Jews; it was also to participate in a hollow, inauthentic modern American culture. Many writers and filmmakers in the latter part of the 20th century, reflecting the social and political trends of their respective decades, used name changing to criticize a corrupt, conformist, sterile, and sexist United States.

In the 1970s, Jewish artists influenced by the civil rights, feminist, and student movements created portraits of name changers not simply as self-hating Jews but as violent bigots and sexists. Joan Micklin Silver's 1975 film *Hester Street* linked name changing to sexism, offering an indelible portrait of Yankl, a callow, cruel Jewish man who changes his name to Jake and begins an affair with a woman after immigrating to the United States without his wife, Gitl.[32] In the 1979 short story "The Woman Who Lost Her Names," Nessa Rappoport described a Jewish woman, Sarah, whose name changes reflect hostile encounters with both American culture and Jewish men, ultimately robbing her of her identity and free will.[33] And in Ira Levin's gothic horror novel *The Stepford Wives* (1972), a name-changing suburbanite is willing to murder his wife in order to gain security and comfort in middle-class America.[34] In the 1970s, not only did name changing signal abandonment of the Jewish community; it was associated with male power and even violence.

Writers in the more conservative 1980s and 1990s offered a slightly different portrait: for them, name changing became a vehicle for the moral bankruptcy that had accompanied Jews' integration into the white middle class in the United States. Portraits of opportunistic name changers who engaged in shady, unethical dealings emerged throughout the 1980s and 1990s in the works of Jewish artists as diverse as Avery Corman, Allegra Goodman, Herb Gardner, and Wendy Wasserstein.[35] In Jon Robin Baitz's *Three Hotels* (1993), name changers were portrayed as Jews who forget their backgrounds and their moral bearings to embrace the lure of American capitalism: "Well of course I changed my name," exclaimed the protagonist of *Three Hotels*, Kenneth Hirshkovitz, who took the surname Hoyle after getting a job at a corporation selling defective formula to women in the developing world. "'Vice President Hirshkovitz'? Are you nuts? I knew the world I was going into."[36] In John Jacob Clayton's short story "Muscles," young Ben admires and fears his arrogant, domineering, name-changing Uncle Cy, who has achieved the American Dream at a price: "Who could be more powerful than Uncle Cy?" Ben wonders. "By the time Ben was born, Cy was a millionaire owning half a city block in the West Forties. No longer a Jew—his name Colburn now—he had made himself into the American *Sport* of his youth."[37] In the 1980s and 1990s, name changing became a symbol of Jews' corrupt bargain with a hollow or destructive American middle class.

Barry Levinson's semiautobiographical film *Avalon* (1990) is perhaps the best-known portrait of Jewish name changers who abandoned the warmth of their Jewish heritage for a sterile consumerist suburbia. The Oscar-nominated film focuses on the journey of the Krichinsky family from their immigrant roots in Baltimore to their suburban lives in the 1960s and 1970s. In the midst of that journey, two cousins, Izzy and Jules, change their names to Kaye and Kirk, because "it's easier to say than Krichinsky," bewildering and angering the family patriarch, Sam, and signaling their spiritual impoverishment. "Who said names are supposed to be easy to say?" Sam explodes upon hearing of the change. "What are you? A candy bar? You've got a name: Krichinsky. . . . This is a family, goddamnit. Krichinsky is the name of the family."[38] The loss of a family name, for Sam Krichinsky (and for Levinson), signaled the loss of family itself. And indeed the Krichinsky family, along with their Jewish heritage, disintegrates by the end of the film, trapped in the flickering meaninglessness of the television screen. *Avalon*'s nostalgic portrait of a cohesive ethnic family in the 1930s and 1940s destroyed by America's complacent individualism and consumerism—symbolized through name changing—reflected the political conservatism of the 1980s, while it also echoed earlier radical anxieties about the sterility, conformity, and bankruptcy of middle-class American life.

The flipside of these harsh portraits of American middle-class life, of course, was the warm nostalgia with which most artists painted "authentic" Jewish life—in Odessa, on the Lower East Side, in the Bronx or Brooklyn, in Baltimore, or in the Catskills. As artists portrayed name changing as a corrupt bargain with modern America, they also offered complementary rosy portraits of an imagined innocent Jewish past, signified by authentic Jewish names. Perhaps the most nostalgic portrait of name changing emerged in the 1982 box-office hit *My Favorite Year,* produced by the filmmaker Mel Brooks. Based loosely on Brooks's experiences as a writer for Sid Caesar's television program *Your Show of Shows,* *My Favorite Year* describes the experiences of the comedy writer Benjy Stone in 1954 when he befriends the weekly guest star on his variety show: Alan Swann, a swashbuckling movie star based on Errol Flynn. Benjy changed his name from Benjamin Steinberg to escape his embarrassing Jewish family from Brooklyn: his aunt wears a wedding dress to meet Alan Swann, and his mother calls him "Swannee": "Mom, he's an actor, not a river," Benjy moans.[39]

Although Benjy's family is painted in broad strokes as ridiculous, they are also the moral force behind the movie. When Benjy's mother invokes the values of family—"Sharing stories, sharing warmth. This is real life, Alan. And this is what you need. A home, and family, and children"— she shames Swann deeply.[40] He later reveals that he too has changed his name, from Clarence Duffy, and that he too is embarrassed of his past—a daughter he has abandoned. By the end of the film, Benjy and Alan are lovingly calling each other Steinberg and Duffy, and Swann has made efforts to see his daughter. Even this sympathetic portrait of name changers, however, reflected painfully and nostalgically on the warm, funny family and cohesive Brooklyn neighborhood that Jews like Stone had left behind as they worked to succeed in American culture. Brooks's film was one of the most popular manifestations of a larger trend: good numbers of Jewish artists in the 1970s, 1980s, and 1990s eulogized Jewish life from earlier eras as authentic and used name changing as a symbol of the hollow, inauthentic American middle-class lifestyle that Jews had eagerly embraced only a few decades earlier.

The movement championing Jewish pride and authenticity spread widely throughout the American Jewish community in the last quarter of the 20th century. Yet it had social, intellectual, and emotional limits. For one thing, as noted earlier, there was no significant movement among Jews to reclaim surnames 40 years after they had been changed. The fact that a 1963 *Jewish Advocate* article actually reported one man's return to the name Sol Goldberg indicates the rarity of such reclamations.[41] To be sure, Jews whose families had changed their names earlier sometimes agonized over those changed names, and there were a few Jews who did change their names back. The Detroit resident Allan Gale, whose family name was changed from Goldfein in the 1950s, noted that by the 1990s, he began to long for a name that expressed his own identity. "I've come to dislike Gale. What does it have to do with me? I can't search my history with the name Gale. . . . Gale is just a meaningless, neutral name. . . . I'm a Goldfein," he insisted, noting that one of his friends actually had changed his name back to Cohen. But Gale never changed his own family's name back to Goldfein, although he considered it; his children resisted a name change, fearing the disruption it would cause in their lives.[42] Calls to appreciate Jewish names as badges of Jewish pride had limits. The benefits of living a white, middle-class lifestyle, unmarked by Jewish difference, often outweighed the authenticity of a reclaimed Jewish name and posed agonizing conflicts for some Jews at the end of the century.

It is understandable that ordinary Jews chose not to shoulder the bureaucratic and psychic burdens of reclaiming stigmatized names that would mark them as different in a white, middle-class world. "I feel slightly lucky that I can keep my minority a secret, and it isn't obvious to everyone who knows my name," testified Sarah Robbins, whose father changed the family surname from Rabinowitz in the 1940s.[43] But it requires more explanation to understand the harsh artistic portraits of Jewish name changers that shaped the cultural landscape at the end of the 20th century. Many artists actually did have intimate understandings of name changing in their own and their families' lives, yet their portraits of name changers typically did not mention the forces that had racialized Jews earlier and led them to change their names. The social, political, legal, and bureaucratic processes through which many Jews had changed their names in the United States were mostly absent from works of art from the 1970s on.

Only a decade earlier, in the 1960s, artists had openly associated name changing with Jews' uncertain racial status. Artists such as Lenny Bruce had addressed name changing in ways that blurred the lines between Jew and non-Jew. Bruce's routine on Barry Goldwater (see chapter 4) ironically compared Bruce's own Jewish identity and changed name with Barry Goldwater's obviously Jewish name, Christian religiosity, and right-wing politics. Leonard Michaels's 1964 short story "Finn" offered a complicated portrait of a college student who calls himself both Finn and Fein, using each name to his advantage when possible; throughout, Michaels is deliberately unclear about the student's actual name and about his true ethnic and religious identity.[44] Artists in the 1960s had used name changing to comment ironically on the problematic status of white Jews in the American racial hierarchy.

But by the 1970s and 1980s, there was little discussion of race or antisemitism in fictional portraits of American Jewish name changers. The fictional representations of name changing during the 1970s and 1980s mentioned earlier mostly imagined name changing as a practice that men used to get ahead.[45] Artists did not mention the discriminatory quotas or help-wanted ads that might have encouraged these characters to improve their families' lives. And the fictional representations of American antisemitism that did emerge from the 1970s through the 1990s typically did not show either men or women changing their names. In books such as *The Launching of Barbara Fabrikant*, Rona Jaffe's *Class Reunion* (1979), and Elinor Lipman's *The Inn at Lake Devine* (1999), authors mentioned quotas and restrictions, but the books did not portray Jews changing their names to navigate those restrictions.[46] For the most part, fictional name changers in the last quarter of the 20th century, such as Kenneth Hoyle, Jules Kaye, and Benjy Stone, operated in a vacuum, without the historical context of discrimination or fear.

Moreover, these characters also operated with little reference to the state. The practical and legal dimensions of name changing that had shaped American Jewish culture and society in the 1940s and 1950s faded from public view, as did the legislative victories of that era. While artists in the 1940s, 1950s, and 1960s had talked about the bureaucratic, legalistic language Jews used to change their names and had referred to the paperwork and the "dues" that made those changes possible, Jewish artists in the 1970s, 1980s, and 1990s tended to treat name changing as a self-willed act of betrayal and corruption, with little legal, governmental, or political context.[47]

Importantly, too, most portraits of name changers at the end of the 20th century focused on men, patriarchs who were responsible for the name changing that disfigured their children's ethnic identity for generations to come. The active and enthusiastic participation of women and children in name changing in the 1930s and 1940s received little attention in American Jewish culture in the 1970s and 1980s.[48] Name changing characters such as Michael King (né Klein) in *Kaaterskill Falls* (1998) and Marty Sterling (né Murray Schlimowitz) in *Isn't It Romantic* (1981) had few female equivalents during their era. And indeed, the authors Allegra Goodman and Wendy Wasserstein purposely contrasted their name-changing male characters with Jewish female heroines who did not change their names. While images of name changers in the first half of the 20th century had highlighted young single females looking for jobs, such as Rachel Wiletsky in the "The Girl Who Went Right," Miss Kapp in *Focus*, and Estelle Walovsky in *Gentleman's Agreement*, by the 1970s and 1980s, these women's experiences were mostly forgotten.

This amnesia may be due in part to shifting images of Jewish women in American Jewish fiction and film. Whereas Jewish women in the 1920s and 1930s were portrayed as "ghetto girls," who wore too much makeup, spoke too loudly, and suggested promiscuity at the workplace, by the 1970s, upward mobility had turned images of Jewish women into "Jewish American Princesses," who did not work or have sex and instead lived off their fathers and husbands.[49] During the 1970s and 1980s, American Jewish fiction and film lost sight of the notion that Jewish women might be hardworking job seekers anxious to improve their own or their families' income and status, and female name changers thus fell out of common discourse. To be fair, American Jewish public discourse by the end of the 20th century also abandoned ugly images of Jewish women as venal, self-hating, social-climbing name changers. Instead it was Jewish men who were blamed for abandoning their names and impoverishing their descendants.

These incomplete portraits of name changing are particularly surprising since many of these artists' works were actually grounded in their own, or their family's, painful experiences. Herb Gardner's father and John Jacob Clayton's uncle had indeed changed their families' names, from Goldberg and Cohon, respectively.[50] Mel Brooks changed his own name from Kaminsky as he entered show business.[51] Ira Levin recalled being rejected from Cornell after being told that he would have a much better chance with a different name.[52] Even as artists themselves understood the complicated process of Jewish name changing at midcentury, they created works at the end of the century that contributed to a cultural amnesia erasing the political, legal, bureaucratic, and social struggles that Jews had faced only a few decades earlier.

We can understand these artists' limited portraits of name changing by exploring more closely their context: the white ethnic revival movement of the 1970s and 1980s. Beginning around the mid-1960s, political and cultural trends toward universalism, integration, and assimilation—trends that had encouraged name changing as a legitimate strategy of upward mobility in the middle of the 20th century—began to shift. Impulses toward cultural nationalism and ethnic pride in the African American civil rights movement led many white ethnics—Jews as well as Italians, Irish, Poles, and the like—to reconsider the choices for assimilation that their family members had made a generation or two earlier. Anxieties surrounding modern mass society—swirling throughout American culture since the 1950s—made premodern ethnic enclaves, such as eastern European shtetls or even 1940s Bronx neighborhoods, seem like oases in the deserts of sterile consumption found in the suburbs of Scarsdale, New York, or Short Hills, New Jersey. These shifting trends emerged at the grassroots as white ethnic groups formed new organizations, such as the Jewish Defense League and the American Italian Historical Association, and in more elite circles, as the study of European immigration to the United States spiraled among American historians and as political candidates such as Michael Dukakis highlighted their immigrant roots in their appeals to voters. Television producers and film directors similarly began to create films, dramas, and situation comedies that moved away from white, ethnically undefined suburban families such as *Leave It to Beaver* and instead centered around the experiences of European immigrants and their children, such as *The Godfather, Ellis Island*, and *Far and Away*.[53] Artists' decisions to cast name changers as symbols of inauthenticity and ruin must be understood within this context of a cultural, political and intellectual movement championing ethnic identity.[54]

Importantly, too, the ethnic-revival movement also encouraged another, more passive image of name changing. If Jews who changed their names were indeed betraying a glowing nostalgic Jewish past, then it might be helpful to imagine that it was not Jews (or other white ethnics) who had even changed their names at all. Rather than focusing on the complicated and perhaps painful history of Jewish families themselves filing name-change petitions at City Court to find jobs and get into college, American Jewish culture began to highlight a different relationship with the state, one that understood its ancestors primarily as innocent and bewildered victims.

By the 1970s and 1980s, the American discourse surrounding name changing centered more frequently on the Ellis Island immigration station and particularly on the government officials who processed incoming immigrants. In American humor, film and fiction, Ellis Island officials became figures of coercion and insensitivity.

Although genealogists and immigration historians have continually argued that Ellis Island officials did not change names and indeed that those officials did not have the power to change names, images of Ellis Island name changing permeate the American cultural landscape.[55] These images became particularly compelling and widespread in the last quarter of the 20th century in the wake of the ethnic-revival movement.

Mentions of Ellis Island name changing are sparse in the most prominent texts about names, name changing, immigration, or Jewish humor written before 1970.[56] The classic joke describing a bewildered Jewish immigrant at Ellis Island being asked his name, saying, "*shayn fergessen*" (I forgot), and becoming Sean Ferguson did not emerge in the literature of Jewish humor or names until around 1970. In earlier books of Jewish humor, multiple jokes about names and name changing appear. But Ellis Island plays little role in those earlier texts, and immigration officials are much less frequently portrayed as the catalysts for Jewish name changing.[57] Indeed, as late as 1969, one Jewish humor book told the Sean Ferguson joke as a joke about Hollywood actors changing their names, not a joke about Ellis Island. In this version, Berel Bienstock, the famous Yiddish actor, came to the United States and was advised by his manager to take a new name. Traveling to Hollywood, he worked to find a new name, but when confronted by an impatient movie producer, he forgot his new American name and could only confess, "*Schoen fer-*

gessen" "And a new star was born when the producer wrote down the man's name—'Sean Ferguson.'"[58] Although stories of Ellis Island officials changing immigrant names existed earlier, mostly in unpublished Jewish folklore, Ellis Island name changing did not become an important image in published literature until around 1970.[59]

And indeed that makes sense, since Ellis Island itself took on growing symbolism in American culture in the 1970s and 1980s, as the station transformed from an abandoned, rat-infested set of administrative buildings in 1965 to a national landmark, refurbished and established as a museum in 1990.[60] Throughout those 25 years, Ellis Island became far more central to ordinary Americans' understanding of the immigration process. At the same time, the white ethnic revival movement helped to make Ellis Island name changing an important symbol of white ethnics' struggles.

One 1994 children's book, *If Your Name Was Changed at Ellis Island*, highlighted the belief that officials changed immigrants' names on the island, noting that some immigrants were detained and deported, while others remained, making their new names "the beginning of a new life."[61] A popular 1979 historical text about Ellis Island described officials as "casual and uncaring on the matter of names," sometimes even "capriciously chang[ing] names, with little or no concern for the feelings of those they were mishandling."[62] Perhaps most famously, the Oscar winner for best picture of 1974, *The Godfather, Part Two*, showed the organized-crime boss Vito Andolini as a young, isolated boy encountering impatient, unfriendly officials at Ellis Island and having his name changed to Corleone, his hometown.[63] The contrast between this image of coercive government name changing and the portrait of active Jewish name changing as a response to antisemitism in *Gentleman's Agreement*, the Oscar winner for best picture 27 years earlier, is particularly striking.

Texts from the 1970s, 1980s, and 1990s tended to highlight European immigrants' name changing as a symbol of the damage that the US government had inflicted and that those immigrants had had to overcome. In the wake of civil rights movements charging the US government with enslavement and genocide, antiwar movements attacking US prosecution of the Vietnam War, and the exposures of corruption and abuse of power at Watergate, Americans in the 1970s and 1980s were increasingly alienated from their own government. Within this political, cultural, and social context, it is understandable that Jewish artists embraced a vision of Jewish name changing that reimagined the legal and bureaucratic history of the practice. If having your name changed by an Ellis Island official was not equivalent to the enslavement or genocide that had devastated people of color in the United States, it was nonetheless a story of disempowerment and cultural dispossession that animated American Jewish culture in the 1970s. Portraying Ellis Island officials as villains who destroyed Jewish identity may have been easier than grappling with the fact that Jewish families themselves actively used the government to elide antisemitism and battle racism, while also establishing themselves as members of the white middle class.

It is important to note that some Jews did actually try to grapple with name changing in a more historically informed way—and their openness might help us to consider both what the community gained during the name-changing phenomenon and what it lost. In 1982, in order to "choose to come out, be visible" instead of remaining "silent when queer or anti-Semitic jokes are told," the poet-activist Melanie Kaye/Kantrowitz incorporated into her surname the name her father had abandoned in the 1940s.[64] In deciding to inscribe the history of her father's name change within her own, Kaye/Kantrowitz highlighted the antisemitism that had impelled his name change, but she also kept the name Kaye to remember the name change itself and its significance in American Jewish history. "Kaye is both history and closet. History of a kind of closet," she wrote in 1981.[65] Like many of the artists of the ethnic revival movement, Kaye/Kantrowitz wanted a name that reflected her Jewish identity in an era when that identity became more vibrant and meaningful in American culture. Unlike many of those artists, however, Kaye/Kantrowitz rejected nostalgia about her Jewish name and acknowledged both the antisemitism and the complicated racial identities that had led Jews to change their names.

And it was not just prominent activists such as Kaye/Kantrowitz who struggled with this dilemma. Jews such as the writer and editor Sarah Flint Erdreich also grappled with both the privileges and the losses that their new names brought them and their families. After Flint uncovered the family secret that her grandfather had changed his name from Finkelstein to Flint, she grappled with the antisemitism that he had faced and its legacy for her own identity: "Was it wrong to keep a neutralized name? Was I perpetuating the fear that had driven so many to change their names?" Acknowledging obliquely that she did not want to take back the stigmatized name Finkelstein, Flint instead took on her mother's original Jewish surname while keeping her grandfather's changed surname. Four months later, Flint Erdreich's sister made the same decision, though she chose the last name Marx, a different Jewish name in her mother's family.[66] For at least a few Jews, their families' erased Jewish names led them to think deeply about their identities as white Americans and Jews and about their commitment to social justice. Ironically— and tellingly—Flint Erdreich's story about her grandfather's painful decision to erase the name Finkelstein was promoted on the front cover of *Lilith* magazine with the headline "Undoing Ellis Island." By the end of the 20th century, American Jewish culture had mostly embraced portraits of name changers as callous Ellis Island officials, domineering Jewish patriarchs, and callow young Jewish men, while saying little of the historical relationships between Jewish men, Jewish women, Jewish families, and the US government throughout the century.

The ethnic revival movement after 1965 and the turn toward Jewish cultural pride had an important impact on ordinary Jews' lives, discouraging many from changing their distinctive Jewish names. But the movement had social, cultural, intellectual, and political limits. Although American Jewish culture abounded with Jewish names in the 1970s, 1980s, and 1990s, the very abundance of those names led many American Jewish artists to forget the antisemitism that had impelled name changing in the first place. For the most part, movies, books, and theater during these years typically portrayed name changing either as a venal effort made by men to get ahead in a corrupt American system or as an insensitive act of xenophobia committed by the US government at Ellis Island. Artists rarely mentioned the bureaucratic antisemitism that had prevented Jews' social mobility in the first place, even when they had firsthand knowledge of that antisemitism. They gave little consideration to the complicated racial status of Jews in the United States only twenty years earlier, said little about the enthusiastic name changing of women and children, and rarely addressed the complicated covering that had enabled Jews to remain connected to Jewish families and communities, despite their name changes. Jewish name changing did not simply decline in the 1960s and 1970s; its textured history and complex experiences were mostly forgotten in American Jewish culture by the new millennium.

6

"Not Everyone Is Prepared to Remake Themselves"

Jews and Other Name Changers in the 21st Century

In 2011, ten years after the September 11 attack on the World Trade Center, the Jewish American writer Amy Waldman published the critically lauded novel *The Submission*, about a competition to create a 9/11 memorial won by a Muslim American architect, Mohammad Khan. Names figure heavily in Waldman's novel. Survivors seek their loved ones' names on the memorial, and Khan's full name inspires chaos and controversy after he wins, even though he uses the Americanized name "Mo" as a nickname throughout. The Jewish lawyer who chairs the competition jury, Paul Rubin, faces Islamophobic pressure to rescind Khan's selection, and when he meets with Khan over lunch to encourage him to bow out of the competition, name changing becomes a fraught topic of conversation.

> "I could change my name," Khan said. . . .
> "Many architects have," Paul said, "Mostly Jewish ones."
> "It was a joke."
> "My great-grandfather—he was Rubinsky, then my grandfather comes to America and suddenly he's Rubin. What's in a name? Nothing, everything. We all self-improve, change with the times."
> "It's a little more complicated than that, picking a name that hides your roots, your origins, your ethnicity."
> "Rubin hardly hides anything."
> "It reveals less than Rubinsky. Not everyone is prepared to remake themselves to rise in America."[1]

This exchange suggests the lasting impact of Jewish name changing on the American cultural landscape in the 21st century. For one thing, Rubin and Khan's conversation makes clear that Jews are still associated with name changing in New York City. It is not accidental that it is a Jewish character that encourages Mohammad Khan to change his name. Moreover, the author still associates Jewish name changing with assimilation and class mobility, without any reference to antisemitism or to Jews' active engagement with the state: Rubinsky just suddenly became Rubin.

Importantly, however, Waldman's portrait, unlike most of the post-1960s ethnic revival literature, attacks Jewish name changing from a comparative perspective. Waldman purposely contrasts Jewish name changing to the choices made by nonwhite immigrants from the Middle East. Since the 1960s, hundreds of thousands of immigrants from all over the world have moved to New York City, but far fewer of those immigrants, from Africa, Asia, Latin and South America, and the Middle East, have chosen to change their names in order to achieve upward mobility than did Jewish immigrants 70 years earlier. Waldman's novel deftly points to that social change, portraying Jews' decision as one intended to help them assimilate and become white, but at a cost. Through Paul's voice, she highlights the anxiety that the racial comparison between Jews and Muslims inspired. "Was Khan implying something about the Jews, their assimilations, their aspirations?" Paul worries in the wake of the tense lunch exchange. Despite his fearful anger at Khan's refusal to back out of the competition, Paul cannot help continuing this invidious comparison between Jews and Muslims by privately admitting to himself that he prefers Khan's strength and self-sufficiency to his own son's hapless dependence.[2]

Waldman's suggestive portrait of Jews as weak white assimilators and Muslims as proud resisters of color is problematic, however, and requires more understanding of the social realities of the post-9/11 world. It is primarily the context of the 21st century that shapes nonwhite immigrants' decisions not to change their names, not the inherent weakness or greed of American Jews or the inherent cultural pride or communal resistance of American Muslims or Latinos or Asians. Changing legal, political, cultural, and social realities—including new intersections between race, class, and the state—shaped the decisions that these different groups made. In order to understand what was distinctive about the Jewish name-changing phenomenon of the 20th century, it is important to explore the new name-changing phenomenon now taking place in New York City Civil Court.

Legal name changing today is, for the most part, much less likely to be an act of social mobility undertaken by second-generation ethnic Americans who seek to shield themselves from racial discrimination in employment and education. Instead, name changing in the 21st century is just as likely to be an act of poor or working-class men and women of color who need to fix bureaucratic mistakes in order to receive state benefits or find employment. Name changers today face state surveillance that is far more intense than what Jews faced in the 20th century; they also face definitions of race and class that are far more rigid and less amenable to the name changing that so shaped Jewish identity 70 years ago.

Since the 1940s, name changing has been democratized in extraordinary ways. After decades of decline, the numbers of name-change petitions to the New York City Civil Court exploded in the new century, and the petitioners were much more likely to be poor or working class than they had been in the 20th century, making the practice much less elite and more democratic.

This explosion was partly a response to legal and administrative efforts in New York and throughout the nation to make the legal system more accessible to people with fewer resources. In 1992, the New York State legislature made it easier for individuals to apply for the legal status of "poor person"; this change allowed many more people to waive the administrative costs of filing a petition.[3] Then in 1997, the Civil Court began several new initiatives to provide greater access for poor litigants, reflecting a growing national movement to simplify court procedures and increase people's access to the law.[4] In following years, the court eliminated detailed legal language on the name-change petition form, made it available online, and then introduced a "do-it-yourself" petition using special software specifically designed for people without access to lawyers.[5]

As a result, after decades in which the number of petitions filed in New York City Civil Court had declined to roughly 150 petitions per year, by the 21st century, the court had begun to process more than 1,000 annually. In 2002, 1,547 petitions were submitted. In 2007, 2,627 petitions were submitted, and in 2012, the court received 3,125 petitions, more than doubling the number ten years earlier. These numbers did not reflect a proportional population increase.[6] Name changing had become an important new phenomenon in 21st-century New York City.

The democratic nature of this phenomenon is worth emphasizing. For most of the 20th century, official name changing had been an act for middle-class strivers in large part because of its cost: the administrative, newspaper, and, most significantly, legal fees had discouraged poor and working-class people from officially changing their names. Although the law had never required petitioners to hire lawyers to change their names, the complicated language of the petitions and judicial procedures made hiring a lawyer the norm. In 1946, the anonymous author of "I Changed My Name" wrote that his name change, including lawyers' costs and fees, had cost $60 in total, a sum that would be roughly equivalent to about $730 today.[7]

Eliminating the perceived need for lawyers' services and making it easier to waive administrative fees allowed many poor and working-class people to change their names. In 2012, for example, fully 17 percent of petitioners received a waiver from paying administrative fees, testifying that the $65 fee alone was a hardship for them. There were no such waivers in the files in the years before the 1960s. Indeed, those waivers reflected a radical change from the name-change petitions of the doctors, businessmen, and clerks of the 1930s, 1940s, and 1950s, all of whom had paid what would now be hundreds of dollars in administrative and legal fees combined. The administrative changes at Civil Court profoundly shifted the demographics of name-change petitioners.

Comparing the neighborhoods and incomes of name changers in the 1940s and 1950s with those after 2002 offers further evidence of the class shift in name changing. In 1946, for example, roughly 40 percent of petitioners lived in census tracts where the median income was $3,000 or more. Another 59 percent lived in areas where the median income was between $2,000 and $3,000. Only 1 percent of petitioners lived in areas where the median income fell below $2,000, a threshold for poverty in the late 1940s (see figure 6.1).[8] The vast majority of 1946 petitioners—99 percent—lived in areas with median incomes above the poverty level.[9] The neighborhoods that petitioners lived in, moreover, reflected mostly middle-class status. Joshua Freeman lists a host of working-class neighborhoods in his book on working-class New York after 1945: Sunset Park, Brownsville, and Williamsburg in Brooklyn; Harlem, Chinatown, and Yorkville in Manhattan.[10] But none of these neighborhoods saw substantial numbers of name-change petitioners in 1946. Instead, the

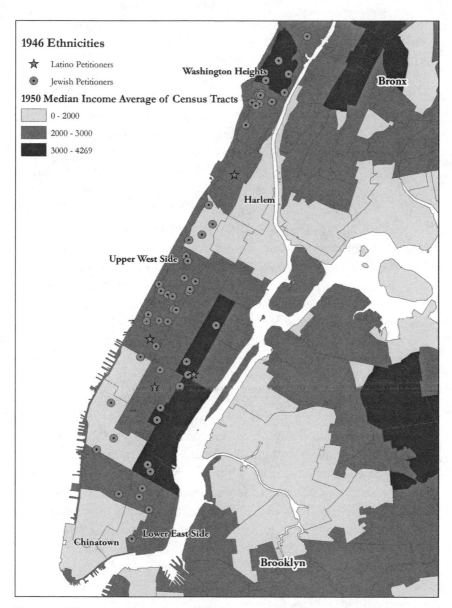

Figure 6.1. This map indicates the middle-class nature of name changing in 1946; only 1 percent of name changers at the time lived in census tracts where the median income was below the poverty level. Source: Name Change Petitions Collection, New York City Civil Court, New York, NY; map made by Amanda Tickner, Michigan State University Library.

neighborhoods that housed the highest percentages of name changers were the middle-class neighborhoods of Washington Heights and the Upper West Side. Not coincidentally, these neighborhoods had significant percentages of Jewish residents as well.[11]

In 2012, however, only 27 percent of petitioners lived in census tracts with the median income of New York City or more—about $50,000.[12] Even more striking, roughly 54 percent of petitioners in 2012 lived in census tracts where the median income fell below the city's poverty level—under $31,000 (see figure 6.2).[13] Priced out of the astronomic Manhattan real estate market, petitioners in 2012 much more typically lived in the poorer outer boroughs, especially Brooklyn or the Bronx.[14] The remaining 19 percent of petitioners lived in neighborhoods that one might categorize as working class or lower middle class in today's New York economy, with a median income between $30,000 and $50,000.

To be sure, median income, like occupation, rent, or neighborhood, is a problematic or at least an incomplete method of determining class status. Residents in these neighborhoods might have easily made more or less than the median; there is no way to know their income for certain. Moreover, and perhaps more importantly, class identity is not shaped by income alone. Class is also shaped by culture, education, gender, ethnicity and race, and it has taken on very different meanings historically.[15]

Nonetheless, taking all this information together, evidence strongly suggests that name changing helped to construct Jewish middle-class identity in the middle of the 20th century. Many in the Jewish community perceived a name-change petition as an important part of upward mobility or at least a means of finding desirable employment. Although not all middle-class Jews changed their names during these years, name changing was a fixture in Jewish neighborhoods where families sought to improve their economic standing by finding white-collar work. It was also part of the cultural milieu of the young second-generation Jewish community, as Jews carefully considered their own names and the names of their children as they made their way in the world. Their reasons for changing their names, recorded on their petitions, made their desires for good jobs, prestigious professions, or higher education clear. Considering together the neighborhoods in which petitioners lived, the median income of their neighborhoods, the occupations that they held or sought in 1946 (a wide range of white-collar professions from physi-

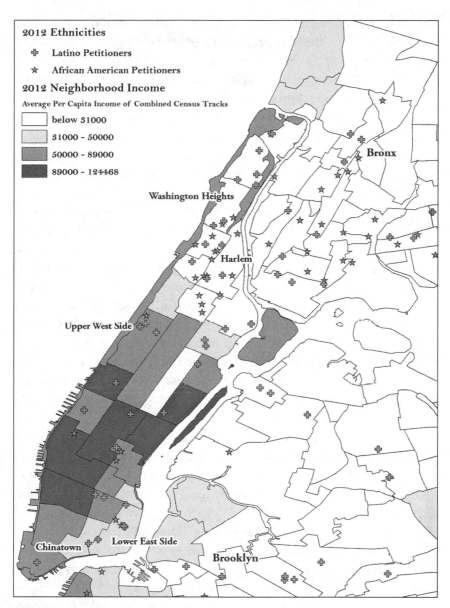

Figure 6.2. This map suggests that name changing in New York City is no longer a middle-class behavior; roughly 54 percent of petitioners in 2012 lived in census tracts where the median income fell below the city's poverty level. Source: Name Change Petitions Collection, New York City Civil Court, New York, NY; map made by Amanda Tickner, Michigan State University Library.

cians to secretaries and from salespeople to artists), and the stated goals of their petitions, the data suggest that overwhelming numbers of mid-century Jewish name changers were in the middle class or lower middle class or that they sought that status. It is possible to go even further to suggest that at that moment, name changing was a practice that helped to shape and define the Jewish middle class, whether individuals actually chose to change their names or simply grappled with the option.

Understanding the class identities of name changers in 2012 is more complicated. The Civil Court's petition forms after 1997 did not require petitioners to give their occupations, making it more difficult to compare class status over generations. The comparatively high percentage of petitioners living in neighborhoods marked by median incomes below the poverty level, however, suggests that name changing by 2012 had become a behavior practiced to a much greater extent than before by poor and working-class New Yorkers. In 2012, poor New Yorkers rarely gave economic or social status as a reason for changing their names, as had middle-class New Yorkers of the mid-20th century, so class identity did not seem to be a factor in their decisions. Instead, many more poor and working-class individuals saw name changing as a part of the system that they could use to support their families and their individual well-being.

The influx of poor and working-class name-change petitions after 2001 does not necessarily signal positive, democratic change. On the one hand, the court demystified the name-changing process, making it more open, affordable, and available to poor and working-class people. On the other hand, however, the tragedy of September 11—a tragedy that unfurled in the immediate vicinity of the Civil Court, killing three of its security officers in the line of duty—inspired a new obsession with security and surveillance, similar to the spike of worry during World War II. After 2001, name-change petitions suggest that it was poor and working-class people who bore the brunt of that anxiety.

This new burden is visible in the significant rise in the numbers of petitioners who sought to correct bureaucratic mistakes on their vital documents in the 21st century. Between 1952 and 1992, roughly 5–11 percent of petitioners changed their names because of bureaucratic error; between 1997 and 2012, 15–25 percent of petitioners changed their names for the same reason. Some of these mistakes were quite significant. Over

7 percent of 2002 petitioners had no first name on their birth certificate at all, simply "Male" or "Female." One petition from a woman whose birth certificate read "Female Eason" requested a name change to Crystal Deanne Bonaparte Dupree, explaining, "because of error at Vital Records in the mid-70s, I have no name and I need it corrected. Please."[16] Other petitioners who did have their first names on their birth certificates indicated that they had used a different last name all their lives and that they possessed many other documents, including Social Security cards, with different last names. Rosa del Valles petitioned to take on the surname Reyes because, she said, "I wanted to get a non driver's ID and wasn't able to because of my name on my birth certificate and other pertinent IDs did not match."[17] These mistakes were significant and clearly required change.

A number of the mistakes that petitioners reported, however, were relatively minor results of typos, mispronunciations, or transliterations that might not have drawn a second look years earlier. Habiba Abdullah requested a change of her first name to Habibah, explaining her reasoning on her petition: "Incorrect spelling of first name. 125 Worth St. Clerk refuses documentation stating it is insufficient."[18] Abdullah's petition offers clear signals of the significance of the growing surveillance state for Arab and Muslim New Yorkers. But in the petitioning process itself, it was not just Arab or Muslim names that were targeted. By 2015, all petitioners were instructed to put every single version of their name that they had ever used on their petition (for example, Linda Joan Smith, aka Linda J. Smith, aka Linda Smith) in order to forestall any bureaucratic questions about their identity.

These petitions offer a window into the growing power of the state in individuals' daily lives in the years after September 11. Although the petitioners' language is usually brief, a reader can discern their annoyance and anger (such as Abdullah's) with a bureaucracy that trapped them into perhaps taking days off work, paying extra money, going from the civil courthouse to the department of health and then back again, waiting on long lines, sometimes in order to claim the name they had always possessed. And in most of these cases, the end goal was yet another bureaucratic document: a passport, a driver's license, a state identification card. Indeed, a number of petitioners simply listed as the reason for their name change the document they sought, rather than the circumstances that led them to request new names. Encarnacion Suarez explained, "Need a new birth certificate, to obtain a new state ID for banks and mortgage application," in her petition to change her first name to Candy.[19]

As Suarez's petition suggests, it is clear that these petitioners were not merely in need of documents but also the benefits that those documents could confer, especially financially. Some explained that they could not get employment or government benefits without matching documents, others that they needed to visit family with a valid passport. Shirley Fay Stewart's petition explained that she wanted to change her surname to Bonilla—the married name that she shared with her husband of 50 years: "I have reached retirement age and have started receiving Social Security retirement checks. However, they are issued in the name Shirley F. Stewart which was my name when I last worked in the 1950s. I have not used that name since then. The name on my bank account is 'Shirley Fay Bonilla' and I cannot deposit my social security checks. Social Security will not issue checks in the name of Shirley Fay Bonilla without a court order."[20] The growing surveillance state was particularly onerous for people who relied on the state for benefits or whose financial activities were more likely to be scrutinized.

The impulse for this surveillance state came in part from growing concerns about illegal immigration, but in large part, especially in New York, the immediate context for much of this scrutiny was the destruction of the Twin Towers only blocks from the civil courthouse. The *9-11 Commission Report* (2004) found that several of the hijackers had entered the country with fake passports, had used credit-card fraud to fund their activities, and had purchased fake driver's licenses to board the airplanes.[21] In response, the federal government investigated documentation procedures in states throughout the country and found that even two years after the attacks, investigators were still successful in acquiring fake driver's licenses in major states such as Michigan, California, and New York.[22] In the wake of these investigations, states rushed to tighten the procedures by which they issued driver's licenses and other important vital documents. New York began cross-checking driver's licenses' Social Security numbers with the federal Social Security Administration and issued a new driver's license with technology designed to prevent fraud.[23] And in 2005, Congress passed the REAL ID Act, which listed new, more rigorous standards for state driver's licenses and other identity documents, although New York was given an extension to meet those standards.[24] Designed to prevent fraud, illegal immigration, and terrorism, these tightened procedures actually wound up trapping innocent men and women in New York City in bureaucratic circles of frustration as they sought to cash checks, open bank accounts, or acquire driver's licenses or state identification.

And it was primarily poor people, who needed identification to cash checks or access government benefits, who seem to have faced the highest level of inspection in this tightened surveillance state. Without the help of university degrees and personnel departments that smoothed daily life for middle-class people with mistakes on their birth certificates, poor and working-class people found themselves unable to access basic things they needed. Whereas in the middle of the 20th century, it had been middle-class people (primarily Jews) who faced high levels of scrutiny in applications for employment and education, by the beginning of the 21st century, it was poor and working-class (predominantly African American and Latino) people whose identities were scrutinized as they struggled to set up bank accounts or find employment. To be sure, there were also middle-class people who were frustrated by the increased stringency of the surveillance state, but the bureaucratic overhaul of the Civil Court that had begun in the late 1990s and the new bureaucratic turn of the post-9/11 world worked together symbiotically, if unintentionally, to make name changing an act of frustration and necessity among large numbers of poor and working-class people in the 21st century.

The second thing that changed dramatically in name-change petitions by the 21st century was the demographic profile of petitioners. As New York City's population changed dramatically, so too did name changers. Beginning with African American migration into the city in the post–World War II era and spiraling in the late 1960s and again in 1990 with expanded immigration from all over the world, New York's population came to encompass hundreds of thousands of new ethnic minorities, with African American, Latino, and Asian populations dramatically increasing and the white population declining to a substantial minority.

We might expect that these large new populations of migrants, immigrants and their children—buffeted by discrimination and seeking to assimilate—took advantage of the name-change petitions at Civil Court in the ways that American Jews did in the 1940s and 1950s. Indeed, widely publicized social scientific literature in the years after 2001 pointed to the economic and educational discrimination faced by ethnic minorities with names that sounded African American, Asian, Latino, or Muslim. It would make sense if the name-change petitions became once again a venue for ethnic New Yorkers to seek upward mobility and perhaps even racial reconstruction.

And for some petitioners—particularly Chinese, Muslim, and Arab Americans—name-change petitions did fulfill that function, in part. But these upwardly mobile New Yorkers were a significant minority at the Civil Court. And although their petitions resembled the petitions of Jews in the 1940s, Chinese, Muslim, and Arab petitions were different from Jewish petitions in enough significant ways (even accounting for their much-smaller populations) to ensure that official name changing in New York City did not become a Chinese or Muslim or Arab phenomenon as it had been a Jewish one.[25]

Instead, as we noted earlier, the vast majority of Latino, Asian, African American, and Muslim and Arabic petitioners kept their ethnically distinct names, even as they may have changed those names to correct bureaucratic mistakes. These surprising findings suggest the refreshing power of multiculturalism as a cultural ideal in the years after 2001, but they also suggest the corrosive power of state surveillance in the post-2001 world. Perhaps most importantly, these findings may also suggest more hardened intersections between race and class in our contemporary society. While aspiring middle-class Jews with white skin and stigmatized names could see in name changing a ticket to upward mobility in an emerging service economy, people of color working at jobs with no room for advancement in a postindustrial economy have not seen economic promise in new names. Instead, name changing has more typically been a means of surviving an increasingly intrusive bureaucracy.

After World War II, New York's population gradually began to encompass more and more people of color. The trend began as white New Yorkers moved to suburbs, while African Americans moved to the city in larger numbers. This increasing diversity was reshaped anew by the Immigration and Nationality Act of 1965 (also known as the Hart-Celler Act), which opened up immigration from Asia, Africa, and Latin America, as well as other successive immigration acts, including the 1990 Immigration and Naturalization Act.[26] In 1940, the white population of New York City had been close to 92 percent, while African Americans represented 6 percent of the population, Latinos were close to 2 percent, and Asians were only 0.24 percent. By 1970, those numbers had changed significantly: the white population had dropped to roughly 63 percent, the black population had risen to 21 percent, Latinos were about 16 percent of the population, and Asians represented roughly 1 percent of New Yorkers.[27] By 2010, the white population of the city was roughly 33 percent, while the African American population was roughly 23 percent, the Latino population was roughly 29 percent, and the Asian population was roughly 12.5 percent.[28] By 2010, then, New York City had become a far different city demographically from the one it had been in the 1940s.

The name-change petitions of the New York City Civil Court reflected those racial and ethnic differences. Unlike the 1940s, when Jews had been the largest white ethnic group in the city and disproportionately dominant in the petitions, in the 2000s, different groups of New Yorkers emerged in the name-change petitions in numbers that roughly reflected their presence in the city.[29] In 2012, roughly 23 percent of petitioners were African, Caribbean, or African American; about 25 percent were Latino; and about 11 percent were Asian. As name changing democratized, it was equally accessible to different groups of New Yorkers.

Then, too, just as no one group dominated name changing, the goal of escaping prejudice that led so many Jews to change their names no longer dominated the petitions filed. This change is particularly surprising when considering that racial discrimination based on ethnic names was highly publicized in academic, popular, and political culture after 2001.

In groundbreaking 2002 research on the impact of race on employment, the economists Marianne Bertrand and Sendhil Mullainathan found that employers were 50 percent more likely to call back job candidates whose names sounded "white" (such as Emily and Greg) than they were to call candidates whose names sounded "black" (such as Lakisha and Jamal).[30] Throughout the next 15 years, social scientists throughout the United States and Europe replicated the authors' research and found similar discrimination based on ethnic names in a host of environments, from elementary school classrooms to college faculty offices to Google search algorithms.[31] These studies were widely publicized, with authors, journalists, and bloggers citing them in best-selling books, YouTube videos, popular websites, and articles in a host of media forums, including the *Root*, the *New York Times*, *Salon*, and National Public Radio. One 2009 series in the *New York Times*, for example, featured African American professionals discussing their decisions to change or hide ethnically distinctive names such as Jabbar or Tahani while searching for jobs, while a widely popular YouTube video featured a young man named José describing the sudden interest he received from potential employers when he dropped the *s* from his name.[32]

These vibrant cultural discussions about ethnic names and economic discrimination might intensify our expectations that New Yorkers in the 2000s changed their ethnic names to avoid stigma and find employment. Those expectations would be misplaced, however. Only about 22 percent of all name-change petitions in 2002 actively sought upward social and economic mobility, a significant drop from the 65–75 percent of similar petitions that sought upward mobility in the middle of the 20th century. Moreover, while there were a few ethnic groups in the 21st century that disproportionately sought upward mobility through name changing, just as Jews had in the 20th century, there were enough significant differences between these groups and Jews to mark Jewish name changing at midcentury as distinct.

Chinese American name changers in the 21st century were in many ways similar to Jewish petitioners 70 years earlier. Chinese petitioners were disproportionate in the New York City Civil Court petitions, filing 13 percent of all petitions in 2012 designed to eliminate ethnic names and/or add Anglo-American ones, even though they represented only 6 percent of all New Yorkers in 2010.[33] Chinese Americans thus erased their ethnic names or took on new "American" names at rates that were roughly double their population in New York City, just as Jews had years earlier.

In many ways, moreover, Chinese American petitioners' reasoning sounded very similar to that of Jewish petitioners in the 1930s and 1940s. In 2002, for example, Bo Long Ma changed his given name to Peter because it was "easier to read."[34] Xiu Ying Chen requested that she be called Lisa Ying Chen because her name was "hard to say."[35] Xin Yan Ye changed her name to Clare Xinyan Ye because she had "been known as Clare for years," and Dongmei Xiao changed her son's name to Danny because "he has been known as Danny to his friends, classmates and teachers."[36] Betty Won Yu Tse petitioned to change her name to Betty Nikki Tse because she wanted "a real American middle name," and indeed many Chinese petitioners similarly—as their Jewish predecessors had previously—requested an "American" name.[37] Complaints about names that were difficult to pronounce, reports of names that had been changed years ago and only now needed to be official, and requests for "American" names reflected the same impulses for name changing that had motivated Jews years earlier.

Yet Chinese and Jewish name changing differed in telling ways. For one thing, although many Chinese parents changed the names of their children after 2001 as Jewish parents had in years past, those parents did not change their own names, and few extended Chinese families changed their names together. The patterns of name changing and family mobility that Jews had innovated became infrequent in the 21st century, and Chinese families did not embrace them.

Additionally, Chinese Americans did nothing to eliminate their own or their children's Chinese surnames. It was only given names and sometimes middle names that they sought to change. Because American racial structure relied so heavily on physical features to categorize Asians as a separate race, Chinese American New Yorkers could not erase employers' perceptions of themselves or their children as Asian simply by eliminating their Chinese names. Chinese American petitioners did not expect their new names to shield them from overt racial discrimination: they only wanted names that did not stand out and that might signal to coworkers, friends, and teachers that they were willing to fit in.

Moreover, a number of Chinese American petitioners tellingly referred to their desire for a new name as a matter of "convenience."[38] New names were not—as they had been for Jewish petitioners—an embrace of an ambiguous racial and ethnic identity that did not automatically announce their background to suspicious outsiders. Instead, Chinese Americans—whose racial identity was announced by their physical appearance—used new names as a convenient tool in an effort to travel more easily through American social and economic life.

The same tendency was true of Latino petitioners, another group found regularly in the name-change petitions in the 21st century. In 2012, Latino petitioners represented a full 25 percent of petitions submitted to erase an ethnic name, but this erasure looked very different

from the Jewish erasures of midcentury. Latin American cultures typically include the mother's maiden name along with the father's name
in individuals' last names; the father's first surname is the child's first
surname, and the mother's first surname is the child's second last name.
These surnames, of course, do not conform to American bureaucratic
forms, which have space for only one surname. Latino people's family
names have frequently been erased by civil servants or misidentified on
bureaucratic documents.[39] In the New York City Civil Court petitions,
numerous Latino petitioners sought to eliminate their mothers' natal
names because the additional names were extraneous in American paperwork and were often confused for surnames. Complaining of "con-
tinuous problems and complaints about signing and typing in names for
documentation," Judy Enriquez petitioned to eliminate her own natal
name, Job, from her 17-year-old son's name, making him Berwyn Ne-
hemiah Enriquez.[40] Many Latino New Yorkers worked to shield their
linguistic difference from American naming culture, hoping to fit into
American culture by erasing the names that highlighted this difference
on bureaucratic applications and forms.

The vast majority of these Latino New Yorkers did not seek to abandon Spanish-sounding names; instead, they typically simply erased one
Spanish-sounding name while adding or leaving another one intact. For
the most part, Latino petitioners did not hope to become unmarked
whites or to adopt an ambiguous racial identity. They sought only to
cover their obtrusive differences, to show other Americans that they
could fit into the United States' bureaucratic expectations for names in
the most convenient ways.

The experiences of both Chinese and Latino petitioners illustrate
that some ethnic Americans in the 21st century still sought to use name
changing to fit into American society and culture but that they faced a
different economic, cultural, and racial landscape. Erasing their ethnic
names entirely—as Jews had done—was not a viable economic strategy
in the 21st-century United States for Asian or Latino New Yorkers. In a
world where their physical appearance announced their racial identity,
these immigrant groups sought not to create an invisible racial identity
but instead to fit better into American culture.

New Yorkers with Muslim- or Arabic-sounding names were a different story. In 2011, *Entertainment Weekly* published an article on Is-

lamophobia in the entertainment industry (featuring the story of one actor who had changed his name), titled "Producers to Middle Eastern Actors: Don't Tell Anyone Your Real Name or You'll Never Work in This Town Again."[41] Other articles similarly reported on individuals who had changed their names to make their coworkers or patients "more comfortable" or to avoid humiliation or harassment.[42] In 2005, the BBC profiled the London public relations executive Daniel Jacob, who had changed his name from Tariq Ahmad to find a job.[43] And some writers—of both fiction and nonfiction—noted the casual and frequent first-name changing that Muslim and Arab Americans used to cover in order to fit into a workplace: "Mohammed becomes 'Mo,' Samiah and Sameer become 'Sam,' Abdullah is 'Abe,' and Walid becomes 'Wally,'" one writer noted in *Al Arabiya*.[44]

In addition to economic discrimination against Muslim and Arab American names, journalists also described new anxieties emerging as the security apparatus in airports and at border checkpoints expanded dramatically. One 2006 *New York Times* article reported that Muslim and Arab Americans feared traveling because their names led security guards to stop them and subject them to invasive searches. "It's a bad time to be named Ahmed right now," joked the comedian Ahmed Ahmed, who was handcuffed in a Las Vegas airport because his name matched that of an Al Qaeda operative.[45] Interviews and memoirs published in the wake of 9/11 described Arab and Muslim Americans being asked if they wanted to change their names during immigration interviews or being suspected during security detention of maintaining false identities because they used simple nicknames.[46] Arab American writers argued that the no-fly list at airports, as well as other post-9/11 security measures, resulted in routine structural racial profiling. Popular and academic writers described the ways that names, as well as clothing (particularly women's veils) and facial hair, had become racial markers for Arab and Muslim Americans and that some people had decided to abandon those markers of difference.[47]

For the most part, writers offered few concrete examples of individuals who had changed their names legally, and none reported that a major name-changing movement among Arab or Muslim Americans was taking place. But many suggested that the subject of name changing had become an important one in Muslim and Arab American communities.

"We've heard that families have packed up and left, that people are think-ing of changing their names. A lot of people now think that if their name is Omar or Mohammed or Osama—something clearly Muslim—they'll never get anywhere in this country anymore," Dahlia Ehissa, a lawyer working for the Arab American Family Support Network in Brooklyn, told the *New York Times* in April 2002.[48] The sociologist Louise Cainkar wrote that many of her Arab and Muslim American informants from Chicago reported discrimination on the basis of their names or reported changing their names to avoid prejudice.[49]

Immediately after 2001, New Yorkers did indeed erase these eth-nically marked names in high percentages, just as Jews had done in midcentury—in 2002, more than 60 percent of all Muslim- and Arabic-sounding names in the New York Civil Court were erased because petitioners feared Islamophobic backlash and sought to find jobs and maintain social connections in the midst of a hostile environment. But this trend did not last, and ten years later, Muslim and Arabic name changers were not tremendously different from other ethnic groups, such as Chinese or Latinos, in their name-changing practices.

In 2002, New Yorkers with Arabic- or Muslim-sounding names used the Civil Court to change their names in different ways from Asian and Latino petitioners and in ways that much more closely echoed Jews' name changing in earlier decades. New Yorkers with Arabic- and Muslim-sounding names reflected roughly 7 percent of the total name-change petitions in 2002 but about 18 percent of the petitions submit-ted to erase ethnic names. These numbers were disproportionately high compared to Arab and Muslim populations in the city; the Arab popu-lation in New York City hovered around 1 percent between 2000 and 2010, and the Muslim population was estimated at around 6.6 percent in 2014.[50] Arab and Muslim New Yorkers, like Jews before them, sought to erase their ethnic names in name-change petitions in numbers that were disproportionate to their population in the city.

Moreover, like Jews in the 1940s, Arab and Muslim Americans sub-mitted petitions with haunting language that revealed fears of discrim-ination, difference, and ostracism. This was particularly true in 2002, when anxiety in the city may have been at its highest—and indeed, Mus-lim and Arab New Yorkers in 2002 expressed that anxiety much more openly than had Jews in 1942. The Algerian immigrant Bouzid Mabarek

Azzem petitioned to change his name to Robert George Marcone because, he said, "I have never felt comfortable with my name because of the difficulty in pronouncing it, and with the backlash against Arabic-sounding names (such as mine) it has only increased my personal stress, anxiety and discomfort."[51] Rayam Azab Youssef, a native-born US citizen, explained why he wanted to change his name to Ray Savant: "to safeguard my liberty in my pursuit of happiness and to best represent my culture and allegiances."[52] The New Jersey–born Ibrahim Antonello Castronovo stated openly the subtext for all of these petitions: "Petitioner prefers the name ROSARIO ANTONELLO CASTRONOVO. The basis for this is that prevailing attitudes and prejudices against persons of Arabic descendancy have been adversely affected as a direct result of the terrorist attacks of September 11, 2001. Petitioner wishes to change his name to a less demonstratively Muslim/Arabic first name."[53] In an era more comfortable with ethnic difference and more concerned about ethnic discrimination, Muslim and Arab Americans were able to voice their anxieties, fears, and anger about growing anti-Muslim and anti-Arab sentiment in the United States in their name-change petitions far more freely than Jews had addressed antisemitism in the 1940s.[54]

However, like many Jews at midcentury, there were still petitioners with Muslim- and Arabic-sounding names in 2002 that did not feel able to be open about their fears of discrimination and hatred. Mostafa Mohamed Abdulaziz wanted to change his name to Tony Abdulaziz because he "has always admired the name proposed and his friends and family have called him Tony since his birth."[55] Bahij Mahmoud El-Tamer petitioned to change his name to Bahij Justin Tamer because he "wanted to choose [his] own middle name" and "because it's easier."[56] The artist Gerard Maurice Bitboul, a Moroccan immigrant, petitioned to change his last name to Mosse, saying that he had "been regularly using the name" and that "his colleagues and clients are . . . accustomed to using" it.[57] The Islamophobia that emerged in the immediate wake of September 11 is clearly visible in the name-change petitions in both veiled and direct language.[58]

Despite these profound similarities to Jewish Americans' earlier petitions, there are differences that indicate substantial change from 1942 to 2012. Most importantly, in 2007 and 2012, more petitioners with Arabic- and Muslim-sounding names sought to correct mistakes in their documents or to emphasize their ethnic or religious backgrounds than sought to erase their ethnic backgrounds. Reflecting the immediate anxieties of September 11, in 2002, a large majority of Arab and Muslim petitioners sought to erase their ethnic and religious markers. But by 2007 and 2012, those anxieties were no longer visible in the petitions, and other concerns, more typical of other ethnic groups in the city, emerged. Samia Ibdo Aljahmi sought to change the spelling of her middle name to Abdo because of a misspelling on official records.[59] Rana H. Attal requested that her father's full name, Hamdy, be included as a middle name in her official legal name to correct a mistake on her birth certificate.[60] In 2012, only one-third of petitioners with Middle Eastern names sought to erase their ethnic names to improve their chances at social mobility; in 1946, 87 percent of all Jewish petitioners had changed their names with the same intent.

Indeed, one group of Muslim New Yorkers consistently *added* names that reflected their minority religion: African Americans. Estimated to reflect as much as one-quarter of the American Muslim population, African Americans who converted to Islam regularly added Muslim names as a part of their religious tradition—even though that might make them targets in a hostile environment. Kenya Brown changed her name to Kenya Shabazz, citing her conversion to Islam, while Avona-cile Muhammad added the names "Muhammad Abdullah" to her grandson's name, Colin Gregory Browne, because, she said, "the child's father and I want him to [have] a Muslim name in addition to an American one."[61] Much more often than we might expect, then, and certainly more often than did Jewish New Yorkers in the mid-20th century, New Yorkers with Arabic and Muslim names after 2001 sought to make their documents conform to their bureaucratic, familial, religious, and cultural needs rather than seeking to fit into a white Christian mainstream.

In the environment of fear that the 9/11 attacks elicited, why did more Arabic and Muslim New Yorkers not submit petitions to change their names and escape discrimination? One possibility is that the backlash to 9/11 erupted quickly and subsided rather quickly, as some observers have suggested.[62] It is perhaps more likely, however, that people with Arabic- and Muslim-sounding names were dissuaded from changing their names by fears of surveillance. In the months after September 11, the New York Police Department (NYPD) began an extensive surveillance operation into New York Muslim communities. With the arrival of a former CIA official, David Cohen, as the NYPD's first civilian intelligence chief in January 2002, the department began to train police officers of Arabic and Muslim backgrounds to work undercover in small ethnic communities, gathering information from cafes, small businesses, student organizations, mosques: anywhere that Arab or Muslim Americans might have conversations or go about their daily business.[63]

The surveillance program was immense, with tentacles throughout the city—including the New York City Civil Court and its name-change petitions. Sometime around 2008, the NYPD began requesting and compiling in databases petitions from individuals changing their names either to or from Arabic or Muslim ones. In 2009, the department began running background checks on Arabic and Muslim individuals changing their names officially and then selecting a handful to conduct interviews. The surveillance might have convinced members of New York's Arab and Muslim populations that Americanizing your name would actually bring you more attention than simply keeping an Islamic-sounding one. The surveillance certainly might have communicated to Muslim and Arab Americans that complaining about discrimination while changing your name might flag you as a potential terrorist and an individual to be more closely watched. Indeed, since police knew "that a would-be terrorist who Americanized his name in hopes of lying low was unlikely to confess as much to detectives," the understood purpose of the program for the NYPD was actually to let members of the Muslim and Arab communities of New York know that they were being scrutinized.[64] There was thus an intentionally chilling effect to this massive surveillance program; it would not be surprising at all if it significantly depressed the numbers of people of Arabic or Muslim descent who wanted to change their names in the years after September 11.[65] The growth of a surveillance state directed specifically at Arab and Muslim Americans shaped the tenor of name changing in New York, making the process a less effective strategy for upward mobility or for escaping discrimination.

Although Arabic and Muslim communities were the only ones who faced this ugly state surveillance, they were not alone in their decision to keep their ethnic names. Name-change petitions after 2001 were submitted primarily by petitioners from Asian, African, Latino, and Middle

Eastern backgrounds who did *not* seek to eliminate the ethnic markers from their names. In fact, some petitioners actually sought to make their names follow the naming cultures of their ethnic origins, ensuring that their names would conform even less to American standards. These re-ethnicizing petitioners were less typical than deethnicizing petitioners, but they were far more typical than they had been in previous years, representing about 5–6 percent of all petitions in 2002. They had represented only 1 percent in 1942. Some Chinese petitioners, for example, sought to add Chinese middle names. Estrella Ying Chang Lai-Yang added Gi Wah to her one-year-old daughter's official records as a middle name, while 25-year-old Hera Yeung sought to include the Chinese name her parents had given her at birth, Yip See, as an official middle name.[66] Similarly, Latino petitioners sometimes sought to reclaim their mothers' maiden names, rather than erasing them. J. Apolinar Varela requested that his ten-year-old daughter Cristal's surname be changed to Varela Perez "to add on mother's last name."[67]

Still other petitioners from Asian, Latino, and Middle Eastern backgrounds sought to reclaim their original names after they or their families had changed them. Michael Andrew Sweet reclaimed his father's original family name, Remez, while the Iranian immigrant Darrius Al Younessy explained that this name had been proposed to him at his interview for citizenship: he wanted to return to his original name, Alireza Younessy.[68] And 57-year-old Patricia Chiang petitioned to take the first name Ching instead: "I no longer wish to use the name Patricia."[69]

The years after 2001 continued the post-1965 multicultural trend in which ethnic names were increasingly accepted in the American mainstream. The election of Barack Obama as president of the United States in 2008 was only its most visible reflection. New York City Civil Court petitions illustrate that petitioners from Asian, Latino, African, and Middle Eastern backgrounds participated in this trend, just as white ethnic New Yorkers had in the late 20th century. Ethnic names became important markers of pride, of family, and of heritage. There was far less of an impulse toward onomastic conformity in these later years, as pride in ethnic difference became a much more important cultural ideal. In many ways, then, 21st-century trends in name changing were quite removed from second-generation Jewish families' methodical use of legal name-change petitions to escape their stigmatized names.

Pride in ethnic difference might help to explain why the New York City Civil Court received almost no name-change petitions from African American New Yorkers seeking to cover their racial identities. Even though many black petitioners took the time, energy, and money to change their names officially, they rarely abandoned either first or last names that might identify their ethnicity to potential employers. Latoya Patrice Brown made the effort to change her last name to Buckram because it had been her name all her life, but she kept her distinctive African American first name.[70] Similarly, although Jamel Sims possessed a distinctive African American name, in 2002, he kept his first name, even as he made the effort to take on the surname of Hopkins, a name he had since birth.[71] The fact that one biracial teenager in Kansas City made headlines by changing her name from Keisha to Kylie in 2013 hints at the rarity of African American efforts to eliminate distinctive names.[72]

Multicultural ideology certainly helps to explain these petitioners' comfort with their distinctive ethnic names—and with those of their children—but it may not be the entire story. African American petitioners, like Asians and Latinos, were marked by their physiognomy. They may have believed (perhaps quite rightly) that a name change would have done little to change their experiences with discrimination, since any employer would immediately have uncovered their racial identity after an interview. Moreover, since many of these African American petitioners were individuals who lived in census tracts with average incomes of under $30,000, it is also possible that they believed (again perhaps quite rightly) that there were many more hurdles they needed to overcome in order to find a good job than simply changing their name. The growth of name-change petitions in New York City from poor people of color—who for the most part did not see name changing as a means of upward mobility—suggest that the intersections between race and class may have become hardened in the 21st century. While middle-class Jews could change their names in the 1930s and 1940s to evade discrimination, to find good jobs, and ultimately to redefine their racial status, that kind of liminality—and the power it enables—is not available to most people of color today.

These hardened racial lines may also extend to Muslim and Arab Americans in New York City, for slightly different reasons. These New Yorkers might seem the most likely to replicate the name-changing phenomenon of Jews in the mid-20th century. As a small minority in the United States with substantial middle-class success, Muslim and Arab Americans do not fall neatly into the black/white divide of American racial categories. Moreover, their physiognomies do not necessarily distinguish them as a distinct race in the United States, nor does their class status necessarily intertwine with their racial status. Finally, especially in the years since 9/11, Muslim and Arab Americans have faced a growing swell of hatred, and they are increasingly perceived as members of an alien religion that conspires to attack and ultimately destroy the nation, just as Jews had been in the 1940s. Given all this, Muslim and Arab American New Yorkers might seem likely to repeat the Jewish name-changing phenomenon of midcentury. Yet, for the most part, they have not. Severe state surveillance has helped to racialize Arab and Muslim New Yorkers more rigidly than was the case for Jews.

Amy Waldman's imagined conversation between Paul Rubin and Mohammed Khan in many ways reflects the social dynamics of name changing in New York City in the 21st century. By 2011, Jews like Rubin were indeed considered fully white. By changing their names, they had gained access to substantial cultural and political capital, while still being able to access Jewish ethnicity when they chose. That success might lead them to imagine that their own history could be repeated by new nonwhite immigrants, asking if (or assuming that) Muslims would pursue the same path that they had taken as Jews. Khan's anger with Rubin's suggestion, and his proud resistance to the assimilation implied within a name change, reflect the multicultural moment in which Waldman's book was written.

Waldman does not fully address, however, the historical context in which these dynamics emerged. Not only were Jews' name changes undertaken within a context of institutional antisemitism that goes unremarked and unnoticed in her novel, but the institutional racism faced by Muslims (and other people of color in New York) is far more severe than a change of name could address. It is not simply multicultural pride like that displayed by Mohammed Khan that leads so many nonwhite Americans to keep their ethnic-sounding names. Intensified state surveillance has racialized Muslim New Yorkers, casting suspicion on avenues of assimilation that worked effectively 60 years ago. At the same time, heightened surveillance has ensnared working-class and poor New

Yorkers of color, requiring them to waste hours working through bureaucracy in order to change minor spelling errors in their names to receive government benefits or find jobs. And intertwined racial and economic inequality have severely limited the economic opportunities available to many African American and Latino New Yorkers, with or without a name change.

I hope this book will replace mythical images of Hollywood movie stars and hapless Ellis Island immigrants with more nuanced portraits of American-born Jewish families escaping antisemitism at midcentury. But I do not want to create new mythical images of Jews triumphing over racism with assimilatory strategies that other ethnic groups might be encouraged to model. Understanding Jewish name changing at midcentury should not mask the harsh racial and economic inequalities that exist today; it should instead offer insight into those inequalities. Jews' past possibilities of escaping racism and achieving a white identity with a name change are much less available to African American, Chinese, Latino, Asian, or Muslim men and women today. Official name changes today reflect the burgeoning multiculturalism of our increasingly diverse society, but they also reflect the impact of a more rigid racial structure, intensified state surveillance, and growing economic inequality—all of which intersect with one another and emerge in ordinary people's decisions in New York City Civil Court each day.

Epilogue

Although this story is grounded in archival and published material, it is expressed best in the lives of ordinary people, whose personal, familial, and communal identities have been reshaped and rewritten by the social and cultural forces described here. Indeed, the rise and fall of Jewish name changing is encapsulated in fascinating ways in the story of one family that began in New York in the 1930s.

Reuben Litowitz was a young Jewish New Yorker who matriculated at George Washington University in Washington, DC, in 1937, under the name Raymond Litowitz. Until he was 18, Litowitz had lived a life of struggle in New York City. His father had abandoned the family, and his mother was committed to a mental institution, leaving Reuben and his sisters to be raised in the Hebrew Orphan Asylum of New York. The orphanage paid for Litowitz's higher education, and he attended George Washington so that he could live with an aunt in the DC area. He excelled as a college student, developing a close relationship with one of his professors. As Litowitz neared graduation in 1941, his professor counseled him to change his name in order to find a job. His efforts to apply for professional school had already proven fruitless because of quotas, and his professor believed that a new name would be necessary to build a career as a CPA. Together, Litowitz and his mentor "sat down and worked out the name."[1] The result, Raymond Edward Lang, was a name the men determined would allow Litowitz to build a highly successful career working both for the federal government and as a private accountant for government employees.[2] Since "Jews were not getting jobs in the government at all," Lang always saw this name as instrumental to his success.[3] Litowitz's experience was typical of Jewish name changing in the 1930s and 1940s: his desire to attain social mobility through a middle-class profession, his frustrating search for education and work with a Jewish-sounding name, his employment of a generic "American-sounding" name with initials that mirrored his own, his decision to change his name as he graduated, and even the fact that the government played a role in his new name were all common experiences found throughout thousands of Jewish name-change petitions in New York City.

In 1941, when Lang changed his name, he married another Jewish New Yorker, Sylvia Bach, whom he had met at the Hebrew Orphan Asylum. After some time in Chicago, the two of them began a life together in the Washington, DC, suburbs in the late 1940s, ultimately raising a son and two daughters. Like other name-changing Jews, the Langs firmly remained part of the Jewish community, even as their names helped them to integrate into the white, middle-class world they now inhabited. The Lang family maintained good relationships with relatives who had not changed their names, and they identified unequivocally as Jewish: they celebrated Jewish holidays, lit candles on Friday evenings, and attended synagogue, and Sylvia was active in Jewish women's groups in suburban Virginia. The Lang family had not "passed" into the non-Jewish world—they remained committed to their Jewish identity—but they did shield their Jewishness from the non-Jews with whom they lived and worked. "I knew we were Jewish, but I knew it was something they didn't talk about. They compartmentalized it very well," Trish, their middle daughter, remembered.[4]

Just as name changing remained something of an open secret in the larger Jewish community, in the Lang family the name change also took on a mysterious air for their children throughout much of their lives, somehow becoming connected to the vague sense of shame their parents communicated about their upbringing as poor orphans in New York. Trish remembered feeling like an "actress" who needed to pretend that her life was perfect. And as a college student at the Ohio State University from 1965 through 1969, she did exactly that. She rushed the sorority Kappa Alpha Theta, becoming one of only two Jewish girls in the entire sorority, although few of her sisters were even aware of the fact. As a pretty coed, with a non-Jewish boyfriend and the name Patricia Lang and even a willingness to help decorate the sorority house for Christmas, she effortlessly became a member of the group: "I was passing. I never hid it per se, but it was never brought up. I looked like all the other sorority sisters," she remembered.[5]

Yet when Trish began getting involved with civil rights work, teaching in a predominantly African American school in Ohio as part of her education degree, she brought her Jewish background into the spotlight. When Kappa Alpha Theta asked her to stop her civil rights work, she quit and criticized the sorority's national president for her anti-Jewish tokenism. If Trish "passed" as a part of life in college in the 1960s, it was not a permanent identity shift, nor was it a conscious and purposeful effort to leave the Jewish community. Instead, her name helped her to shield herself from embarrassment and to accomplish the social integration she sought. As soon as the sorority interfered with her own set of values, she openly brought up her Jewish background.

Trish married James Kent, a Jewish man whose father had changed his family name from Katz. As an immigrant in Toronto, James's father, Charles, and his mother, Ida, wanted to establish a pharmacy, but they found little success before changing the brand name to Kent. Like the Langs and many other Jewish families, the Kent family saw the name change as the root of their middle-class success: "Katz was going nowhere, and Kent is nationwide," was the family lore. Then, too, like the Langs and like so many other name-changing families, the Kent family remained deeply rooted within the Jewish community of Toronto, living in a Jewish neighborhood, becoming leaders of local Jewish organizations, and maintaining networks of Jewish friends and family: "In the years that I knew the family, I don't think I ever saw a non-Jew come in the door," Trish recollected. "That was their way of protecting themselves."[6] The Lang and Kent families got along famously, in part because they shared the same Jewish background and the same narrative of triumph over their impoverished childhoods.

Trish and James Kent raised their children—Joanna, Marjorie, and Steven—as Jews in the suburbs of Fairfax County, Virginia, in the 1980s and 1990s. The family belonged to the Reform synagogue, attended services, and celebrated holidays, and the children had bar and bat mitzvah ceremonies. Trish became the president of the Northern Virginia Jewish Community Center, and they had large circles of Jewish family friends.

Yet the Kent siblings were still the only Jews in their elementary school. As Trish had, they felt like outsiders in a non-Jewish world, initially proud when they could pass as non-Jews. "When I was younger, I was told that I didn't look Jewish. . . . It was given as a compliment, it was taken as a compliment," Dove Kent (then called Marjorie) remembered. But being raised in the 1980s and 1990s, in a different world in which

Jewish identity was less fraught, Joanna and Marjorie never felt that they needed to shield themselves from scrutiny or that they needed to be silent about their identities or their family's name change. "I know that at various points for me and my siblings, there were opportunities for passing for Christian or non-Jewish, though we had no interest. People were often surprised to know that I was Jewish. The name Marjorie Kent doesn't sound Jewish at all," Dove Kent explained, noting that she "came out" as Jewish to people on more than one occasion.[7]

As young adults in the 2000s, both Joanna and Marjorie became deeply dissatisfied with names that did not encompass their Jewish identities. In 2007, Joanna made the decision to officially reclaim her grandfather's distinctive Jewish name, while keeping the name Kent as well. Since graduating from college in 1999, she had gone to Seattle, come out as gay, and gotten involved in the antiracist movement. But while she was energized by her political group's efforts to critique and challenge whiteness, she had felt intimidated and silenced by their unwillingness to talk about other ethnic identities. She began meeting in secret with another Jewish woman in the group to talk about the intersections between their Jewishness, whiteness, and antiracist commitments.

Joanna became connected with Jews for Economic and Racial Justice, went to New York, and interviewed Jewish women who were also thinking about intersections between Jewishness and whiteness. When she came back, she said, "I wanted to be out as a Jew. I wanted Jews to identify me. I would say I was Jewish, and people would say, 'You don't look Jewish' or 'Your name is Kent: you're not a real Jew.' [I wanted] to be included as a Jew." Earlier, she had read Melanie Kaye/Kantrowitz's essays on her name change, on being a queer Jewish woman who had reclaimed her family's Jewish name while also maintaining the changed name as a marker of her own white privilege, and she had been inspired: "I thought that was absolutely brilliant, and I wanted to do that. And I did." In an essay that she sent to her family after she had changed her name officially in 2007, Kent Katz explained,

> I want to recognize what my white skin, my height, my straight hair, my blue eyes, and a non-Jewish name has offered me. I want to illuminate my history of having the privilege to create my own safety, choosing when to out myself as a Jew and when to keep my Jewishness invisible. . . .

And I want to make apparent my culture, my heritage, my relationship with beautiful spiritual and cultural traditions. I want to claim my connections to Jewish values and teachings and to generations of Jews who have worked towards justice with determination, compassion, and reflection as I strive to do.

As a social justice educator, Kent Katz has traveled around the country to give workshops on antiracism and the Jewish community using the story of her name as a part of her work.[8]

Marjorie Dove Kent made a slightly different decision. Working as a Jewish professional with Jews for Economic and Racial Justice, Kent acknowledged that she would be "much more comfortable" if she had a name that was "unquestionably Jewish": "I would always include my middle name because it was a part of a Jewish name. I would always put it in there just so people would say, 'Oh, that's a Jewish name.'" Although she considered the idea of taking back her father's Jewish surname, she decided against it: "My life had been the result of all sorts of assimilation into whiteness. Kent was a more true marker of my life experience, the conditions that I'd had," Dove explained of her decision. Instead, in 2014, Marjorie Dove dropped her first name and adopted her middle name, becoming Dove Kent: "I have interestingly felt more comfortable having the name Dove. Now I pass as a Jewish man, at least on paper, which is closer, getting there."[9]

After the ethnic revival movement, Jews such as Dove and Joanna were proud to claim their Jewish identities, uncomfortable explaining their generic American-sounding names, and interested in signaling their Jewishness to both Jews and non-Jews around them. At the same time, at least some of these same Jews struggled not only with the ways their names insufficiently communicated Jewishness but also with the ways that their names had allowed them white privilege, giving them an invisibility and an option to claim ethnicity on their own terms.

The story of the Litowitz-Lang-Katz-Kent family is exceptional: only a minority of American Jews changed their names; fewer still reverted to their family's original name decades later; and in general, few Jewish families experienced quite so much name changing over the course of three generations. Nonetheless, even just one individual's decision to change his or her name led to substantial ramifications for family members generations later. This family's struggles with their names offer a valuable window into the meaning of name changing in the past 75 years.

As Raymond Lang's experiences suggest, name changing in the 1930s and 1940s was an unexceptional, normal behavior for Jews in New York City and, indeed, the United States. It is not surprising that an authority figure at a key moment in this young man's life might have seen it as a kindness or even as a professional duty—not an imposition or an insult—to suggest that he help his mentee find a new name.[10] If everyone in the community did not change their name, the vast majority of Jews knew someone who did or had been counseled to do so or had struggled with the decision whether to do so or had seen some sort of cultural representation of Jewish name changing. We need to revise our standard vision of name changing as the behavior of exceptional movie stars or confused immigrants. Name changing was the province of ordinary Jewish men and women, and it hovered in the background of many middle-class Jews' daily experiences.

The Kent-Lang family story also suggests for us the importance of family and community in name changing. Reuben Litowitz and Charlie Katz did not decide as lone individuals to change their names, nor did their decisions have impact on these men alone. Litowitz and Katz worked together with family members and trusted friends to change their names. More significantly, their name changes affected a broad web of family members. Both Lang's and Kent's decisions had lasting impact on the women and children who were a part of their families, as well as their descendants. Ida Kent decided along with Charlie to change their names for their shared goals of starting a pharmacy. Lang's wife, Sylvia, took on the name Lang, as well as the family secret that it represented: it was Trish's mother, not her father, who explained to Trish as a child why their names were different from their cousins' names. And to be sure, as a college student under 21, Lang was probably still identified as a child himself when he began planning to change his name. Women and children were actively involved in and deeply affected by name changing, something that American culture frequently and surprisingly forgets or ignores. If our standard vision of name changing is of an isolated man changing his name alone to make his way in the world, we need to reshape that vision to consider the active participation of women and children in name changing, both alone and in family units. Indeed, it was frequently networks of men, women, and children working together who filled out name-change petitions. Name changing was a family behavior, and it affected families for generations to come.

Raymond Lang's work in the federal government offers us insight into still another element of name changing that might seem exceptional but nonetheless hints at something quite normal. If Ellis Island officials did not impose new names on Jews, name changing was nonetheless aided and abetted by the state. New York Jews turned to local city courts to help them change names, and they did so in an environment in which the government was expanding its reach into individuals' daily lives, providing jobs and benefits and monitoring personal identity in ways it never had before. At the same time, the government allowed to thrive a private system of racial discrimination that used Jews' personal names to label, segregate, and exclude them. Indeed, Lang's story—like those of a few of the petitions found at the New York City Civil Court—suggests that the federal government itself participated in this system of discrimination. In the United States, Jews' names were not determined or limited by the state, as they were in Europe, and Jews faced no legal state racism, as did nonwhite minorities in the United States. Nonetheless, in a host of ways, the US government created conditions that subtly encouraged Jews to change their names, illustrating both the ways that voluntarism has shaped the US state more broadly and the ways that US state policies have intersected with racial identity. Moreover, if nations from Germany to Russia to Israel have historically instituted more coercive policies shaping Jews' personal and racial identities through their names, the example of American Jewish name changing allows us to understand a wider spectrum of state interest in Jewish names than historians have previously explored.

Litowitz's name change to Lang further highlights how much name changing was bound up with middle-class status for Jews in the United States. To be sure, most Jews reached the middle class without changing their names. But Litowitz's story shows how important some Jews believed name changing was for their middle-class aspirations. Reuben Litowitz—like so many name-changing Jews in the 1930s and 1940s—had entered college as a poor young man. He wanted to use his college education to join a prestigious profession that would assure his family of a comfortable life. He received multiple rejections from medical school, suggesting evidence of discrimination. Government work and accounting seemed to promise an equally comfortable life, and indeed they did, giving Raymond Lang a rewarding lifelong career and his family a comfortable home in the suburbs, like so many Jews of the postwar era. Name changing was an important part of class mobility in the mid-20th century—not a requirement but a significant aid, especially for Jews such as Lang who wanted to join a profession or live in a middle-class neighborhood that incorporated significant numbers of non-Jews. Our understandings of Jewish middle-class mobility have not always considered the impediments to that mobility. Litowitz's story reminds us of the obstacles that Jews faced and the losses they suffered as they advanced in the middle class.

If Raymond Lang saw his name change in terms of class mobility, the experiences of his daughter, Trish, and her daughters, Joanna and Dove, make clear the racial and ethnic meaning that underlay the surface of their family's changed name—and many other Jews' changed names as well. On the one hand, the Lang family clearly maintained its Jewish identity, rather than attempting to convert or abandon the community or to pass into a non-Jewish world. Yet the name change shielded the family from being openly different from the non-Jews of their community. With the name Lang, the family tried to become invisible, eliminating differences that might be embarrassing or humiliating, either for Raymond at work or for Trish and her siblings at school. By the time Trish arrived at the Ohio State University, she was expert in acting like a non-Jew, even if she never denied her Jewishness. Her name helped to shape her whiteness in the suburbs and at school—a whiteness that did not lead her to abandon the Jewish community but that allowed her to use her Jewishness only when she wanted to. Indeed, she drew on her Jewish identity to defend her own work in civil rights and ultimately to quit her sorority. Trish hid her Jewishness when she needed to, but she also wielded it as a weapon when she wanted to; this ability both to hide and to deploy ethnic identity has been identified by many sociologists as the essence of whiteness. As was true for many Jews with changed names by the 1960s and 1970s, Jewishness and whiteness went hand in hand, rather than opposing each other, as our historical conversations have too typically suggested.

Dove's and Joanna's stories, however, illustrate the frustrations and struggles of contemporary Jews to come to terms with their changed names—to find ways to be identified as Jewish with generic names in a multicultural world, while nonetheless grappling with both the anti-semitism and the white privilege that their generic names reflect. Not all Jews today struggle with their changed names as fundamentally as have Dove Kent and Joanna Kent Katz, but even the existence of some men and women questioning and thinking deeply about their Jewish and changed names and their meanings suggests an important reckoning with the past.

Indeed, perhaps the most important message inherent in the story of the Litowitz-Katz-Lang-Kent family is the emotional meaning of name changing. Even though Raymond and Sylvia Lang and Charlie and Ida Kent celebrated their success in selecting these new names and relished their new comfortable lives, they and their families struggled with those new names throughout the years. The older names became tied to painful family secrets, to shame and regret and loss. They became a burden that older generations felt they needed to shoulder alone: although Trish Kent knew about her family's changed last name as a child, she was devastated to learn, only after her father's death decades later, that he had also changed his first name to Raymond. Other oral histories and memoirs have described how new names sometimes created fissures between name changers and family members or friends who were suspicious of their access to non-Jewish worlds or angered by their perceived betrayal or amused by their pretensions at a non-Jewish identity.[11] Name changing may have been the foundation of generations of good Jewish jokes, but it has also been the source of confusion and sorrow for many ordinary Jews.[12] Name changing had emotional ramifications in the lives of Jews in the 20th century and beyond.

Looking at name-change petitions over the past 100 years gives insight into our culture and society. Long overlooked as historical sources, name-change petitions offer an important window into the shifting dynamics between the state on one hand and race, ethnicity, class, and gender on the other. Name changing has served as an important tool for racial reconstruction and economic advancement for some people, while it has also served as an agent of state surveillance and bureaucratic aggravation for others.

We typically think about our names as private and individual, while we frequently forget their tremendous social, economic, cultural, and political valence. Shakespeare's question "what's in a name?" plays on these assumptions, encouraging audiences to imagine temporarily that Romeo and Juliet's love can overcome the differences inscribed in their family names. But of course, Shakespeare intended a very different ultimate message: names indicate family, status, community, and culture, and they have significant impact on our lives. Jews in the middle of the 20th century—men, women, and children—understood that their names had serious consequences, and many of them devoted time, energy, and resources to erasing those names from public view. Similarly, African Americans, Latinos, Asian Americans, and Muslim Americans today celebrate the power of their names, even as they struggle with the impact of those names on their own and their families' economic and social well-being.

Individual Jews' decisions to change their names in the 20th century were not really individual: they typically involved networks of family and friends, they inspired Jewish groups to reconsider their definitions of community, and they sparked legislative and judicial responses that ultimately helped to reshape racial identity in the United States. The state was also closely implicated in these individual Jewish decisions to change names—if not as a coercive Ellis Island official, then as a city court clerk processing name-change paperwork, a military sergeant purposely mispronouncing Jewish names, a civil rights commissioner checking application blanks for discriminatory questions, or a judge ruling that racism can be a subtle and hidden process.

The goal of this book has been to recover the struggles of ordinary men, women, and children in a world that judged them for their names. I want to restore our understandings of those struggles and the decisions these people made to change their names in the face of those struggles. Portraits of name changers as shallow traitors have dominated American Jewish (and American) culture, and I want to upend those portraits, to allow us to understand the forgotten history of name changing and its meaning for Jewish individuals, as well as for the American Jewish community. What does it mean when we laugh at a name such as Sheldon or Lipschitz or tell a joke in which the name changer is the butt of the humor? The phenomenon of Jewish name changing in the middle of the 20th century offers us insight into the very real pain that those jokes have masked for years.

We need to look more closely at names, not as trivial labels or jokes but as gateways into the personal and political, familial and cultural, public and private dimensions of our lives. The stories of Reuben Litowitz, Charlie and Ida Katz, Joanna Kent, and Marjorie Kent—as well as the stories of Max Greenberger, Dora Sarietzky, and Elias Biegelman, and the stories of Bo Long Ma, Latoya Patrice Brown, and Ibrahim Antonello Castronovo—all demand to be told as a part of history, even as those names have become history themselves.

ACKNOWLEDGMENTS

It is fitting (if a bit too on the nose) that I end this book about names with a long list of names.

As the book suggests, though, names are not just superficial labels to be listed. These names are deeply meaningful, embedded in relationships, and crucial to our understanding of history. There would indeed be no book at all without the people whose names are listed in these pages. It goes without saying, of course, that if there are errors in this book, the people whose names are listed here are in no way responsible. I am the one who will need to change my own name out of embarrassment. I will probably change it to Rosenberg.

First and most importantly, I need to thank Ernesto Belzaguy, Michael Boyle, James Lopez, Rochelle Klempner, Carol Alt, Alia Razzaq, and many others who have worked at the New York City Civil Court. Too many years ago, when I first began work on this project, Ernesto Belzaguy, who was then First Deputy Chief Clerk at the Court, graciously brought me into his office, showed me the hundreds of boxes of name-change petitions housed in the building, and offered me full access to them. His generosity was unparalleled, and it made this volume possible. Mike Boyle and James Lopez helped me navigate files and find office space and provided good cheer and company as I worked. Over the course of years of research, I relied on many others at the Civil Court for needs both large and small, and they were always unfailingly helpful, giving me a great appreciation for the hard work of New York City civil servants.

Three women at Michigan State University were instrumental in helping me with the quantitative, geocoding, and legal research techniques necessary to analyze my research. I am grateful to the university for providing me with their invaluable services and even more grateful to them for their kind willingness to go out of their way to help me. Sarah Hession at the MSU Center for Statistical Training and Consulting showed me how to analyze my raw data and to understand what was statistically significant in my findings. Barbara Bean at the MSU Law Library helped me navigate New York State civil rights law, explore the culture of the legal profession in the 1920s and 1930s, and find judicial decisions regarding name changing throughout the 20th century. Amanda Tickner at the MSU Main Library helped me to construct the book's maps and, even more significantly, to analyze the relationship between neighborhoods and class in New York City. All of these amazing women put in hours of their own time and energy to offer me assistance, enthusiasm, and support when it was badly needed.

I also need to thank the archivists and librarians who facilitated my archival research. At the Center for Jewish History, where I conducted most of my research, Fruma Mohrer and Ettie Goldwasser at YIVO and Tanya Elder, Susan Malbin, Boni Jo Koelliker, and Elizabeth Hyman at the American Jewish Historical Society were extremely helpful. Marion Smith at the National Archives gave me important clues at the beginning of my search. I am also grateful to archivists and librarians at the New York State Archives and Library in Albany; Princeton University Rare Books and Special Collections; University Archives, Rare Book & Manuscript Library at Columbia University in the City of New York; University of Mississippi Archives and Special Collections; the Hagley Museum and Library; the American Jewish Committee Archives; and the Ellis Island Archives.

I received generous funding from a number of institutions, including the Jean and Samuel Frankel Institute for Advanced Judaic Studies at the University of Michigan, the Association for Jewish Studies, the YIVO Institute for Jewish Research, the MSU Humanities and Arts Research Program, the MSU Provost Undergraduate Research Initiative, and the MSU History Department and Jewish Studies Program. I also participated in a number of seminars and workshops where many talented colleagues commented on my work: the Frankel Institute for Advanced Judaic Studies; the Newberry Seminar on Women and Gender; the Jews in Postwar America seminar at the 2014 AJS conference; the Posen Summer Seminar on Approaches to Jewish Secularism; the Milstein Family Research Fellowship Conference at the YIVO Institute for Jewish Research; the Myth of Silence Conference at the University of California–Los Angeles; and the MSU-CIC Midcareer Faculty Seminar on Race and Ethnicity.

Undergraduate and graduate students did much of the important grunt work of locating published materials and even worse: data entry. Many also helped me creatively with developing websites or reading the materials in ways I had not seen before. Many thanks to these graduate and undergraduate student assistants (some of them now friends and colleagues in the field of history) for their hard work, clear thinking, and good cheer: Allan Amanik, Allie (Browe) Dennis, Emily Calabrese, Rebecca Koerselman, Sylvia Marques, Sebastian Mercier, Katherine Moilanen, Micaela Procopio, Allison Rosen, Lauren Rouff, Justin Rowe, Emmy Walters, and Connor Yeck.

I owe a tremendous debt to the people who were willing to speak with me or send me information about their own experiences with name changing. I need to thank in particular Trish Kent, Dove Kent, and Joanna Kent Katz for their willingness to open up the story of their family for this book; and many thanks to Marsha Heller and Danielle Feris for introducing us. And I would like to thank the many other people who offered me their own stories either at public talks, over email, or in oral histories. Special mention goes to friends and family members such as Reva Blum, Miranda DuClair, Max Ferm, Jay Gold, Marcia Horan, Stuart Marvin, and Steve Rayburn. Perhaps most crucially, I need to acknowledge the people whose name-change petitions I have relied on in writing this book. Their petitions are public information, but they shared details that were personal and intimate. I hope that these men and women and their descendants feel I have done justice to their difficult decisions and complicated lives.

A number of editors helped greatly as I refined and developed my arguments: Edward Linenthal, John Bukowczyk, and Wendy Rose Bice. Reviewers at the *Journal of American History*, the *Journal of American Ethnic History*, and NYU Press were also instrumental in offering sharp and invaluable comments.

Thanks to New York University Press for its work publishing this volume. Hasia Diner has been supportive of this project since I first mentioned it to her years ago, and she has continued in her unfailing support. Eric Zinner worked to acquire the book and bring it to production. Lisha Nadkarni, Cecilia Cancellaro, Mary Beth Jarrad, Dolma Ombadykow, and many others at the press all helped to make it a finished product.

Staff members in the Department of History and Jewish Studies Program at MSU—Debra Greer, Elyse Hansen, Jeanna Norris, and Viki Gietzel—helped me navigate bureaucracy and get reimbursements for needed research and conference trips. I truly appreciated their help.

Friends and colleagues diligently scoured memoirs and obituary pages for name-change stories for me or directed me to useful secondary or primary sources, let me bounce ideas off of them, helped me with the publishing process or digital sources or funding, came to my workshops and lectures, and/or provided needed moral support. Many thanks to Michael Alexander, Mark Bauman, Max Baumgarten, Marc Bernstein, Costanza Biavaschi, Linda Borish, Lizabeth Cohen, Emily Conroy-Krutz, Amy DeRogatis, Anne Dohrenwend, Ian Dworkin, Judith Dworkin, Jodi Eichler-Levine, Carrie Euler, Sara Fingal, Aleisa Fishman, Joshua Furman, Stephanie Ginensky, Susan Glenn, Steve Gold, Eric Goldstein, Rachel Gordan, Cheryl Greenberg, Sheryl Groden, Steve Haider, Walter Hawthorne, Daniel Horowitz, Sarah Klimek, Shira Kohn, Rachel Kranson, Jonathan Krasner, Miriamne Krummel, Josh Lambert, Christine Levecq, Mary Lewis, Brandon Locke, Deborah Margolis, Keren McGinity, Adam Mendelsohn, Tony Michels, Dan Mishkin, Leslie Moch, Deborah Dash Moore, Francesca Morgan, Ken Muir, Avigail Oren, Sean Pager, Matt Pauly, Josh Perelman, Sara Pugach, Christine Root, Jonathan Sarna, Kevin Schultz, Ethan Segal, the late Tanya Sigal, Nancy Sinkoff, Bobby Smiley, Judith Smith, Daniel Soyer, Keely Stauter-Halsted, Ronen Steinberg, Kim Stone, Alon Tal, Chantal Tetreault, Britt Tevis, Nick Underwood, Margot Valles, Helen Veit, Naoko Wake, Kerry Wallach, Ken Waltzer, Steve Weiland, David Weinstein, and Erica Windler. Kirsten Danis and Bob Kolker get a special shout-out for the support and sympathy, for the professional advice, and of course, for the beautiful Park Slope apartment that was essentially mine for research trips whenever I needed it.

I am grateful to the amazing friends and colleagues who read and commented on portions of this book: Sarah Bunin Benor, Allison Berg, Jessica Cooperman, Lisa Fine, Karla Goldman, Ronnie Grinberg, Rebecca Kobrin, Andrea Louie, and Terese Monberg. And for those rare friends and family members who actually suffered through the whole manuscript, there is a special spot in heaven (with lots of chocolate) for you all: Lois Fermaglich, Jonathan Gold, Melissa Klapper, Mindy Morgan, and Anna Pegler-Gordon.

I have been fortunate to have loving and supportive family members throughout my life, including the Fermaglich-Abrams family, the Sunter family, the extended Gold family, and the Hochman-Jackson family. I miss especially my aunt, the late Sondra Schaare, and both my grandmothers, Gene Fermaglich and Pearl Gelber, and wish that they were here to read this book. Danny, Lois, and Lewis Fermaglich have been among my greatest supporters throughout my career and especially in writing this book. They not only gave me couches to sleep on but attended my public talks, gave me pep talks when I hit roadblocks, forwarded me obituaries and newspaper articles, conducted an oral history or two (after getting IRB training, of course), gathered some documents in the archives, and asked important questions about my work. Going above and beyond the call of duty, my mother, Lois, actually came to the Civil Court to help me finish my research one crazy week in 2015, proving that maternal love really does last a lifetime. I am so grateful.

Finally, there are the immediate members of the Gold-Fermaglich family. For Jon Gold, there are not enough words to say thank you. And most of them would be clichés anyway, and you would scorn them. From every extra hour you spent watching children or washing dishes to each evening you dedicated to reading or editing my work and cheering wholeheartedly every small success: this book would not, could not exist without you. For Raphael Benjamin Fermaglich Gold and Dalia Gene Gold Fermaglich, on the other hand, there are probably too many words. This book might have shown up a lot earlier without you. But it would be nowhere near as meaningful. You are both so beautiful and precious—more beautiful even than the very long names we took months to choose for you. I dedicate this book to you as a testament to my love for you and as final evidence that I do not actually change people's names for a living.

NOTES

INTRODUCTION

1. Petition N533-1942, Name Change Petitions Collection, New York City Civil Court, New York, NY. All name-change petitions are from this source.
2. Petition N129-1946.
3. Petition N884-44C-1957.
4. See, for example, Ewa Morawska, "In Defense of the Assimilation Model," *Journal of American Ethnic History* 13 (Winter 1994): 83–84; Gary Gerstle, *American Crucible: Race and Nation in the Twentieth Century* (Princeton, NJ: Princeton University Press, 2001), 165–66. For folkloric descriptions of name changing, see, for example, Robert M. Rennick, "Hitlers and Others Who Changed Their Names and a Few Who Did Not," *Names* 17 (September 1969): 199–207; and Rennick, "Judicial Procedures for a Change-of-Name in the United States," *Names* 13 (September 1965): 145–68.
5. For discussions of assimilation, see Russell A. Kazal, "Revisiting Assimilation: The Rise, Fall, and Reappraisal of a Concept in American Ethnic History," *American Historical Review* 100 (April 1995): 437–71; Michael R. Olneck, "Assimilation and American National Identity," in *A Companion to American Immigration*, ed. Reed Ueda (Malden, MA: Wiley Blackwell, 2006), 202–24; and Susan K. Brown and Frank D. Bean, "Assimilation Models, Old and New: Explaining a Long-Term Process," *Migration Information Source*, October 2006, www.migrationinformation.org. For a classic statement on the construction of ethnicity, see Kathleen Neils Conzen, David A. Gerber, Ewa Morawska, George E. Pozzetta, and Rudolph J. Vecoli, "The Invention of Ethnicity: A Perspective from the U.S.A.," *Journal of American Ethnic History* 12 (Fall 1992): 3–41. For the complex dynamics between mobility and discrimination, see, for example, George Sánchez, *Becoming Mexican American: Ethnicity, Culture, and Identity in Chicano Los Angeles, 1900–1945* (New York: Oxford University Press, 1993); and Nancy C. Carnevale, *A New Language, A New World: Italian Immigrants in the United States, 1890–1945* (Urbana: University of Illinois Press, 2009).
6. Costanza Biavaschi, Corrado Giulietti, and Zahra Siddique, "The Economic Payoff of Name Americanization" (Discussion Paper No. 7725, Institute for the Study of Labor, Bonn, November 2013).
7. Mary Antin, *The Promised Land*, 2nd ed. (Princeton, NJ: Princeton University Press, 1969), 187–88.

8. For some of the basic texts that have helped to build this narrative, see Robert Michael, *A Concise History of American Antisemitism* (Lanham, MD: Rowman and Littlefield, 2005); Leonard Dinnerstein, *Antisemitism in America* (New York: Oxford University Press, 1994); and David A. Gerber, ed., *Anti-Semitism in American History* (Urbana: University of Illinois Press, 1986). For more detailed monographs on some of these subjects, see Laura B. Rosenzweig, *Hollywood's Spies: The Undercover Surveillance of Nazis in Los Angeles* (New York: NYU Press, 2017); Victoria Saker Woeste, *Henry Ford's War on Jews and the Legal Battle Against Free Speech* (Stanford, CA: Stanford University Press, 2012); Stephen H. Norwood, "Marauding Youth and the Christian Front: Antisemitic Violence in Boston and New York during World War II," *American Jewish History* 91, no. 2 (2003): 233–67; Donald I. Warren, *Radio Priest: Charles Coughlin, Father of Hate Radio* (New York: Free Press, 1996); Alan Brinkley, *Voices of Protest: Huey Long, Father Coughlin, and the Great Depression* (New York: Knopf Books, 1982); Marcia Graham Synnott, *The Half-Opened Door: Discrimination and Admissions at Harvard, Yale, and Princeton, 1900–1970* (Westport, CT: Greenwood, 1979).

9. For a criticism of American Jewish historians for avoiding American antisemitism, see Hasia Diner and Tony Michels, "Considering American Jewish History," *OAH Newsletter* 35, no. 4 (2007): 9–18.

10. I am indebted to David A. Gerber's description of American antisemitism as "insidious." See Gerber, "Anti-Semitism and Jewish-Gentile Relations in American Historiography and the American Past," in Gerber, *Anti-Semitism in American History*, 19.

11. Petition N1608-1937.

12. For discussion of exclusion following Jews' success, see Marcia Graham Synnott, "Anti-Semitism and American Universities: Did Quotas Follow the Jews?," in Gerber, *Anti-Semitism in American History*, 233–71.

13. For a criticism of this lack of attention to economic obstacles and even failures, see, for example, Rebecca Kobrin, "Destructive Creators: Sender Jarmulowsky and Financial Failure in the Annals of American Jewish History," *American Jewish History* 97, no. 2 (2013): 105–37.

14. Petitions N159255-1937 and N57-1942. See also, for example, Petition N649-1946.

15. For oral histories that describe Jews' belief that a name change would help their chances in business, see, for example, Joy Anne Friedler, email communication with author, March 17, 2015; Sarah Beth Robbins (now Weers), email communication with author, February 8, 2015; Jay Gold, interview by author, digital recording, July 14, 2014.

16. See, for example, Kobrin, "Destructive Creators"; Rebecca Kobrin, ed., *Chosen Capital: The Jewish Encounter with American Capitalism* (New Brunswick, NJ: Rutgers University Press, 2012); Adam D. Mendelsohn, *The Rag Race: How Jews Sewed Their Way to Success in America and the British Empire* (New York: NYU Press, 2015); and Eli Lederhendler, *Jewish Immigrants and American Capitalism,*

1880–1920: From Caste to Class (New York: Cambridge University Press, 2009). For an exception to this trend, see Hasia Diner, Roads Taken: The Great Jewish Migrations to the New World and the Peddlers Who Forged the Way (New Haven, CT: Yale University Press, 2015). For a criticism of the trend, see Riv-Ellen Prell, "The Economic Turn in American Jewish History: When Women (Mostly) Disappeared," unpublished essay in author's possession. Many thanks to Riv-Ellen Prell for allowing me to cite this piece.

17. Sherwin B. Nuland, Lost in America: A Journey with My Father (New York: Knopf, 2003), 141.

18. Melanie Kaye/Kantrowitz, "Some Notes on Lesbian Jewish Identity" (1982), in The Issue Is Power: Essays on Women, Jews, Violence, and Resistance (San Francisco: Aunt Lute Books, 1992), 80.

19. For criticisms of women's oppression in surname-change expectations, see, for example, Una Stannard, Mrs. Man (San Francisco: GermainBooks, 1977); Omi [Morgenstern Leissner], "Jewish Women's Family Names: A Feminist Legal Analysis," Israel Law Review 34 (2000): 560–99; Elizabeth F. Emens, "Changing Name Changing: Framing Rules and the Future of Marital Law," University of Chicago Law Review 74 (2007): 761–863; Kelly Snyder, "All Names Are Not Equal: Choice of Marital Surname and Equal Protection," Washington University Journal of Law & Policy 30 (2009): 560–87, http://openscholarship.wustl.edu/law. See also my own work on women and gender in the New York City name-change petitions, "I'm the Sole Provider and Caretaker" (in progress); and "Married Names, Middle Names, Maiden Names: Gender and Name Changing in the New York City Civil Court in the 20th Century," paper presented at the Newberry Seminar on Women and Gender, Chicago, IL, February 19, 2016.

20. See, for example, Brian P. Luskey, On the Make: Clerks and the Quest for Capital in Nineteenth-Century America (New York: NYU Press, 2010), Daniel J. Walkowitz, Working with Class: Social Workers and the Politics of Middle-Class Identity (Chapel Hill: University of North Carolina Press, 1999); and Pierre Bourdieu, Distinction: A Social Critique of the Judgement of Taste, trans. Richard Nice (Cambridge, MA: Harvard University Press, 1984).

21. See, for example, Michael Rogin, Blackface, White Noise: Jewish Immigrants in the Hollywood Melting Pot (Berkeley: University of California Press, 1996); Karen Brodkin, How Jews Became White Folks and What That Says About Race in America (New Brunswick, NJ: Rutgers University Press, 1998); Matthew Frye Jacobson, Whiteness of a Different Color: European Immigrants and the Alchemy of Race (Cambridge, MA: Harvard University Press, 1998); Eric L. Goldstein, The Price of Whiteness: Jews, Race, and American Identity (Princeton, NJ: Princeton University Press, 2006).

22. See, for example, Richard Dyer, "White," Screen 29, no. 4 (1988): 44–64; Dyer, White: Essays on Race and Culture (New York: Routledge, 1997); Ruth Frankenberg, White Women, Race Matters (Minneapolis: University of Minnesota Press, 1993); Frankenberg, "Introduction: Local Whitenesses, Localizing Whiteness,"

in *Displacing Whiteness*, ed. Frankenberg (Durham, NC: Duke University Press, 1997), 1–33; Birgit Brander Rasmussen, Eric Klinenberg, Irene J. Nexica, and Matt Wray, introduction to *The Making and Unmaking of Whiteness*, ed. Rasmussen, Klinenberg, Nexica, and Wray (Durham, NC: Duke University Press, 2001), 1–24. Note that the introduction by Rasmussen et al. and Ruth Frankenberg's essay in the same volume ("The Mirage of an Unmarked Whiteness," 72–96) critique notions of whiteness's invisibility, particularly for nonwhites. Although these criticisms are important interventions, they do not negate the perspectives of Jews who longed for an erasure of racial markings.

23. See, for example, Richard Alba, *Ethnic Identity: The Transformation of White America* (New Haven, CT: Yale University Press, 1990), 295; Mary C. Waters, *Ethnic Options: Choosing Identities in America* (Berkeley: University of California Press, 1990).

24. Stuart Svonkin, *Jews Against Prejudice: American Jews and the Fight for Civil Liberties* (New York: Columbia University Press, 1997), 190; Cheryl Lynn Greenberg, *Troubling the Waters: Black-Jewish Relations in the American Century* (Princeton, NJ: Princeton University Press, 2006), 166. Michael Rogin suggests changes to Jewish racial identity through both civil rights activism and racial masquerade, see Rogin, *Blackface, White Noise*, 209-268.

25. Elias Tobenkin, "Why I Would Not Change My Name," *American Legion Monthly* 8, no. 1 (1930): 7.

26. Fred L. Israel, email communication with author, December 23, 2015.

27. Nathaniel Zalowitz, "Why Should Levy Become Lee and Rabinowitz Robins?," *Jewish Daily Forward*, March 7, 1926.

28. Clement Greenberg, "Under 40: A Symposium," *Contemporary Jewish Record*, February 1, 1944, 32. See also Lionel Trilling, ibid., 15–16; Stanley M. Elkins, interview by author, audio recording, February 2, 1998.

29. For an important discussion of this cultural phenomenon, see Susan A. Glenn, "The Vogue of Jewish Self-Hatred in Post–World War II America," *Jewish Social Studies: History, Culture, Society*, n.s. 12, no. 3 (2006): 95–136.

30. Petitions N237-1942 and N129-1946.

31. "Big Charitable Gifts: Where Donors Have Given $1 Million or More," *Chronicle of Philanthropy*, accessed January 25, 2018, http://philanthropy.com; Jane Levere, "Featured Philanthropist: Transammonia's Ronald Stanton Discusses Two Loves: Opera and Philanthropy," *Forbes*, September 17, 2011, www.forbes.com; Zach Wichter, "Ronald P. Stanton, Trammo Founder Who Shared His Fortune, Dies at 88," *New York Times*, September 28, 2016.

32. For more on Grant, see "University Musical Society Receives $1,000,000 Gift as Part of U-M Victors for Michigan Campaign," press release, University of Michigan, January 16, 2015; and *Building New York: New York Life Stories with Michael Stoler* (aired June 24, 2013).

33. Beverly Winston to David L. Cohn, May 24, 1948, David L. Cohn Collection, University of Mississippi, Oxford, MS; see also, for example, Petition N11978-1932.

34. J. Alvin Kugelmass, "Name-Changing—and What It Gets You," *Commentary* 14 (1952): 145–50.

35. Reva Blum, telephone interview by author, digital recording, March 29, 2018.

36. For Garland's identification as a Jew, see, for example, Uriel Heilman, "Inside the Jewish Life of Supreme Court Nominee Merrick Garland," *Jerusalem Post*, March 20, 2016, www.jpost.com. For Larry King's identification as a Jew, see, for example, Gaby Wenig, "Q and A with Larry King," *Jewish Journal*, November 3, 2003, www.jewishjournal.com.

37. For a call for "dispersionist" rather than "communalist" American Jewish history, see David Hollinger, "Communalist and Dispersionist Approaches to American Jewish History in an Increasingly Post-Jewish Era," *American Jewish History* 95, no. 1 (2009): 1–32, as well as responses by Hasia Diner, Alan Kraut, Paula Hyman, and Tony Michels in the same volume.

38. Daniel F. Littlefield, Jr., and Lonnie E. Underhill, "Renaming the American Indian: 1890–1913," *American Studies* 12, no. 2 (1971): 33–45. See also Thomas Biolsi, "The Birth of the Reservation: Making the Modern Individual Among the Lakota," *American Ethnologist* 22, no. 1 (1995): 28–53.

39. Anna Pegler-Gordon, *In Sight of America: Photography and the Development of U.S. Immigration Policy* (Berkeley: University of California Press, 2009), 24.

40. Una Stannard, "Manners Make Laws: Married Women's Names in the United States," *Names* 32, no. 2 (1984): 114–28.

41. See, for example, Richard L. Kagan and Abigail Dyer, eds., *Inquisitorial Inquiries: Brief Lives of Secret Jews and Other Heretics* (Baltimore: Johns Hopkins University, 2011); Kevin Ingram, ed., *The Conversos and Moriscos in Late Medieval Spain and Beyond* (Boston: Brill, 2009); Linda Martz, *A Network of Converso Families in Early Modern Toledo: Assimilating a Minority* (Ann Arbor: University of Michigan Press, 2003), 76–80.

42. See, for example, Dietz Bering, *The Stigma of Names: Antisemitism in German Daily Life, 1912–1933*, trans. Neville Plaice (Ann Arbor: University of Michigan Press, 1992), esp. 27–33; Eugene M. Avrutin, *Jews and the Imperial State: Identification Politics in Tsarist Russia* (Ithaca, NY: Cornell University Press, 2010), 148–50; and Gerard Noiriel, "The Identification of the Citizen: The Birth of Republican Civil Status in France," in *Documenting Individual Identity: The Development of State Practices in the Modern World*, eds. Jane Caplan and John Torpey (Princeton, NJ: Princeton University Press, 2001), 36–37. For broader considerations of surnames as measures of social control in Europe, with specific attention to Jews, see Steven Wilson, *The Means of Naming: A Social and Cultural History of Naming in Western Europe* (London: UCL Press, 1998), 243–46; Jane Caplan, "'This or That Particular Person': Protocols of Identification in Nineteenth Century Europe," in Caplan and Torpey, *Documenting Individual Identity*, 49–66; and James C. Scott, *Seeing like a State: How Certain Schemes to Improve the Human Condition Have Failed* (New Haven, CT: Yale University Press, 1998), 64–71. For useful discussion of the relationship between Jews and the state in Emancipation throughout

Europe and in the United States, see Pierre Birnbaum and Ira Katznelson, *Paths of Emancipation: Jews, States, and Citizenship* (Princeton, NJ: Princeton University Press, 1995).

43. See, for example, Avrutin, *Jews and the Imperial State*; Bering, *Stigma of Names*.

44. See Robert M. Rennick, "The Nazi Name Decrees of the Nineteen Thirties," *Names* 18 (1970): 65–88.

45. See Efrat Neuman, "In the Name of Zionism, Change Your Name," *Ha'aretz*, April 17, 2014, www.haaretz.com; Omi (Naomi) Morgenstern Leissner, "A Jewish Rose by Any Other Name: Thoughts on the Regulation of Jewish Women's Personal Names," *Women in Judaism: A Multidisciplinary Journal* 14, no. 1 (2017): 16–19.

46. See, for example, Scott Baird, "Anglicizing Ethnic Surnames," *Names* 54, no. 2 (2006): 173–92; Marian L. Smith, "American Names: Declaring Independence," *Immigration Daily*, accessed January 26, 2018, www.ilw.com.

47. See, for example, Edward J. Bander and Lawrence G. Greene, *Change of Name and Law of Names* (Dobbs Ferry, NY: Oceana, 1973), 1–4; *Laws of New York* (Albany, 1893), chapter 366, title X, section 2410, p. 722.

48. See Scott, *Seeing like a State*, 64–71; James C. Scott, John Tehranian, and Jeremy Mathias, "The Production of Legal Identities Proper to States: The Case of the Permanent Family Surname," *Comparative Studies in Society and History* 44, no. 1 (2002): 4–44.

49. See, for example, John Torpey, *The Invention of the Passport: Surveillance, Citizenship and the State* (Cambridge: Cambridge University Press, 2000), 93. For criticisms of the idea of the United States as a weak state, see William J. Novak, "The Myth of the 'Weak' American State," *American Historical Review* 113 (June 2008): 752–72; and essays by John Fabian Witt, Gary Gerstle, Julia Adams, and William J. Novak in "*AHR* Exchange: On the 'Myth' of the 'Weak' American State," *American Historical Review* 115 (June 2010): 766–800.

50. See, for example, Susan J. Pearson, "'Age Ought to Be a Fact': The Campaign against Child Labor and the Rise of the Birth Certificate," *Journal of American History* 101 (March 2015): 1144–65; Jessica Wang, "Dogs and the Making of the American State: Voluntary Association, State Power, and the Politics of Animal Control in New York City, 1850–1920," *Journal of American History* 98, no. 4 (2012): 998–1024; and Christopher Capozzola, *Uncle Sam Wants You: World War I and the Making of the Modern American Citizen* (New York: Oxford University Press, 2008).

51. See Deborah Dash Moore, *At Home in America: Second Generation New York Jews* (New York: Columbia University Press, 1981); Beth Wenger, *New York Jews and the Great Depression: Uncertain Promise* (Syracuse, NY: Syracuse University Press, 1999); and Jeffrey Gurock, *Jews of Gotham: New York Jews in a Changing City, 1920–2010*, vol. 3 of *City of Promises: A History of the Jews of New York*, ed. Deborah Dash Moore (New York: NYU Press, 2012).

52. For information on New York's growing white-collar economy and Jews within that economy, see Joshua B. Freeman, *Working-Class New York: Life and Labor*

since World War II (New York: Free Press, 2000); Moore, *At Home in America*; Wenger, *New York Jews and the Great Depression*; Gurock, *Jews in Gotham*; and Miriam Cohen, *Workshop to Office: Two Generations of Italian Women in New York City, 1900–1950* (Ithaca, NY: Cornell University Press, 1992), 161–62.

53. Wenger, *New York Jews and the Great Depression*; Martha Biondi, *To Stand and Fight: The Struggle for Civil Rights in New York City* (Cambridge, MA: Harvard University Press, 2003).

54. Leonard Broom, Helen P. Beem, Virginia Harris, "Characteristics of 1,107 Petitioners for Change of Name," *American Sociological Review* 20, no. 1 (1955): 33–39.

55. Judith B. Kramer and Seymour Leventman, *Children of the Gilded Ghetto: Conflict Resolutions of Three Generations of American Jews* (New Haven, CT: Yale University Press, 1961), 86–87.

56. "Name Changing: R. Brown, St. Louis, Missouri," folder 1, box 72, collection C0246, Louis Adamic Papers, Princeton University Library, Princeton, NJ. This folder indicates the geographical range of name changing in the 1930s and 1940s.

57. Mrs. Hubert H. Lowe to David L. Cohn, May 25, 1948, David L. Cohn Collection. See other letters in the folder for the wide geographical reach of these essays.

58. Michael J. Collier to Laura Z. Hobson, July 14, 1947, folder: "Gentleman's Agreement: Correspondence, Fan Mail 1947," box 20, Laura Z. Hobson Collection, Rare Book & Manuscript Library, Columbia University, New York. See this box for the geographic range of Hobson's readers and audiences.

59. Meyer Levin, *The Old Bunch* (Secaucus, NJ: Citadel, 1937), 328–30; Edna Ferber, "The Girl Who Went Right" (1918), in *America and I: Short Stories by American Jewish Women Writers*, ed. Joyce Antler (Boston: Beacon, 1990); Budd Schulberg, *What Makes Sammy Run?* (New York: Random House, 1941), 218–20; Burke Davis, *Whisper My Name* (New York: Rinehart, 1949); Jack Ansell, *The Shermans of Mannerville* (New York: Arbor House, 1971).

60. Paul Rudd, "Alfred Uhry," *BOMB—Artists in Conversation* 60 (Summer 1997), http://bombmagazine.org.

61. Between 1887 and 1962, New Yorkers submitted name changes to City Court. In 1962, City Court and Municipal Court merged to become Civil Court. Residents of the Bronx, Brooklyn, Queens, and Staten Island could also change their names in separate borough courts, and residents of all five boroughs could also change their names at the Court of Common Pleas before 1895 and in State Supreme Court after 1895. Furthermore, immigrants could officially change their names on naturalization petitions after 1906. For more, see Arthur Scherr, "Change-of-Name Petitions of the New York Courts: An Untapped Source in Historical Onomastics," *Names* 34 (September 1986), 284–302; and the New York State Unified Court System, "Civil Court History," accessed January 25, 2018, http://nycourts.gov.

62. Note that I also gathered and analyzed petitions from 1918 and 1946. These years did not fit into my systematic pattern (that is, they did not fall every fifth year),

but the large numbers of petitions during these two years suggested that they were historically relevant—following both world wars—and that they needed to be analyzed.

63. For more on Sephardic names, see Guilherme Faiguenboim, Paulo Valadares, and Anna Rosa Campagno, eds., *Dicionario Sefaradi de Sobrenomes: Inclusive Cristaos-novos, Conversos, Marranos, Italianos, Berberes e sua História a Espanha, Portugal e Italia / Dictionary of Sephardic Surnames: Including Christianized Jews, Conversos, Marranos, Italians, Berbers, and Their History in Spain, Portugal and Italy*, 2nd ed. (Rio de Janeiro: Avotaynu, 2003).

64. For stigma surrounding Jewish names after Emancipation, see Bering, *Stigma of Names*.

65. See Alexander Beider, *A Dictionary of Jewish Surnames from the Kingdom of Poland* (Teaneck, NJ: Avotaynu, 1996), 33, 37–38.

66. Ibid., 8–14.

67. See Alexander Beider, *A Dictionary of Ashkenazic Given Names: Their Origins, Structure, Pronunciation, and Migrations* (Bergenfield, NJ: Avotaynu, 2001), 1–11. For criticism of the absence of girls' names from Jewish law, see Leissner, "Jewish Rose by Any Other Name."

68. See Stanley Lieberson, *A Matter of Taste: How Names, Fashions, and Culture Change* (New Haven, CT: Yale University Press, 2000), 208–22; and Susan Cotts Watkins and Andrew S. London, "Personal Names and Cultural Change: A Study of the Naming Patterns of Italians and Jews in the United States in 1910," *Social Science History* 18 (Summer 1994): 169–209. For a similar phenomenon taking place in Europe, see Bering, *Stigma of Names*, 44–75; and Ernest Maass, letter to the editor, *Commentary*, January 1956, www.commentarymagazine.com.

69. See, for example, Avrutin, *Jews and the Imperial State*, 152–53; Bering, *Stigma of Names*, 78–79.

70. For comparison with French name legislation and name changing, see Nicole Lapierre, *Changer de nom* (Paris: Stock, 1995).

71. See, for similar analysis, Henry Bial, *Acting Jewish: Negotiating Ethnicity on the Stage and Screen* (Ann Arbor: University of Michigan Press, 2005).

72. William Haefeli, cartoon, *New Yorker*, November 9, 2009, www.newyorker.com.

CHAPTER 1. "MY NAME PROVED TO BE A GREAT HANDICAP"

1. Petition N5454-1932.

2. Note that I did not have access to the actual petitions for the years 1907 to 1927; they are missing from the Civil Court of the City of New York records. Instead, I used court orders to gather data on petitioners during these years. Petitions contained the reasons for the name change; court orders gave only names of petitioners and the judge's decision. My data here are thus necessarily incomplete for 1907 through 1927.

3. Because the records for these years are incomplete, I can only quantify reasons for name changing for the 1930s.

4. For the Jewish population of New York, see C. Morris Horowitz and Lawrence J. Kaplan, *The Estimated Jewish Population of the New York Area, 1900–1975* (New York: Federation of Jewish Philanthropies, 1959), 22–23. Researchers for this study used the Yom Kippur method of calculating Jews—that is, they calculated the numbers of children absent from public schools on Yom Kippur, the holiest day of the year. The method, of course, has flaws: it links Jewish identity to Jewish religious practice, and it tends to understate Jewish population where the population is small (and probably overstate Jewish population where the population is large).

5. See Nathan Glazer and Daniel Patrick Moynihan, *Beyond the Melting Pot: The Negroes, Puerto Ricans, Jews, Italians, and Irish of New York City* (Cambridge, MA: MIT Press, 1963), 185–86. See also John Horace Mariano, *The Second Generation of Italians in New York City* (Boston: Christopher, 1921), 11–15; and William B. Shedd, *Italian Population in New York* (New York: Casa Italiana Educational Bureau, 1934), 3.

6. See Lawrence G. Greene, *How to Change Your Name, and the Law of Names* (New York: Oceana, 1954), 7, 76; Bander and Greene, *Change of Name and Law of Names*, 1, 73. See also *Laws of New York*, vol. 1 (Albany, 1893), chapter 366, title X, section 2410, p. 722.

7. For the importance of kin networks in finding working-class jobs, see, for example, John Bodnar, *The Transplanted: A History of Immigrants in Urban America* (Bloomington: Indiana University Press, 1985), 61–64. For a description of working-class women's bodies being appraised when seeking domestic service, see, for example, Ella Baker and Marvel Cooke, "The Slave Market," *Crisis* 42 (November 1935): 330–31, 340.

8. For these working-class name changers, see, for example, Petitions N4155-1932, N3362-1932, N160532-1937, and N158737-1937.

9. For Jews' prominence in the middle class by the 1930s, see Wenger, *New York Jews and the Great Depression*, 15–17.

10. Jacobson, *Whiteness of a Different Color*, 171–99; Goldstein, *Price of Whiteness*, 35–50.

11. Archibald MacLeish, "Jews in America," *Fortune* 13 (February 1936): 141; see also Heywood Broun and George Britt, *Christians Only: A Study in Prejudice* (New York: Vanguard, 1931), esp. 126–61.

12. J. X. Cohen, *Jews, Jobs, and Discrimination: A Report on Jewish Non-employment* (New York: American Jewish Congress, 1937), 11. See also Dinnerstein, *Antisemitism in America*, 88–89; Broun and Britt, *Christians Only*, esp. 125–245; and Carey McWilliams, *A Mask for Privilege: Anti-Semitism in America* (Boston: Little, Brown, 1948), 28, 151–59.

13. J. X. Cohen, *Towards Fair Play for Jewish Workers: Third Report on Jewish Non-employment* (New York: American Jewish Congress, 1938), 8.

14. Rudolf Glanz, *The Jew in Early American Wit and Graphic Humor* (New York: Ktav, 1973); Matthew Baigell, *The Implacable Urge to Defame: Cartoon Jews in the*

American Press, 1877–1935 (Syracuse, NY: Syracuse University Press, 2017); Broun and Britt, *Christians Only*, 244.

15. Petition N159255-1937.
16. Petition N19438-1932.
17. Petition N11978-1932.
18. Petition N52738-1932.
19. Petition N157584-1937.
20. It is clearly possible that if Kaminsky and Goldkopf were Roman Catholic, then others whom I type as Jews in my study may not have been Jewish; this might point to a problem with my methodology. Nonetheless, I believe that the vast majority of people with two Jewish-identified names (e.g., Julius Kaminsky) were, in fact, Jewish. I may be identifying a few Gentiles as Jews with my methodology, but I am also probably missing many other Jews who did not possess two Jewish-identified names. In the end, I believe my methodology is more likely to underestimate, rather than overestimate, the numbers of Jews.
21. Petition N159255-1937.
22. Petition *N11-1937.
23. See, for an example of a request for an "American" name, Petition N15404-1937.
24. Petition N16315-1932.
25. See, for example, Petitions N240-1922, N1161-1922, N1410-1922, N1411-1922, and N1892-1922.
26. For discrimination against Jews in the legal profession, see Jerold S. Auerbach, *Unequal Justice: Lawyers and Social Change in Modern America* (New York: Oxford University Press, 1976), 100–29; Auerbach, "From Rags to Robes: The Legal Profession, Social Mobility and the American Jewish Experience," *American Jewish Historical Quarterly* 66, no. 2 (1976): 249–84; Kenneth DeVille, "New York City Attorneys and Ambulance Chasing in the 1920s," *Historian* 59, no. 2 (1997): 291–310.
27. For Jewish lawyers working within Jewish communities and changing their own names, see Louis Anthes, *Lawyers and Immigrants, 1870–1940: A Cultural History* (Levittown, NY: LFB, 2003), esp. 131–216; and Edward M. Benton, recollection, in Howard Simons, *Jewish Times: Voices of the American Jewish Experience* (Boston: Houghton Mifflin, 1988), 86–87.
28. For fragments of evidence regarding Jewish lawyers drawing up their own paperwork and that of relatives, see, for example, Arnold Forster, *Square One: A Memoir* (New York: Donald R. Fine, 1988), 39; Nuland, *Lost in America*, 143–45. For law students concerned about making their name changes official, see Petitions N5255-1932 and N159254-1937.
29. See, for example, Petitions N898-1932, N1533-1932, and N1986-1932.
30. Petition N12095-1932.
31. See also, for example, Judith E. Smith, *Family Connections: A History of Italian and Jewish Immigrant Lives in Providence, Rhode Island, 1900–1940* (Albany: SUNY Press, 1985); Wenger, *New York Jews and the Great Depression*, 33–53.

32. Petition N158150-1937.
33. Petition N159250-1937.
34. For the concept of "managing stigma," see Erving Goffman, *Stigma: Notes on the Management of Spoiled Identity* (New York: Prentice-Hall, 1963).
35. Petition N2835-1932; see also, for example, Petitions N176-1942 and N159256-1937.
36. Petition N2904-1937.
37. Morris Freedman, "The Jewish College Student: 1951 Model," *Commentary*, October 1951, 312.
38. See, for example, Petitions N10661-1932 and N13852-1932. See also Martin W. Horan, "Autobiography of Martin W. Horan," photocopy, ca. 2002, 24, in author's possession; Benton, recollection, in Simons, *Jewish Times*, 86–87.
39. Petition N11492-1932.
40. Petition N160533-1937; see also Petitions N159105-1937 and N158450-1937.
41. Petition N886-1937.
42. Petition N31219-1932.
43. See, for example, Petitions N9018-1932, N3607-1932, N55340-1932, N160302-1937, *N11-1937, and N160026-1937.
44. Jo Sinclair, *Wasteland, a Novel* (New York: Harper, 1946), 78.
45. Note that observed percentages in the 1930s fluctuate greatly in comparison to those of other years under study. Because only one in ten petitions were gathered in these years and because only about 300 people submitted petitions during each of these years, the sample sizes of 1932 and 1937 are markedly smaller than those of other years.
46. Petition N6060-1932.
47. Petition N1608-1937.
48. Petition N49169-1932.
49. Petition *N11-1937.
50. For white-collar opportunities available to women in the interwar years, see, for example, Lois Scharf, *To Work and to Wed: Female Employment, Feminism, and the Great Depression* (Westport, CT: Greenwood, 1980); Susan Ware, *Holding Their Own: American Women in the 1930s* (Boston: Twayne, 1982); Alice Kessler-Harris, *Out to Work: A History of Wage-Earning Women in the United States* (New York: Oxford University Press, 1982).
51. See Cohen, *Workshop to Office*, 135–46; Riv-Ellen Prell, *Fighting to Become Americans: Assimilation and the Trouble between Jewish Women and Jewish Men* (Boston: Beacon, 1999), 107–10.
52. Alfred Luverne Severson, "Nationality and Religious Preferences as Reflected in Newspaper Advertisements," *American Journal of Sociology* 44, no. 4 (1939): 542–44.
53. Julia Weber, "Have You a Pleasing Voice?," *American Jewish News*, July 26, 1918, 368, quoted in Prell, *Fighting to Become Americans*, 47.
54. Ferber, "Girl Who Went Right," 58–61, originally published in Ferber, *Cheerful by Request* (New York: Doubleday, Page, 1918).

55. Arthur Miller, *Focus* (1945; repr., Syracuse, NY: Syracuse University Press, 1997), 17; see also 13, 28–36.

56. Petition N9908-1937.

57. Petition N160533-1937.

58. Petition N160287-1937; see also Petition N159105-1937.

59. Note that there was a different well-publicized story of a Harry Kabotchnik who changed his name to Cabot during these same years. The famous Cabot family of New England sued him for the use of their name and lost. See Justin Kaplan and Anne Bernays, *The Language of Names* (New York: Simon and Schuster, 1997), 60–61.

60. Louis Adamic, "The Importance of Being Yourself," *Los Angeles Times*, August 17, 1941, H2, reprinted in Adamic, *What's Your Name?* (New York: Harper, 1942), 3–8.

61. See, for example, Prell, *Fighting to Become Americans*, 92–103; Paula E. Hyman, *Gender and Assimilation in Modern Jewish History: The Roles and Representation of Women* (Seattle: University of Washington Press, 1995), 44–50, 134–69.

62. Petition N184-1942; see also Petition N10755-1937.

63. See Allyson Hobbs, *A Chosen Exile: A History of Racial Passing in American Life* (Cambridge, MA: Harvard University Press, 2014); Daniel J. Sharfstein, *The Invisible Line: Three American Families and the Secret Journey from Black to White* (New York: Penguin, 2011); and Martha A. Sandweiss, *Passing Strange: A Gilded Age Tale of Love and Deception across the Color Line* (New York: Penguin, 2009). For literary discussions of the phenomenon, see, for example, Elaine K. Ginsberg, ed., *Passing and the Fictions of Identity* (Durham, NC: Duke University Press, 1996); Gayle Wald, *Crossing the Line: Racial Passing in Twentieth-Century U.S. Literature and Culture* (Durham, NC: Duke University Press, 2000); Kathleen Pfeiffer, *Race Passing and American Individualism* (Amherst: University of Massachusetts Press, 2003); Steven J. Belluscio, *To Be Suddenly White: Literary Realism and Racial Passing* (Columbia: University of Missouri Press, 2006).

64. For the possibilities of Latinos to officially redefine themselves as "Spanish," or "white," see, for example, Albert M. Camarillo, "Navigating Segregated Life in America's Racial Borderhoods, 1910s–1950s," *Journal of American History* 100, no. 3 (2013): 655–56; Geraldo L. Cadava, *Standing on Common Ground: The Making of a Sunbelt Borderland* (Cambridge, MA: Harvard University Press, 2013), 96–97, 106; and Thomas A. Guglielmo, "Fighting for Caucasian Rights: Mexicans, Mexican Americans, and the Transnational Struggle for Civil Rights in World War II Texas," *Journal of American History* 92 (March 2006): 1212–37.

65. N11978-1932; see also Petition N237-1942.

66. Justice [Aaron J.] Levy, "Supreme Court, Special Term, Part II," *New York Law Journal* 78, no. 94 (1928): 1965, quoted in Rennick, "Judicial Procedures," 156–57.

67. Quoted in Rennick, "Judicial Procedures," 157. See also "Goldstein Would Be Golding, but Judge Goldstein Says No," *Jewish Telegraphic Agency*, February 6, 1930, www.jta.org.

68. Rennick, "Judicial Procedures," 156–57.

69. Petition N47151-1932.
70. Petition N168-1942.
71. For another petition to return to a former Jewish name, see Petition N158449-1937; for a petition of a convert to Judaism seeking to adopt a more Jewish name for the sake of his new family members after marriage to a Jew, see Petition N15733-1932.
72. Zalowitz, "Why Should Levy Become Lee and Rabinowitz Robins?," 3.
73. Jacob C. Rich, "Why I Changed My Name to Sound More American," *Jewish Daily Forward* (English section), April 4, 1926, 3. See also Irwin Edman, "Reuben Cohen Enters American Life," *Menorah Journal* 12 (June–July 1926): 247, cited in Daniel Greene, "Reuben Cohen Comes of Age: American Jewish Youth and the Lived Experience of Cultural Pluralism in the 1920s," *American Jewish History* 95, no. 2 (2009): 172.
74. Adamic, *What's Your Name?*, 86.
75. Quoted ibid., 85–86.
76. Tobenkin, "Why I Would Not Change My Name," 52.
77. Ibid., 7.
78. Adamic, *What's Your Name?*, 144.
79. Ibid., 86. For letters to Adamic focusing on antisemitism, see, for example, P. N. Root to Louis Adamic, July 11, 1939; Robert Rubin, "Some of the Problems Facing Second Generation Jews in Current American Life"; and Edith M. Stern to Louis Adamic, April 20, 1939, all in folder 1, box 62, Adamic Papers.
80. For mainstream interwar texts that addressed name changing as a response to antisemitism, see George E. Sokolsky, *We Jews* (Garden City, NY: Doubleday, Doran, 1935), 82–118; Broun and Britt, *Christians Only*, 199, 244–45.
81. *The Jazz Singer*, directed by Alan Crosland (Warner Bros., 1927).
82. *The Younger Generation*, directed by Frank Capra (Columbia Pictures, 1929); Fannie Hurst, "The Gold in Fish," *Cosmopolitan*, August 1925, reprinted in *The Stories of Fannie Hurst*, ed. Susan Koppelman (New York: Feminist Press at the City University of New York, 2004), 254–81; Hurst, *It Is to Laugh*, directed by Rollo Lloyd (New York, 1927).

CHAPTER 2. "WHAT'S UNCLE SAM'S LAST NAME?"

1. Petition N237-1942.
2. The numbers of petitions in the years before World War I, during the interwar years, during the 1940s, and after 1948 are from my data set.
3. For the Jewish population of New York, see Horowitz and Kaplan, *Estimated Jewish Population*, 15, 22–23.
4. Gene Fein, "For Christ and Country: The Christian Front in New York City, 1938–1951" (Ph.D. diss., City University of New York, 2006); Dinnerstein, *Antisemitism in America*, 112–22; Norwood, "Marauding Youth and the Christian Front"; Brinkley, *Voices of Protest*. On the America First Committee, see, for example, Wayne S. Cole, *America First: The Battle Against Intervention, 1940–1941*

(New York: Octagon Books, 1971), 131–54; and Cole, *Charles A. Lindbergh and the Battle Against American Intervention in World War II* (New York: Harcourt Brace Jovanovich, 1974), 171–85. For antisemitic rhetoric from members of Congress and their constituents, see, for example, David S. Wyman, *The Abandonment of the Jews: America and the Holocaust, 1941–1945* (New York: Pantheon Books, 1984), 12–14.

5. Gerald B. Winrod, *Antichrist and the Tribe of Dan* (Wichita, KS: Defender, 1936), 24, Hathi Trust Digital Library, http://hdl.handle.net; and US Congress, House, Special Committee on Un-American Activities, *New Dealers in Office: With Their Red Front Personnel; The Amazing Roster of Persons with Strange Names Ascending into Vital Federal Positions since 1933, Together with Those Holding Memberships in Red Front Organizations as Alleged by the Dies Committee, 1940* (Indianapolis: Fellowship Press, 1941).

6. "Refu-Jews Go Back! Jer U.S.A. lem!" (New York: Nationalist Press Association, n.d.). Thanks to Sarah Klimek for this source.

7. Petition N57-1942. On petitioners who were not quite so explicit, see Petition N124-1942. See also, for example, Petitions N66-1942, N77-1942, N109-1942, N110-1942, N523-1942, N533-1942, N22-1946, N39-1946, N649-1946, and N191-1947.

8. Jessard A. Wisch, "My Experiences and Observations as a Jew in World War II," n.d., 5, folder 3, box 1, YIVO essay contest, Memoirs of American-Jewish Soldiers, RG 110, YIVO Institute for Jewish Research, New York, NY; Joseph W. Bendersky, *The "Jewish Threat": Anti-Semitic Politics of the U.S. Army* (New York: Basic Books, 2000), 297–300.

9. Petitions N150-1942 and N186-1942.

10. Petition N72-1942. See also Petition N1036-1942; "Westchester Einsteins Deny Naval Academy Officers Advised Son to Change Name," *Jewish Telegraphic Agency*, June 16, 1939, www.jta.org; "Easton Saves the Navy," *Opinion* 9 (September 1939): 9; and Adamic, *What's Your Name?*, 86.

11. The comparison of petitioners in 1942 and 1946 comes from my data set; "I Changed My Name," *Atlantic* 181, no. 2 (1948): 72.

12. For Jewish soldiers reporting charges of cowardice and profiteering, see Deborah Dash Moore, *GI Jews: How World War II Changed a Generation* (Cambridge, MA: Harvard University Press, 2006), 80–81; Bendersky, *"Jewish Threat,"* 295–97; Alexander Shatton, "My Experiences and Observations as a Jew in World War II," n.d., 2–4, folder 34, box 2, YIVO essay contest, Memoirs of American-Jewish Soldiers; Julian Scheineson, "My Experiences and Observations as a Jew in World War II," n.d., 11, folder 52, box 2, YIVO essay contest, Memoirs of American-Jewish Soldiers; Jack Salomon, "My Experiences and Observations as a Jew in World War II," n.d., 2, folder 33, box 2, YIVO essay contest, Memoirs of American-Jewish Soldiers. For rumors of Jewish doctors labeling Jews 4-F, see Army and Navy Public Relations Committee, National Jewish Welfare Board, *Combatting Rumors: A Positive Public Relations Program for Community Leaders* (New York: National Jewish Welfare Board, 1942), 20–29. For rumors linking Jews to the prosecution of

the war, see James T. Sparrow, *Warfare State: World War II Americans and the Age of Big Government* (New York: Oxford University Press, 2011), 89–94. For Jews fighting despite stereotypes of Jewish cowardice, see Derek Penslar, *Jews and the Military: A History* (Princeton, NJ: Princeton University Press, 2013).

13. "Subject: Anti-Semitic Literature in Military Establishments," December 29, 1943, folder 20, box 1, Richard C. Rothschild Papers, American Jewish Committee Archives, New York, NY. For other versions of "The First American," see Lois Judith Meltzer, "Anti-Semitism in the United States Army during World War II" (M.A. thesis, Baltimore Hebrew College, 1977), 97; Dinnerstein, *Antisemitism in America*, 139; and Moore, *GI Jews*, 169. On other widely circulated poems, see "Subject: Anti-Semitic Literature in Military Establishments," n.p.; Meltzer, "Anti-Semitism in the United States Army," 37–44, 96–101; Dinnerstein, *Antisemitism in America*, 141. Tracy Sugarman to June Sugarman, February 23, 1945, in Tracy Sugarman, *My War: A Love Story in Letters and Drawings* (New York: Random House, 2000), 173–74, quoted in Moore, *GI Jews*, 169, 171.

14. David A. Levine, "My Experiences and Observations as a Jew in World War II," n.d., 10, folder 10, box 1, YIVO essay contest, Memoirs of American-Jewish Soldiers; Shatton, "My Experiences and Observations," 2.

15. Wisch, "My Experiences and Observations"; Petition N162-1942. For Elias Biegelman's biography, see Elias Begelman Papers, Tamiment Library and Robert F. Wagner Labor Archives, New York, NY; and Abraham Lincoln Brigade Archives, "Elias Begelman," accessed March 9, 2018, www.alba-valb.org. In the name-change petition, Biegelman spelled his name with an *i*, but in his other papers, his name is spelled without the *i* as "Begelman." For other descriptions of soldiers who sought to hide their identity, including with changed names, see H. Ziglin, "My Experiences and Observations as a Jew in World War II," n.d., 7–10, folder 31, box 2, YIVO essay contest, Memoirs of American-Jewish Soldiers; Harold Heifetz, "My Experiences and Observations as a Jew in World War II," n.d., 6, folder 48, box 2, YIVO essay contest, Memoirs of American-Jewish Soldiers; and Gerstle, *American Crucible*, 225–26.

16. For others who claimed to fear anti-German sentiment, see also Petitions N224-1942, N744-1942, N574-1942, N136-1942, N317-1942, N129-1946, N255-1946, and N333-1946. Helen P. Wulbern, "The How and Why of Name Changing," *American Mercury* 64 (June 1947): 718; Patricia Kollander with John O'Sullivan, *"I Must Be a Part of This War": A German American's Fight against Hitler and Nazism* (New York: Fordham University Press, 2005), 86–87; Tom Frazier with Delphine Frazier, *Between the Lines: The Story of a German Boy Raised in Nazi Times Who Returns to His Homeland as an American Soldier in WWII—Passionately Fighting for the Ideals of His Adopted Country While Suffering over What His Fatherland Had Become* (Oakland, CA: Regent, 2001).

17. See, for example, Russell A. Kazal, *Becoming Old Stock: The Paradox of German-American Identity* (Princeton, NJ: Princeton University Press, 2004), 264–65; Carnevale, *New Language*, 163–64. For an alternative perspective, see Timothy J.

Holian, *The German-Americans and World War II: An Ethnic Experience* (New York: P. Lang, 1996). The finding that 30 percent of name-change petitions were distinctive Jewish names comes from my data set. For the quote, see Petition N148-1942. See, for similar claims, Petitions N207-1942 and N129-1946.

18. See, for example, "Report of Subcommittee on Discrimination against Aliens," n.d., folder 8, box 2, Papers of the Coordinating Committee of Jewish Organizations on Employment Discrimination in Defense Industries, 1940–1945, RG I-169, American Jewish Historical Society (AJHS), Boston, MA, and New York, NY. See also Ernest Maass, "Integration and Name Changing among Jewish Refugees from Central Europe in the United States," *Names* 6 (September 1958): 132–39.

19. For a petitioner whose experience with antisemitism in Europe in the 1920s and 1930s motivated her name change, see Petition N16315-1932. For the Solomon Goldfarb quote, see Petition N155-1942. For the Victor Aguschewitsch quote, see Petition N67-1942. See also Petition N186-1942. On the persistence of these claims after the war, see, for example, Petitions N39-1946, N186-1946, N230-1946, and N191-1947.

20. On the World War I rumors and survey, see "Historical Note," finding aid, Records of the National Jewish Welfare Board—Bureau of War Records, 1940–1969, accessed March 8, 2018, http://search.cjh.org. For criticism of the World War I effort, see editorial, *Jewish Ledger*, April 9, 1943, folder 5, box 90, Records of the National Jewish Welfare Board—Bureau of War Records, 1940–1969, RG-152, AJHS (hereafter NJWB-BWR Records).

21. S. C. Kohs to Jeanne Gerber, May 20, 1946, Aaron-Abelia folder, box 117, NJWB-BWR Records; Milton Weill, untitled speech, n.d., 8, folder 8, box 1, Milton Weill Papers, RG P-34, AJHS. For Berkley and Coleman, see, for example, Petitions N431-1942 and N564-1947. On the JWB's materials, see Jewish Welfare Board, *Suggested Topics for New Speakers on the Necessity of Compiling War Records for Jewish Men and Women in World War II* (prepared for the Speakers' Bureau in the Philadelphia Jewish War Record Drive, February–March 1943), cited in Abraham G. Duker, "Emerging Culture Patterns in American Jewish Life," *American Jewish Historical Society Publications* 39 (June 1950): 386n88.

22. S. C. Kohs to Uriah Z. Engelman, April 2, 1946, folder: "Distinctive Jewish Names," box 10, NJWB-BWR Records. For the origins and process of the DJN method, see ibid. For the continued use of the DJN method, as well as controversy surrounding its usage, see, for example, Fred Massarik, "New Approaches to the Study of the American Jew," *Jewish Journal of Sociology* 8, no. 2 (1966): 175–91; Barry A. Kosmin and Stanley Waterman, "The Use and Misuse of Distinctive Jewish Names in Research on Jewish Populations," in *Papers in Jewish Demography, 1985: Proceedings of the Demographic Sessions Held at the 9th World Congress of Jewish Studies, Jerusalem, August 1985,* ed. U. O. Schmelz and Sergio Della Pergola (Jerusalem, 1985), 1–9; Barry R. Chiswick, "The Rise and Fall of the American Jewish PhD," and Jonathan Sarna, "What's in a Name? A Response to Barry Chiswick," *Contemporary Jewry* 29 (April 2009): 67–90.

23. For the rough figure of DJNs as 15 percent of the Jewish population of any city, see Jerome Shuchter to Samuel Abramson, January 29, 1947, folder 7, box 82, NWJW-BWR Records; and Jerome Shuchter to Joshua Marcus, December 16, 1946, ibid.

24. For more on the Institute for American Democracy as an intermediary organization used by Jewish organizations, see Svonkin, *Jews against Prejudice*, 42–49; for the advertisement, see Stanley Musicant to Frank L. Weil, October 10, 1944, folder 11, box 1, Weill Papers. For the song, see Eddie Cantor to Milton Weill, June 9, 1943, folder 11, box 1, Weill Papers. For more on Cantor and his politics, see David Weinstein, *The Eddie Cantor Story: A Jewish Life in Performance and Politics* (Hanover, NH: Brandeis University Press, 2017).

25. Samuel Calmin Kohs, "Romance of Statistics," handwritten note, May 2, 1945, folder: "Anti-Semitism," box 4, Samuel Calmin Kohs Papers, RG P-90, AJHS.

26. See, for example, Howard F. Barker, "How the American Changes His Name," *American Mercury* 36, no. 141 (1935); H. L. Mencken, *The American Language: An Inquiry into the Development of English in the United States*, 4th ed. (New York: Knopf, 1965), 474–505.

27. The finding that 75 percent of name-change petitions were submitted by native-born Americans comes from my data set.

28. Shane Landrum, "Undocumented Citizens: The Crisis of U.S. Birth Certificates, 1940–1945," paper delivered at the annual meeting of the American Historical Association, San Diego, CA, January 8, 2010, accessed March 8, 2018, at Landrum's website, http://cliotropic.org. For the emergence of state control over identity through the birth certificate earlier in the 20th century, see Pearson, "Age Ought to Be a Fact."

29. Torpey, *Invention of the Passport*, 93–121; John Torpey, "The Great War and the Birth of the Modern Passport System," in Caplan and Torpey, *Documenting Individual Identity*, 256–70; Frederick C. Luebke, *Bonds of Loyalty: German-Americans and World War I* (DeKalb: Northern Illinois University Press, 1974), 250–55, 270–73, 282–83; Capozzola, *Uncle Sam Wants You*, 173–205.

30. The numbers of petitions in 1913–18, as well as the comparison of numbers in the 1930s and in 1942, come from my data set.

31. Petition N116-1942. See, for other examples, Petitions N123-1942, N87-1942, N95-1942, N50-1942, N242-1942, and N875-1942. The finding that 70 percent of petitions in 1942, 1946, and 1947 were submitted to formalize an earlier informal name change comes from my data set. For the postwar era, see, for example, Petitions N409-1946, N204-1947, and N534-1947.

32. Morris Fishbein, "What's in a Name?," *Hygeia* 22 (March 1944): 173; see also, for example, Bergen Evans, "The Personal Appellation," *Saturday Review of Literature*, August 12, 1950, 15; Adamic, *What's Your Name?*, xi.

33. For Italian, Slavic, and Greek name changes, see, for example, Petitions N367-1942, N420-1942, N1046-1942, N40-1946, N44-1946, and N313-1946.

34. See Gerstle, *American Crucible*, 165–67.

35. Petitions N1083-1942, N624-1942, N169-1942. For other examples of Italian and German name changes, see Petitions N166-1942, N37-1946, and N1030-1946. For a contemporary journalist who identified name changing among Germans and Italians, as well as Jews, see Wulbern, "How and Why of Name Changing," 718.

36. Petitions N239-1942 and N293-1942. For Polish petitioners with non-Jewish names who similarly referred to their names as "foreign," see Petition N146-1942. See also, for example, Petitions N136-1942, N181-1942, and N410-1942. On the identification of these names as "foreign-sounding" after hostilities had ended, see, for example, Petitions N54-1946, N78-1946, N333-1946, N18-1946, and N208-1947.

37. "Subject: Anti-Semitic Literature in Military Establishments," 2.

38. Minutes, May 1, 1942, folder 3, box 1, Papers of the Coordinating Committee of Jewish Organizations on Employment Discrimination in Defense Industries, 1940–1945; "Memorandum on Discrimination against Jews in Defense Industries," February 2, 1942, memo, folder 1, box 2, ibid. For more on the FEPC, see Merl E. Reed, *Seedtime for the Modern Civil Rights Movement: The President's Committee on Fair Employment Practice, 1941–1946* (Baton Rouge: Louisiana State University Press, 1991); and Daniel Kryder, *Divided Arsenal: Race and the American State during World War II* (New York: Cambridge University Press, 2000).

39. Office of War Information, *Government Information Manual for the Motion Picture Industry* (Washington, DC: Office of War Information, 1942). For a discussion of the Office of War Information, see Clayton R. Koppes and Gregory D. Black, *Hollywood Goes to War: How Politics, Profits, and Propaganda Shaped World War II Movies* (New York: Free Press, 1987), 69. See also Kenneth D. Rose, *Myth and the Greatest Generation: A Social History of Americans in World War II* (New York: Routledge, 2008), 164; Jeanine Basinger, *The World War II Combat Film: Anatomy of a Genre* (Middletown, CT: Wesleyan University Press, 2003), 56–57.

40. War Manpower Commission, "Americans All," 1942, poster, Prints and Photographs Division, Library of Congress, Washington, DC, www.loc.gov; Council against Intolerance in America, *Calling All Americans: A Handbook of National Unity* (New York: Council against Intolerance in America, 1941). This handbook was not produced under the auspices of the government but instead by the intercultural organization, the Council against Intolerance in America. See "The Stab of Intolerance," *New York Times*, July 10, 1941, 18.

41. Howard Chandler Christy, "Americans All! Victory Liberty Loan," 1919, poster, Prints and Photographs Division, Library of Congress, Washington, DC, www.loc.gov; Gerstle, *American Crucible*, 84. For the government's use of this image to "nationalize" white ethnic immigrants, see Lucy E. Salyer, "Baptism by Fire: Race, Military Service, and U.S. Citizenship Policy, 1918–1935," *Journal of American History* 91(December 2004): 847–76, esp. 853–54; and Nancy Gentile Ford, *Americans All! Foreign-Born Soldiers in World War I* (College Station: Texas A&M University Press, 2001), 15.

42. See "Subject: Anti-Semitic Literature in Military Establishments," 2.

43. The decline of name-change petition numbers after 1948 and the return to pre–World War II numbers in the 1980s comes from my data set. See Richard Polenberg, "The Good War? A Reappraisal of How World War II Affected American Society," *Virginia Magazine of History and Biography* 100 (July 1992): 295–322.

CHAPTER 3. "I CHANGED MY NAME"

1. "I Changed My Name," 73, 74.
2. David L. Cohn, "I've Kept My Name," *Atlantic Monthly* 181, no. 4 (1948): 44, 43, 41–42; Harold U. Ribalow, *Mid-Century: An Anthology of Jewish Life and Culture in Our Time* (NY: Beechhurst Press, 1955).
3. See, for example, Jonathan Sarna, *American Judaism* (New Haven, CT: Yale University Press, 2004); Arthur A. Goren, *The Politics and Public Culture of American Jews* (Bloomington: Indiana University Press, 1999); Edward Shapiro, *A Time for Healing* (Baltimore: Johns Hopkins University Press, 1992). For perspectives that suggest anxiety among American Jews during this era, see Susan A. Glenn, "The Jewish Cold War: Anxiety and Identity in the Aftermath of the Holocaust," David W. Belin Lecture in American Jewish Affairs 24 (Jean & Samuel Frankel Center for Judaic Studies, University of Michigan, 2014); Hasia Diner, *The Jews of the United States, 1654–2000* (Berkeley: University of California Press, 2004).
4. For other discussions of antisemitism in the postwar era, see Art Simon, "The House I Live In: Albert Maltz and the Fight against Anti-Semitism," in *"Un-American" Hollywood: Politics and Film in the Blacklist Era*, ed. Frank Krutnik, Steve Neale, Brian Neve, and Peter Stanfield (New Brunswick, NJ: Rutgers University Press, 2007), 169–83; Kelly King-O'Brien, "'Names and Appearances Are Often Indeterminate': Quandaries over Identifying Jews in Chicago, 1953–1961," *Journal of the Illinois State Historical Society* 110, no. 1 (2017): 9–58.
5. Isaiah M. Minkoff, "Inter-Group Relations," *American Jewish Year Book* 49 (1947–48): 196.
6. Committee on Employment Discrimination of the National Community Relations Advisory Council, *FEPC Reference Manual* (New York: National Community Relations Advisory Council, 1948), 6–7. See also National Community Relations Advisory Council, *Post-war Employment Discrimination against Jews, 1946* (New York: National Community Relations Advisory Council, 1946), 6.
7. Ruth G. Weintraub, *How Secure These Rights? Anti-Semitism in the United States in 1948: An Anti-Defamation League Survey* (Garden City, NY: Doubleday, 1949), 77–79.
8. Albert Weiss, "Jews Need Not Apply," in *Barriers: Patterns of Discrimination against Jews*, ed. Nathan C. Belth (New York City: Friendly House, 1958), 44–45; see also Benjamin R. Epstein and Arnold Forster, *"Some of My Best Friends . . ."* (New York: Farrar, Straus and Cudahy, 1962), 232. For a valuable historical appraisal of continued antisemitic employment discrimination in the 1950s, with issues of bureaucracy and identification at the heart of the discrimination, see King-O'Brien, "Names and Appearances Are Often Indeterminate."

9. Weiss, "Jews Need Not Apply," 46.

10. Epstein and Forster, "*Some of My Best Friends*," 210–14, 244–46. See also Bernard Simon, "Insurance, Banking, Public Utilities," in Belth, *Barriers*, 48–51.

11. Epstein and Forster, "*Some of My Best Friends*," 193–94; King-O'Brien, "Names and Appearances Are Often Indeterminate."

12. Kramer and Leventman, *Children of the Gilded Ghetto*, 146.

13. David S. Berkowitz, "Inequality of Opportunity in Higher Education: A Study of Minority Group and Related Barriers to College Admission," in *A Report of the (New York State) Temporary Commission on the Need for a State University* (Albany, NY: Williams, 1948), 111–22.

14. American Council on Education, *On Getting into College: A Study Made for the Committee on Discriminations in College Admissions* (Washington, DC: American Council on Education, 1949), 62–63, cited in Weintraub, *How Secure These Rights?*, 43.

15. Weintraub, *How Secure These Rights?*, 46–48.

16. *New York Post*, August 7, 1945, quoted in Dan W. Dodson, "College Quotas and American Democracy," *American Scholar* 15, no. 3 (1946): 270.

17. See Jerome Karabel, *The Chosen: The Hidden History of Admission and Exclusion at Harvard, Yale, and Princeton* (Boston: Houghton Mifflin, 2005), 238.

18. For details on these acts, see Milton R. Konvitz and Theodore Leskes, *A Century of Civil Rights: With a Study of State Law against Discrimination* (New York: Columbia University Press, 1961), 225–30.

19. Karabel, *Chosen*, 297.

20. For estimated percentages of Jewish students at the Ivy League schools in 1961–62, see Dan A. Oren, *Joining the Club: A History of Jews and Yale* (New Haven, CT: Yale University Press, 1985), 196.

21. Konvitz and Leskes, *Century of Civil Rights*, 232–33. See also Forster, "*Some of My Best Friends*," 143–44.

22. Weintraub, *How Secure These Rights?*, 65.

23. Harold Braverman, "Medical School Quotas," in Belth, *Barriers*, 74–76.

24. Quoted in "Bias against Dentistry Seen," *New York Times*, February 7, 1945, 19.

25. For continued racism in higher-education admissions, see, for example, Karabel, *Chosen*.

26. Arnold Forster and the staff of the Civil Rights Division League of the Anti-Defamation League of B'nai B'rith, *Anti-Semitism in the United States in 1947* (New York: Anti-Defamation League of B'nai B'rith, 1948), 28.

27. Ibid., 38.

28. Anti-Defamation League of B'nai B'rith, *Not the Work of a Day: The Story of the Anti-Defamation League of B'nai B'rith* (New York: Anti-Defamation League of B'nai B'rith, 1965), chap. 5.

29. Weintraub, *How Secure These Rights?*, 25–33.

30. Harold Braverman, "Bigotry and Hotels," in Belth, *Barriers*, 29–30; Forster and Epstein, "*Some of My Best Friends*," 45–51.

31. Albert Weiss, "Resorts: A National Survey," in Belth, *Barriers*, 26–27.

32. For Holiday Inns, see Dinnerstein, *Antisemitism in America*, 158.

33. McWilliams, *Mask for Privilege*, 124.

34. Vance Packard, *The Status Seekers* (New York: David McKay, 1959), 264.

35. E. Digby Baltzell, *The Protestant Establishment: Aristocracy and Caste in America* (New York: Random House, 1964), 381.

36. Because only one out of ten petitions was actually examined and because more than one petitioner could file on each petition, this methodology cannot indicate exactly how many individuals actually changed their names during these years. The guess of 1,000 is a conservative one; over 2,500 petitions were submitted during these three years, and sampled petitions suggest that Jews represented a bit more than one-half of petitioners each year.

37. Petition N149-1946.

38. Petition N649-1946.

39. Petition N375-1952.

40. See, for example, Petitions N766-1946, N85-1947, N191-1947, N248-1947, N264-1947, N504-1947, and N21-1952.

41. Petition N10801-1957.

42. Petition N485-1952.

43. Petition N5557-1957.

44. Petition N21-1952.

45. Petition N1944-1957.

46. Petition N284-1952; see also Petition N244-1952.

47. Petition N6311-1957.

48. Mrs. Harry Snyderman to David L. Cohn, June 24, 1948, David L. Cohn Collection.

49. Nuland, *Lost in America*, 140–46.

50. Glenn, "Vogue of Jewish Self-Hatred."

51. David Bernstein, "Jewish Insecurity and American Realities," *Commentary* 6 (January 1, 1948): 125.

52. Milton Steinberg, *A Partisan Guide to the Jewish Problem* (Cornwall, NY: Cornwall, 1945), 124.

53. Hobbs, *Chosen Exile*. For a different discussion of the relationship between Jewish and African American passing during an earlier era, see Daniel Itzkovitz, "Passing like Me," *South Atlantic Quarterly* 98, nos. 1–2 (1999): 35–57. European discourses over Jewish visibility and invisibility, conversion and assimilation, may have also shaped American Jewish perceptions of the practice of passing. See, for example, Kerry Wallach, *Passing Illusions: Jewish Visibility in Weimar Germany* (Ann Arbor: University of Michigan Press, 2017); Todd Endelman, *Leaving the Jewish Fold: Conversion and Radical Assimilation in Modern Jewish History* (Princeton, NJ: Princeton University Press, 2015); and Deborah Sadie Hertz, *How Jews Became Germans: The History of Conversion and Assimilation in Berlin* (New Haven, CT: Yale University Press, 2007).

54. Sinclair, *Wasteland*; Davis, *Whisper My Name*; Herman Wouk, *Marjorie Morningstar* (Garden City, NY: Doubleday, 1955). See also Merle Miller, *That Winter* (New York: William Sloane, 1948); Martha Gellhorn, *The Wine of Astonishment* (New York: Scribner, 1948); Henry J. Berkowitz, *Boot Camp* (Philadelphia: Jewish Publication Society, 1948); Abraham Bernstein, *Home Is the Hunted* (New York: Dial, 1947); Joseph Wechsberg, "The Rules of the Game," *New Yorker*, October 1, 1949, 28–33; and Bernard Malamud, "The Lady of the Lake," in *The Magic Barrel* (New York: Random House, 1958), 105–34.

55. Baltzell, *Protestant Establishment*, 360–61; Epstein and Forster, *"Some of My Best Friends,"* 2–5; John W. Stevens, "Rector Is Praised for Stand on Bias," *New York Times*, January 16, 1961, 24.

56. Baltzell, *Protestant Establishment*, 348.

57. Petition N9105-1957.

58. Petition N-B53-1962.

59. Petition N22-1967.

60. Oren, *Joining the Club*, 268–69.

61. David Hollinger, *Science, Jews, and Secular Culture* (Princeton, NJ: Princeton University Press, 1996), 13.

62. Broom, Beem, and Harris, "Characteristics of 1,107 Petitioners," 37–39.

63. "I Changed My Name," 73–74.

64. "Letters to and from the Editor," *Atlantic* 181, no. 6 (1948): 20–21.

65. Goffman's uncle was a bookie, his sister was an actress, and his wife was a schizophrenic. See testimonies and published sources, including Dmitri Shalin, "Interfacing Biography, Theory, and History," *Symbolic Interaction* 37, no. 1 (2013): 2–40, accessed April 1, 2018, at the Erving Goffman Archives, http://cdclv.unlv.edu/ega/.

66. Erving Goffman, *Stigma: Notes on the Management of Spoiled Identity* (New York: Simon and Schuster, 1963), 60, 100–101.

67. Ibid., 102–3.

68. Ibid., 103.

69. For an important discussion of covering in the 21st century, see Kenji Yoshino, *Covering: The Hidden Assault on Our Civil Rights* (New York: Random House, 2006).

70. Petition N345-1952; see also Petitions N18-1946, N30-1946, N95-1947, N159-1947, N365-1952, N375-1952.

71. See, for example, Petitions N6279-1957 and N6311-1957.

72. Petition N55-1947.

73. See, for example, Petitions N85-1947, N248-1947, N191-1947, N304-1947, N504-1947.

74. Beverly Winston to David L. Cohn, May 24, 1948, David L. Cohn Collection.

75. Mrs. Harry Snyderman to David L. Cohn, June 24, 1948, David L. Cohn Collection.

76. Kramer and Leventman, *Children of the Gilded Ghetto*, 87.

77. Ibid., 89.

78. Kugelmass, "Name-Changing," 150.

79. Ibid., 147.

80. Ibid., 145, 148.

81. Bernstein, *Home Is the Hunted*, 38.

82. Ibid.

83. Ibid., 61.

84. Lenny Bruce, *The Essential Lenny Bruce*, ed. John Cohen (New York: Bell, 1970), 65–66, quoted in David E. Kaufman, *Jewhooing the Sixties: American Celebrity and Jewish Identity* (Waltham, MA: Brandeis University Press, 2012), 114.

85. Albert Goldman (from the journalism of Lawrence Schiller), *Ladies and Gentlemen, Lenny Bruce!!* (New York: Ballantine Books, 1974), quoted in Kaufman, *Jewhooing the Sixties*, 107.

86. Bruce, *Essential Lenny Bruce*, 65–66, quoted in Kaufman, *Jewhooing the Sixties*, 114.

87. Kugelmass, "Name-Changing," 145.

88. Charles Silberman, *A Certain People* (New York: Summit Books, 1985), 60.

89. Gerhart Saenger and Norma S. Gordon, "The Influence of Discrimination on Minority Group Members in Its Relation to Attempts to Combat Discrimination," *Journal of Social Psychology* 31 (1950): 101.

90. Kugelmass, "Name-Changing," 149.

91. Daniel Horowitz, email communication with author, September 22, 2006.

92. Nuland, *Lost in America*, 146.

93. "Repartee: Letters to and from the Editor," *Atlantic Monthly* 181, no. 6 (1948): 20. See, for antisemitism at privileged resorts, Jon Sterngass, *First Resorts: Pursuing Pleasure at Saratoga Springs, Newport, and Coney Island* (Baltimore: Johns Hopkins University Press, 2001), 106–10. Sterngass does not specifically address antisemitism in Newport, but he does address antisemitism at Saratoga Springs and Coney Island.

94. "Repartee," 20–23.

95. John Bainbridge, "Little Magazine," *New Yorker*, cited in John Heidenry, *Theirs Was the Kingdom: Lila and DeWitt Wallace and the Story of the "Reader's Digest"* (New York: Norton, 1993). The series was in five parts. For suggestions of antisemitism, see "I—Wally," November 17, 1945, 39; and "V—Dr. Wallace's Magic Formula," December 15, 1945, 46–48.

96. Joshua Bloch, "The Year's Bookshelf: A Survey of American Jewish Books in English for 1947–48," *Jewish Book Annual* 7 (1948–49): 27–28.

97. Sinclair, *Wasteland*; Davis, *Whisper My Name*; Bernstein, *Home Is the Hunted*; Miller, *That Winter*; Gellhorn, *Wine of Astonishment*; Berkowitz, *Boot Camp*; Wechsberg, "Rules of the Game,"; Wouk, *Marjorie Morningstar*; Malamud, "Lady of the Lake."

98. Miller, *That Winter*, 253.

99. Bernstein, *Home Is the Haunted*, 90.

100. Bruce, *Essential Lenny Bruce*, 65–66, quoted in Kaufman, *Jewhooing the Sixties*, 114.

101. Laura Z. Hobson, *Gentleman's Agreement* (1947; repr., New York: Avon Books, 1968), 128.

102. Hobson, *Gentleman's Agreement*, 57; for Phil looking Jewish, see Susan A. Glenn, "Funny, You Don't Look Jewish," in *Boundaries of Jewish Identity*, ed. Susan A. Glenn and Naomi B. Sokoloff (Seattle: University of Washington Press, 2010), 73–74. For another reading that highlights Phil looking white, see Jacobson, *Whiteness of a Different Color*, 125–31.

103. Hobson, *Gentleman's Agreement*, 86.

104. For the text of the speech, see 80 Cong. Rec. H10792 (1947). For a text that highlights the importance of the actors' changed names in the films' reception in the midst of Cold War anxieties, see Marjorie Garber, *Symptoms of Culture* (New York: Routledge, 1998), 84–86; for a text that also focuses on the importance of Phil's name (but suggests mistakenly that he actually identifies himself as Greenberg), see Baz Dreisinger, *Near Black: White-to-Black Passing in American Culture* (Amherst: University of Massachusetts Press, 2008), 59–60.

105. Laura Z. Hobson, *Laura Z: A Life* (New York: Arbor House, 1983), 7; for Hobson's changing names, see 146–47; for her speech to employers about her Jewish name, see 81–82.

106. See also Laura Mount (Laura Z. Hobson), "The Perfect Man," *New Yorker*, April 23, 1932, 19–21.

107. Laura Z. Hobson, *Laura Z: A Life, Years of Fulfillment* (New York: Donald I. Fine, 1986), 74–75.

CHAPTER 4. "HAVE YOU BEEN KNOWN BY ANOTHER NAME?"

1. Shlomo Katz, "So You Changed Your Name," *Congress Weekly* 15, no. 5 (1948): 9.

2. Cohn, "I've Kept My Name," 43.

3. Katz, "So You Changed Your Name," 8–9.

4. Application for Admission, Columbia University, n.d., folder 3, box 330, "Historical Subject Files Collection," University Archives, Rare Book and Manuscript Library, Columbia University, New York, NY. Many thanks to archivist Jocelyn Wilk for finding this document.

5. The term "problem" is Keppel's; see Harold Wechsler, *The Qualified Student: A History of Selective College Admission in America* (New York: Wiley, 1977), 133–68, esp. 135.

6. Ibid., 150–55.

7. Ibid., 156.

8. "Oppose Dr. Butler," *New York Times*, December 9, 1917, 20.

9. For more on Harvard's quotas, see Synnott, *Half-Opened Door*, 58–124, esp. 95, 112; and Karabel, *Chosen*, 77–109.

10. Broun and Britt, *Christians Only*, 74.

11. Synnott, *Half-Opened Door*, 258n24. Yale did not ask about name changing but did ask for mother's maiden name. See Oren, *Joining the Club*, 47, 55.

12. Synnott, *Half-Opened Door*, 94–95.

13. Wechsler, *Qualified Student*, 163–64.
14. Although the book focuses on blue-collar workers, see David R. Roediger and Elizabeth D. Esch, *The Production of Difference: Race and the Management of Labor in U.S. History* (New York: Oxford University Press, 2012), esp. 139–69.
15. See J. X. Cohen, *Who Discriminates and How?* (New York: American Jewish Congress, 1946), 9. For samples of application blanks with questions about citizenship, race, parents' birthplaces, or maiden names published in trade magazines and handbooks, see "Samples of Effective Administration Procedure," *Systems* 7, no. 2 (1944); and Eileen Ahern, *Handbook of Personnel Forms and Records*, Research Report 16 (New York: American Management Association, 1949), 34, 42, 46, 51.
16. Miller, *Focus*, 17.
17. Richard L. Abel, *American Lawyers* (New York: Oxford University Press, 1989), 85–86.
18. See Auerbach, *Unequal Justice*, esp. 40–73, 94–101. See also Auerbach, "From Rags to Robes"; De Ville, "New York City Attorneys"; and Anthes, *Lawyers and Immigrants*.
19. For the especially restrictive application process in Pennsylvania, but elsewhere as well, see Auerbach, *Unequal Justice*, 126–29. It is not clear whether state law boards developed their restrictive policies independently or whether they were influenced by the college admissions practices of schools such as Harvard and Columbia.
20. Anthes, *Lawyers and Immigrants*, 202.
21. Weintraub, *How Secure These Rights?*, 67.
22. For other treatments of Jewish racialization during this era that do not address bureaucracy or names, see, for example, Jacobson, *Whiteness of a Different Color*; Goldstein, *Price of Whiteness*; and Brodkin, *How Jews Became White Folks*.
23. See Konvitz and Leskes, *Century of Civil Rights*; Anthony S. Chen, *The Fifth Freedom: Jobs, Politics, and Civil Rights in the United States, 1941–1972* (Princeton, NJ: Princeton University Press, 2009); Oliver Cromwell Carmichael, *New York Establishes a State University: A Case Study in the Processes of Policy Formation* (Nashville, TN: Vanderbilt University Press, 1955).
24. For details on the CLSA, see Svonkin, *Jews against Prejudice*, 79–85; see also Marc Dollinger, *Quest for Inclusion: Jews and Liberalism in Modern America* (Princeton, NJ: Princeton University Press, 2000), esp. 132–33, 143–47; and Greenberg, *Troubling the Waters*, esp. 114–46.
25. For more on this liberal postwar coalition, see Chen, *Fifth Freedom*, 9–15, 40–46; Greenberg, *Troubling the Waters*, 114–68; and Biondi, *To Stand and Fight*, 15–16.
26. See Cohen, *Who Discriminates and How?*, 21–24, cited in Miyuki Kita, "Breaking the 'Gentleman's Agreement': Jews and the 1945 Fair Employment Practices Act," in *New York and the American Jewish Communal Experience*, ed. Fruma Mohrer and Ettie Goldwasser (New York: YIVO Institute for Jewish Research, 2013), 87–89. For Cohen's testimony, see New York State, Temporary Commission Against Discrimination, *Public Hearings*, vol. 3, November 27, November 28, November

29, November 30, December 4, December 5, December 6, 1944, 1293–94, cited in Kita, "Breaking the 'Gentleman's Agreement,'" 87–89.

27. For descriptions of reports conducted in 1947 and 1948, see Will Maslow to Ordway Tead, October 8, 1947, 4, folder 18, box 407, RG I-77, American Jewish Congress Papers, AJHS (hereafter AJCongress Papers); and Alvin Johnson, "This Business of Admissions," *Survey Graphic* 36 (November 1947): 629, folder: "CLSA Subject Files: Discrimination in Education, NYS Committee for Equality in Education," box 407, ibid.; Theodore Leskes, "Survey of College Application Blanks—June 1948," 4, folder 4, box 74, RG 347, American Jewish Committee Papers, YIVO.

28. Weintraub, *How Secure These Rights?*, 48–55. See also, for example, Philadelphia JCRC [Jewish Community Relations Council], "Survey of Application-for-Admission Forms Used by Pennsylvania Colleges and Universities 1953," folder 4, box 74, American Jewish Committee Papers.

29. Maslow to Tead, October 8, 1947, 4.

30. Johnson, "This Business of Admissions," 2.

31. *Laws of New York* (Albany, 1945), chapter 118, article 12, section 131, subsection 3, p. 461.

32. See, for example, "Minutes of October 22, 1945," 5, "Minutes of June 21, 1946," 1, and "Minutes of July 26, 1946," 1, State Commission Against Discrimination (SCAD) Minutes, 19283-07, State Archives of New York, Albany, NY.

33. New York State Commission Against Discrimination, *1949 Report of Progress* (Albany: State of New York, 1949), 20; New York State Commission Against Discrimination, *1950 Report of Progress* (Albany: State of New York, 1950), 22–24.

34. See, for AJCongress pressure on SCAD for rulings on unlawful questions, "Minutes of November 28, 1945," 2, SCAD Minutes, 19283-07.

35. For 1948 rulings, see New York State Commission Against Discrimination, *1948 Report of Progress* (Albany: State of New York, 1948), 57–60.

36. "Minutes of April 5, 1951," 1–2, and "Minutes of April 12, 1951," 1–2, Appendix A, SCAD Minutes, 19283-07.

37. Stephen S. Wise to Chancellor William J. Wallin, March 26, 1949, Education File, AJCongress Papers, quoted in Biondi, *To Stand and Fight*, 109.

38. State Education Department, University of the State of New York, *Education in New York State 1949: Preliminary Annual Report of the Education Department for the School Year Ending June 30, 1949* (Albany: University of the State of New York, 1949).

39. State Education Department, University of the State of New York, *Forty-Seventh Annual Report of the Education Department for the School Year Ending June 30, 1950*, vol. 1 (Albany: University of the State of New York, 1952), 46.

40. *Holland v. Edwards et al.*, 307 N.Y. 38, 119 N.E.2d 581 (1954).

41. New York State Commission Against Discrimination, "Decision and Order, Finding of Fact and Conclusions of Law," Complaint Case No. C-2833-51 (*Rue Lehds v. Helena Holland d/b/a/ Holland Vocational Service*), mimeographed, August 4,

1952, 4, quoted in Jay Anders Higbee, *Development and Administration of the New York State Law against Discrimination* (University: University of Alabama Press, 1966), 173.

42. *Holland v. Edwards et al.*, 116 N.Y.S.2d 264 (1952).

43. *Holland v. Edwards*, 282 A.D. 353, 122 N.Y.S.2d 721 (1953).

44. *Holland v. Edwards*, 307 N.Y. 38, 119 N.E.2d 581 (1954).

45. For one case that cited *Holland v. Edwards* as precedent and that did address questions about maiden names as part of racial discrimination, see *State Division of Human Rights v. Gorton*, 32 A.D.2d 933 (1969).

46. See, for example, *Browning v. Slenderella Systems of Seattle*, 54 Wash. 2d 440 (1959); *US v. Texas Education Agency*, 532 F.2d 380 (1976); and *Bodaghi v. Department of Natural Resources*, 995 P.2d 288 (2000). See also *Dobbins v. Local 212, International Brotherhood of Elec. Workers, AFL-CIO*, 292 F.Supp. 413 (1968).

47. See, for example, *K-Mart Corp. v. West Virginia Human Rights Commission*, 181 W.Va. 473 (1989); *State Division of Human Rights on Complaint of Cottongim v. County of Onondaga Sheriff Department*, 71 N.Y.2d 623 (1988); *Bodaghi v. Department of Natural Resources; People of the State of New York v. McCray*, 57 N.Y.2d 542 (1982). For historians who have addressed *Holland v. Edwards* briefly but have not addressed its significance in highlighting the subtlety of discrimination or the case's origins in name changing, see Konvitz and Leskes, *Century of Civil Rights*, 207–10; Higbee, *Development and Administration*, 172–73; and Paul D. Moreno, *From Direct Action to Affirmative Action: Fair Employment Law and Policy in America, 1933–1972* (Baton Rouge: Louisiana State University Press, 1997), 131–32.

48. For frustrations with state commissions in the late 1960s, though no specific reference to *Holland v. Edwards*, see Duane Lockard, *Toward Equal Opportunity: A Study of State and Local Antidiscrimination Laws* (New York: Macmillan, 1968), 73–101.

49. Alfred W. Blumrosen, "Strangers in Paradise: *Griggs v. Duke Power Co.* and the Concept of Employment Discrimination," *Michigan Law Review* 71 (1972–73): 66.

50. For an example of a case that cited *Holland v. Edwards* but called for affirmative action as a remedy, see *Brown v. Gaston County Dyeing Mach. Co.*, 457 F.2d 1377 (1972). For recent criticisms of "color-blind" ideology and legal theory, see, for example, Eduardo Bonilla-Silva, *Racism without Racists: Color-Blind Racism and Racial Inequality in Contemporary America*, 3rd ed. (Lanham, MD: Rowman and Littlefield, 2010); Charles A. Gallagher, "Color-Blind Privilege: The Social and Political Functions of Erasing the Color Line in Post-Race America," in "Special Edition on Privilege," ed. Abby L. Ferber and Dena R. Samuels, *RCC Journal* 10, no. 3 (2003); Lani Guinier and Gerald Torres, *The Miner's Canary: Enlisting Race, Resisting Power, Transforming Democracy* (Cambridge, MA: Harvard University Press, 2002); and Patricia J. Williams, *Seeing a Color-Blind Future: The Paradox of Race* (New York: Noonday / Farrar, Straus, and Giroux, 1998).

51. See, for example, Shana Bernstein, *Bridges of Reform: Interracial Civil Rights Activism in Twentieth Century Los Angeles* (New York: Oxford University Press, 2011);

Kita, "Breaking the 'Gentleman's Agreement'"; Greenberg, *Troubling the Waters*; Dollinger, *Quest for Inclusion*; Svonkin, *Jews against Prejudice*.

52. For some examples of prominent Jewish civil rights activists who changed their names (or whose families changed their names), see Murray Friedman, "John Slawson (1896–1989)," *American Jewish Year Book* 91 (1991): 557; Forster, *Square One*, 39; Dennis Hevesi, "Will Maslow, 99, Lawyer Who Fought Discrimination, Dies," *New York Times*, February 27, 2007, A17; *In the Matter of the Application of Isadore Polier, for leave to change his name to Shad Polier*, January 30, 1940, folder 1, box 8, RG P-572, Shad Polier Papers, AJHS.

53. Saenger and Gordon, "Influence of Discrimination," 96, 101, 102.

54. For a compelling portrait of Jewish civil rights activists seeking to make Jewish religious identification private, see Kevin M. Schultz, *Tri-Faith America: How Catholics and Jews Held Postwar America to Its Protestant Promise* (Oxford: Oxford University Press, 2011), 159–78.

55. For the structure of SCAD, as well as activists' frustrations, see Biondi, *To Stand and Fight*, 98–106; Chen, *Fifth Freedom*, 113–14; Moreno, *From Direct Action to Affirmative Action*, 107–61; and Lockard, *Toward Equal Opportunity*, 73–101.

56. American Jewish Congress, "Montgomery, Ala. Negro Leader Asks Support in 'Crusade for Citizenship' in South; Dr. Israel Goldstein, AJCongress President, Advances Program to 'Save America's Good Name' in Struggle for Full Equality," press release, February 7, 1958, folder 7, box 160, AJCongress Papers.

57. See, for example, the AJCongress battle against Levittown's policies discriminating against African Americans and against segregated schools in New York City. AJCongress, "AJCongress Calls on New Jersey Senators to Halt Construction of All-White Levittown Project," press release, June 13, 1958, folder 27, box 160, AJCongress Papers; AJCongress, "Two All-White Housing Units in N.J. Must Face Charges of Discrimination, American Jewish Congress Hails Ruling," press release, February 17, 1959, folder 30, box 161, AJCongress Papers; AJCongress, "American Jewish Congress Charges Segregation in New York Schools; Urges Action to End Discrimination," press release, February 2, 1959, folder 12, box 161, AJCongress Papers.

58. See, for example, Greenberg, *Troubling the Waters*, 166–67.

59. See, for example, Greenberg, *Troubling the Waters*; Svonkin, *Jews against Prejudice*; Dollinger, *Quest for Inclusion*.

60. Forster, *Square One*, 53–54.

61. Ibid., 39.

62. Ibid., 37–38.

63. Ibid., 48.

64. Ibid., 39, 48.

65. Ibid., 40.

66. Ibid., 20.

CHAPTER 5. "MY RESENTMENT OF ARBITRARY AUTHORITY"

1. David Wallechinsky, "David Wallace: The Underachiever," in *What Really Happened to the Class of '65?*, by Michael Medved and David Wallechinsky (New York: Random House, 1976), 266.
2. See, for example, Petitions N22-1967, N185-1967, N385-1967, N196-1972, N346-1972, N42-1977, N115-1977, N203-1977, N246-1977, N287-1977, N296-1977, N45-1982, N65-1982.
3. Petition N115-1967.
4. Petition N236-1977.
5. Petition N278-1977; see also, for example, Petitions N145-1976, N213-1977, N277-1977, N12-1982.
6. UJA-Federation of New York, *Jewish Community Study of New York* (New York: UJA-Federation of New York, 2011), 39, www.ujafedny.org.
7. Paul Ritterband, "Counting the Jews of New York, 1900–1991: An Essay in Substance and Method," in *Papers in Jewish Demography*, eds. Sergio DellaPergola and Judith Even (Jerusalem: Hebrew University, 1997), 199–228. The same trend is visible in other cities, such as Detroit and Boston. See, for example, Gerald Gamm, *Urban Exodus: Why the Jews Left Boston and the Catholics Stayed* (Cambridge, MA: Harvard University Press, 1999); Lila Corwin Berman, *Metropolitan Jews: Politics, Race, and Religion in Postwar Detroit* (Chicago: University of Chicago Press, 2015).
8. During these years, between 58 and 77 percent of petitions were submitted with other family members. These numbers exclude petitions that mentioned mothers remarrying and adopting new husbands' names but include underage children whose mother petitioned for their name change (regardless of the reason for the name change).
9. In the last two decades of the 20th century, only 17 to 38 percent of all petitions indicated families changing their names together.
10. Freeman, *Working-Class New York*, 256–87; Kim Phillips-Fein, *Fear City: New York's Fiscal Crisis and the Rise of Austerity Politics* (New York: Metropolitan Books, 2017).
11. See, for example, Petitions N935-1942, N945-1942, N1005-1942, N1025-1942, N1036-1942, N1074-1942, N5-1946, N7-1946, N36-1946, N62-1946, N63-1946, N65-1946, N74-1946, N76-1946, N98-1946, N220-1946, N303-1946, N323-1946, N371-1946, N495-1946, N534-1946, N634-1946, N766-1946, and N853-1946.
12. Levin, *Old Bunch*, 329.
13. Alfred J. Kolatch, *These Are the Names* (New York: Jonathan David, 1948), 30. See also Cynthia Ozick, "Geoffrey, James, or Stephen," *Midstream* 3 (1957): 70–76. For the argument that advice authors sought to blend Jewish and American names, see Joshua Furman, "'Jew and American in the Making': Education and Childrearing in the American Jewish Community, 1945–1967" (Ph.D. diss., University of Maryland, 2015).

14. See, for example, Alfred J. Kolatch, *Complete Dictionary of English and Hebrew First Names* (Middle Village, NY: Jonathan David Books, 1981); Anita Diamant, *What to Name Your Jewish Baby* (New York: Summit Books, 1989); Diamant, *The New Jewish Baby Book: A Guide for Today's Families* (Woodstock, VT: Jewish Lights, 1993), 15–84; Linda Rosenkrantz and Pamela Redmond Satran, *Beyond Sarah and Sam: An Enlightened Guide to Jewish Baby Naming* (New York: St. Martin's, 1992). Joshua Furman comments on the small numbers of Jewish baby-naming books in the immediate postwar years. See Furman, "'Jewish Education Begins at Home': Training Parents to Raise American Jewish Children," in *Mishpachah: The Jewish Family in Tradition and in Transition*, ed. Leonard J. Greenspoon (West Lafayette, IN: Purdue University Press, 2016), 175–96.

15. Diamant, *What to Name Your Jewish Baby*, 26–27.

16. For the popularity of names, see the website of the Social Security Administration, which has a search engine devoted to names over the past century: www.ssa.gov.

17. Social Security Administration, "Popularity of Name Sarah," accessed March 6, 2018, www.ssa.gov.

18. Lieberson, *Matter of Taste*, 217–21.

19. Sarah Bunin Benor and Steven M. Cohen, "Survey of American Jewish Language and Identity," Hebrew Union College—Jewish Institute of Religion, 2009, 10, accessed March 5, 2018, at Berman Jewish Policy Archive, www.bjpa.org.

20. Diamant, *What to Name Your Jewish Baby*, 27.

21. For data on baby names in New York State, see "State-Specific Data," on the Social Security Administration website, accessed September 24, 2017, www.ssa.gov.

22. Sarah Bunin Benor, "On Jewish Languages, Names, and Distinctiveness," *Jewish Quarterly Review* 106, no. 4 (2016): 440–49. See also Benor, "When Harry and Sally Became Chaim-Dov and Sara-Bracha," presentation at the American Name Society conference, Boston, MA, January 2013. Many thanks to Sarah Bunin Benor for providing me with the text of her presentation.

23. Linda Rosenkrantz and Pamela Redmond Satran, *Beyond Ava and Aiden: The Enlightened Guide to Naming Your Baby* (New York: St. Martin's, 2009), 184.

24. Stephanie Ginensky describes this trend as a "literature of return." See Ginensky, "And These Are the Names: An Onomastic Approach to American-Jewish Literature" (Ph.D. diss., Tel Aviv University, 2015).

25. Henry Roth, *Call It Sleep* (1934; repr., New York: Cooper Square, 1964); Clifford Odets, *Awake and Sing: A Play in Three Acts* (New York: Random House, 1935); Levin, *Old Bunch*; Irwin Shaw, *The Young Lions* (New York: Random House, 1948). See also, for example, Tillie Olsen, *Tell Me a Riddle* (Philadelphia: Lippincott, 1961); Hobson, *Gentleman's Agreement*; Norman Mailer, *The Naked and the Dead* (New York: Rinehart, 1948).

26. Philip Roth, "Eli the Fanatic" and "Epstein," in *Goodbye, Columbus* (Boston: Houghton Mifflin, 1959); Roth, *Portnoy's Complaint* (New York: Random House, 1969).

27. On Roth's ambivalence about being called a Jewish writer, see, for example, Judith Thurman, "Philip Roth Is Good for the Jews," *New Yorker*, May 28, 2014, www. newyorker.com. By 1981, Roth had published *Zuckerman Unbound* (New York: Farrar, Straus and Giroux, 1981).

28. See the author's discussion of the controversy in Philip Roth, "Writing about Jews," *Commentary*, December 1, 1963, www.commentarymagazine.com.

29. Gail Parent, *Sheila Levine Is Dead and Living in New York* (1972; repr., New York: Overlook Duckworth Books, 2004); Louise Blecher Rose, *The Launching of Barbara Fabrikant* (Philadelphia: McKay, 1974); Edith Konecky, *Allegra Maud Goldman* (1976; repr., New York: Feminist Press of the City University of New York, 1990); and Sarah Schulman, *The Sophie Horowitz Story* (New York: Naiad, 1984).

30. Parent, *Sheila Levine Is Dead*, 8.

31. Schulman, *Sophie Horowitz Story*, 59–61.

32. *Hester Street*, directed by Joan Micklin Silver (Midwest Films, 1975). The film is an adaptation of an Abraham Cahan novella; the original story includes the name change but not the indictment of Yankl's sexism. See Abraham Cahan, *Yekl: A Tale of the New York Ghetto* (New York: Appleton, 1896).

33. Nessa Rapoport, "The Woman Who Lost Her Names," in *The Woman Who Lost Her Names: Selected Writings by American Jewish Women*, ed. Julia Wolf Mazow (New York: Harper and Row, 1980), 135–42.

34. The main character Joanna's best friend, Bobbie Markowe, is clearly designated as a Jew with a changed name: "'Markowe' is upward mobile for 'Markowitz.'" Bobbie's death at the hands of her husband and other Stepford men signals to Joanna the danger she herself faces. Ira Levin, *The Stepford Wives* (New York: Random House, 1972), 23.

35. See, for example, Avery Corman, *The Old Neighborhood* (New York: Simon and Schuster, 1980); Philip Roth, *American Pastoral* (Boston: Houghton Mifflin, 1997); Allegra Goodman, *Kaaterskill Falls* (New York: Dial, 1998); Herb Gardner, *Conversations with My Father* (Garden City, NY: Fireside Theater, 1993); Wendy Wasserstein, *Isn't It Romantic* (New York: Dramatists Play Service, 1998; orig. produced 1981); and Wasserstein, *The Sisters Rosensweig* (New York: Harcourt Brace Jovanovich, 1993).

36. Jon Robin Baitz, *Three Hotels* (New York: Available Lights Production, 1990), 10. For an analysis that highlights name changes in this play and others, see Julius Novick, *Beyond the Golden Door: Jewish American Drama and Jewish American Experience* (New York: Palgrave Macmillan, 2008), 69–70; 124–28.

37. John J. Clayton, "Muscles," in *Wrestling with Angels: New and Collected Stories of John J. Clayton* (New Milford, CT: Toby, 2007), 268, 269; originally published in *Tri-Quarterly* (Spring 1985).

38. *Avalon*, directed by Barry Levinson (TriStar, 1990).

39. *My Favorite Year*, directed by Richard Benjamin (MGM, 1982).

40. Ibid.

41. "Regrets Name Change, Switches Back," *Jewish Advocate*, February 28, 1963, 13.

42. Allan Gale, telephone interview by author, digital recording, April 27, 2016.

43. Robbins, email communication with author.

44. Leonard Michaels, "Finn," in *Going Places* (New York: Farrar, Straus and Giroux, 1964), 165–77.

45. Herb Gardner's *Conversations with My Father* is an exception. See Gardner, *Conversations with My Father*, 64–66, 79–80, 85–86.

46. Rose, *Launching of Barbara Fabrikant*; Rona Jaffe, *Class Reunion* (New York: Dell, 1986); Elinor Lipman, *The Inn at Lake Devine* (New York: Vintage, 1999).

47. There are a few exceptions: John Jacob Clayton refers briefly to the cost of his family's name change, and Herb Gardner describes the language of his father's name-change petitions. See Clayton, "Waiting for Polly Adler," in *Wrestling with Angels*, 182–83; and Gardner, *Conversations with My Father*, 26.

48. In *Hester Street*, the heroine Gitl's decision to call her son Joey is an exception.

49. See, for example, Prell, *Fighting to Become American*, 177–208.

50. For Gardner's father's name change from Goldberg, see "Herb Gardner," IMDb, accessed October 2, 2017, www.imdb.com; and Joseph Berger, "Chasing a Name Lost to Time," *City Room* (blog), *New York Times*, July 2, 2011, https://cityroom.blogs.nytimes.com. For Clayton's uncle's name change from Cohon, see John Jacob Clayton, "My Father's Humiliation," *Commentary*, February 16, 2017, www.commentarymagazine.com.

51. Charles M. Young, "Seven Revelations about Mel Brooks," *Rolling Stone*, February 9, 1978, www.rollingstone.com.

52. Ira Levin, *Oral History Memoir*, March 1992, 13, William E. Wiener Oral History Library of the American Jewish Committee at the New York Public Library, accessed April 5, 2018, http://digitalcollections.nypl.org.

53. *The Godfather*, directed by Francis Ford Coppola (Paramount, 1972); *Ellis Island*, directed by Jerry London (CBS, November 11–14, 1984); *Far and Away*, directed by Ron Howard (Imagine, Universal, 1992).

54. Matthew Frye Jacobson, *Roots Too: White Ethnic Revival in Post–Civil Rights America* (Cambridge, MA: Harvard University Press, 2006).

55. For popular references to officials changing names at Ellis Island, see, for example, Barbara Goldberg, "After the War," *Lilith* 42, no. 2 (2017): 11; Paul Sochaczewski, "Back to My Roots," *Tablet*, March 21, 2012, www.tabletmag.com; Philologos, "Last Names, Lost in Translation," *Forward*, March 13, 2008, http://forward.com; Steve Koppman and Lion Koppman, *A Treasury of American-Jewish Folklore* (New York: Jason Aronson, 1998); Kaplan and Bernays, *Language of Names*, 54–55; Bill Severn, *Ellis Island: The Immigrant Years* (New York: Julian Messner, 1971), 99. For criticisms of these portraits, see, for example, Smith, "American Names"; Vincent J. Cannato, *American Passage: The History of Ellis Island* (New York: HarperCollins, 2009), 401–3; Dara Horn, "Jewish Names (Supposedly) Explained," *Mosaic*, January 21, 2014, http://mosaicmagazine.com; Aliza Giammatteo, "Ellis Island Changed Our Name," *Ambassador*, Fall 2012, 13–16, ProQuest; and Alicia Ault, "Did Immigration Of-

ficials Really Change the Names of Immigrants?," *Smithsonian.com*, December 28, 2016, www.smithsonianmag.com.

56. For texts that did not mention Ellis Island (or immigration officials) name changing, see "New Names for East Siders," *New York Tribune*, July 3, 1898, reprinted in *City Life, 1865–1900*, ed. Ann Cook, Marilyn Gittell, and Herb Mack (New York: Praeger, 1973), 78–79; Barker, "How the American Changes His Name"; Adamic, *What's Your Name?*; S. Felix Mendelsohn, *Let Laughter Ring* (Philadelphia: Jewish Publication Society of America, 1941); Theodore Reik, *Jewish Wit* (New York: Gamut, 1962); Mencken, *American Language*, 4th ed.; H. L. Mencken, *The American Language: An Inquiry into the Development of English in the United States: Supplement II* (New York: 1962); Moses Rischin, *Promised City* (New York: Corinth, 1964); Leo Rosten, *The Joys of Yiddish* (New York: McGraw-Hill, 1968); Rudolf Glanz, "German Jewish Names in America," *Jewish Social Studies* 23 (1961), and Glanz, "Jewish Names in Early American Humor," *Max Weinreich Festschrift*, 1964, both reprinted in Glanz, *Studies in Judaica Americana* (New York: Ktav, 1970), 278–313; and Ralph L. Woods, *The Joy of Jewish Humor* (New York: Essandess Special Editions, 1969). For brief suggestions of immigration officials, though not Ellis Island, name changing, see George E. Sokolsky, *We Jews* (Garden City, NY: Doubleday, Doran, 1935), 99; A. A. Roback, "Name-Changing among American Jews," *Chicago Jewish Forum* 19, no. 2 (1960–61): 124; and Robert M. Rennick, "The Folklore of Curious and Unusual Names," *New York Folklore Quarterly* 22, no. 1 (1966): 5–14.

57. See, for example, Mendelsohn, *Let Laughter Ring*, 31–32, 175, 176, 180, 192–93, 207; Henry D. Spalding, ed., *Encyclopedia of Jewish Humor* (New York: Jonathan David, 1969), 21, 46, 52, 59, 66, 349, 374, 433, 443; Harry Golden, *The Golden Book of Jewish Humor* (New York: Putnam, 1972), 53, 90–91, 136, 141, 188–91, 216, 218.

58. Spalding, *Encyclopedia of Jewish Humor*, 267–68.

59. For Jewish folklore in the 1940s and 1950s identifying Ellis Island officials as name changers, see Beverly Winston to David L. Cohn, May 24, 1948, David L. Cohn Collection; Robert M. Rennick, "The Inadvertent Changing of Non-English Names by Newcomers to America: A Brief Historical Survey and Popular Presentation of Cases," *New York Folklore Quarterly* 26 (1970): 263–82. For Ellis Island as a sympathetic symbol for ethnic Americans in the 1940s and 1950s, not a station of coercive name changing, see Louis Adamic, *Plymouth Rock and Ellis Island: Summary of a Lecture* (New York: Common Council for American Unity, 1940); Robert L. Fleegler, *Ellis Island Nation: Immigration Policy and American Identity in the Twentieth Century* (Philadelphia: University of Pennsylvania Press, 2013).

60. Jacobson, *Roots Too*, 59–60; Cannato, *American Passage*, 391–409; Fleegler, *Ellis Island Nation*, 189–90, 196–97.

61. Ellen Levine, *If Your Name Was Changed at Ellis Island* (New York: Scholastic, 1993), 76–77. Beginning in 2001, a popular public school curriculum that was developed in Iowa, Bringing History Home, included a simulation of the Ellis Island experience that included officials changing children's names. See Bring-

ing History Home, "Ellis Island Simulation," accessed March 28, 2018, www. bringinghistoryhome.org.

62. David M. Brownstone, Irene M. Franck, and Douglass L. Brownstone, *Island of Hope, Island of Tears* (New York: Rawson, Wade, 1979), 177–79.

63. *The Godfather, Part Two*, directed by Francis Ford Coppola (Paramount, 1974).

64. Melanie Kaye/Kantrowitz, "Jews in the U.S.: The Rising Cost of Whiteness," in *Names We Call Home: Autobiography on Racial Identity*, ed. Sandra Thompson and Sangeeta Tyagi (New York: Routledge, 1996), 129. For comparison with a more recent, more personal, and less political discussion of a name change back to the original, see Sochaczewski, "Back to My Roots." .

65. Kaye/Kantrowitz, "Some Notes on Lesbian Jewish Identity," 80.

66. Sarah Flint Erdreich, "Too Jewish? Changing the Family Name," *Lilith* 33, no. 1 (2008): 10–11.

CHAPTER 6. "NOT EVERYONE IS PREPARED TO REMAKE THEMSELVES"

1. Amy Waldman, *The Submission* (New York: Farrar, Straus and Giroux, 2011), 73.

2. Ibid., 73–76.

3. Vincent C. Alexander, "Practice Commentaries," *McKinney's Consolidated Laws of New York Annotated, NY CPLR § 1101*, 3–6. Many thanks to Barbara Bean for helping me to find and work with this text.

4. For changes to the court beginning in 1997, see Civil Court of the City of New York, *A Decade of Change and Challenge in "The People's Court," 1997–2006* (New York: Civil Court of the City of New York, December 2006), www.nycourts.gov. For the broader national concern with access to justice in court procedure, see, for example, American Bar Association, National Conference on Access to Justice in the 1990s, *Civil Justice: An Agenda for the 1990s* (Chicago: American Bar Association, 1991), www.americanbar.org; Mauro Cappelletti and Bryant Garth, eds., *Access to Justice* (Alphen aan den Rijn, the Netherlands: A. Giuffrè, 1978–79).

5. Ernesto Belzaguy, First Deputy Chief Clerk of the Civil Court, email to author, February 19, 2016. Belzaguy remembers making changes to the name-change form after taking a class that emphasized the value of plain language in legal forms to make them more accessible; he does not remember when that class took place. Ernesto Belzaguy and Rochelle Klempner, telephone interview by author, February 16, 2016; Civil Court of the City of New York, *Decade of Change and Challenge*. For more on A2J software, see Institute of Design and Chicago–Kent College of Law, Illinois Institute of Technology, "Access to Justice: Meeting the Needs of Self-Represented Litigants," accessed March 7, 2018, www.kentlaw.iit.edu; and Ny Jon Van, "Computer Program Helps the Poor Get Their Day in Court," *Chicago Tribune*, September 24, 2007.

6. The city's population was slightly more than 8 million in 2000; it grew to slightly less than 8.2 million in 2010: an increase of roughly 685,000 people but not a doubling. See US Census Bureau, 2010 and 2000 Census Public Law 94-171 Files

and 1990 STF1 File, Population Division—New York City Department of City Planning, accessed April 5, 2018, www1.nyc.gov.

7. For the $60 fees, see "I Changed My Name," 72. For the approximation of $60 in today's dollars, I used two inflation calculators: www.usinflationcalculator.com; and www.westegg.com/inflation/.

8. For this historical threshold of poverty, see Gordon M. Fisher, "Poverty Lines and Measures of Income Inadequacy in the United States since 1870: Collecting and Using a Little-Known Body of Historical Material," paper delivered at the Social Science History Association conference, October 17, 1997, accessed March 7, 2018, https://aspe.hhs.gov. Note that this measure was devised in 1948, not 1946, and that it reflects the broader United States and not New York specifically. There were few academic or government efforts to develop poverty thresholds during the late 1940s, so efforts to compare poverty in that era with 2012 will be imperfect and incomplete.

9. Many thanks to Amanda Tickner and the Michigan State University Library for all the mapping that made these conclusions possible. See, for example, although it reflects a slightly later date and a larger national study, US Department of Commerce and Bureau of the Census, *Current Population Reports: Consumer Income* (Washington, DC: US Government Printing Office, 1952), 1.

10. Freeman, *Working-Class New York*, 29.

11. For more discussion of these neighborhoods as middle class—and Jewish—see Moore, *At Home in America*, 65–68.

12. For New York City's median income, see US Census, *QuickFacts*, accessed March 7, 2018, www.census.gov.

13. For the city's poverty threshold in 2012, see New York City Office of the Mayor, *The CEO Poverty Measure, 2005–2012: An Annual Report from the Office of the Mayor* (New York: Office of the Mayor, April 2014), v, www.nyc.gov.

14. Fully 41 percent of petitioners lived in either the Bronx or Brooklyn, boroughs where nearly one-quarter of the population lived in poverty in 2012. Ibid., xi. Note that New Yorkers from the Bronx and Brooklyn also emerge in Civil Court in Manhattan in 2012 far more regularly than in earlier years because of administrative changes to the name-change process that encouraged people from the outer boroughs to change names in Manhattan.

15. See, for example, Jefferson Cowie, *Stayin' Alive: The 1970s and the Last Days of the Working Class* (New York: New Press, 2010); Lisa Fine, *The Story of Reo Joe: Work, Kin, and Community in Autotown, U.S.A.* (Philadelphia: Temple University Press, 2005); Gary J. Kornblith, Seth Rockman, Jennifer L. Goloboy, Andrew Schocket, and Christopher Clark, "Symposium on Class in the Early Republic," *Journal of the Early Republic* 25, no. 4 (2005): 523–64; Burton J. Bledstein and Robert D. Johnston, eds., *The Middling Sorts: Explorations in the History of the American Middle Class* (New York: Routledge, 2001); Walkowitz, *Working with Class*. For some specific discussions of the intersections between Jewish ethnicity and class, see, for example, Rachel Kranson, *Ambivalent Embrace: Jewish Upward Mobil-*

ity in Postwar America (Chapel Hill: University of North Carolina Press, 2017); Lederhendler, *Jewish Immigrants and American Capitalism*; Moore, *At Home in America*.

16. Petition N131-2002; see also, for example, Petitions N793-2002, N1061-2002, N1091-2002, N1111-2002.

17. Petitions N621-2002 and N1438-2007; see also Petition N1131-2002.

18. Petition N108-2007.

19. Petitions N1827-2007 and N781-2007.

20. Petition N1217-2007; see also Petitions N1877-2007 and N51-2007.

21. See, for example, Oriana Zill, "Crossing Borders: How Terrorists Use Fake Passports, Visas, and Other Identity Documents," *Frontline*, PBS, October 2001, www.pbs.org; National Commission on Terrorist Attacks Upon the United States, *The 9/11 Commission Report* (Washington, DC: Government Printing Office, 2004), 243, www.9-11commission.gov; Bob Sullivan, "9/11 Report Light on Theft Issues," *NBCNews.com*, August 4, 2004.

22. US General Accounting Office, *Security: Vulnerabilities Found in Driver's License Application Process*, GAO-03-989RNI (Washington, DC: US General Accounting Office, September 9, 2003); US General Accounting Office, *Security: Counterfeit Identification and Identification Fraud Raise Security Concerns*, GAO-03-1147T (Washington, DC: US General Accounting Office, September 9, 2003); Jennifer 8. Lee, "Two Years Later: Counterfeit Documents; Fake Licenses Are Still Seen as Easy to Obtain," *New York Times*, September 9, 2003, A20; Jonathan Krim, "U.S. Finds Weakness in ID Systems," *Washington Post*, September 9, 2003, E1.

23. See, for example, Nina Bernstein, "Immigrants Face Loss of Licenses in ID Crackdown," *New York Times*, August 19, 2004, B1; Leslie Casimir, "Immigrant Drivers Find a Roadblock," *New York Daily News*, April 12, 2004, 20; Daily Record Staff, "NY Governor Unveils New Design for State License," *Rochester (NY) Daily Record*, August 31, 2005.

24. Real ID Act of 2005, Pub. L. No. 109-13, 119 Stat. 231, 302 (2005).

25. A note on methodology: just as the issue of Jewish names is a complicated subject, so is the issue of Muslim or Arab names. Many Arabs of different faiths have names that sound Muslim because of their countries and cultures of origin; similarly, many Muslim individuals may have names that are Arabic, Asian, or North African because of their ethnic backgrounds. Because the Civil Court petitions do not inquire about petitioners' religion, I do not know whether petitioners are Muslim (unless they state it voluntarily on the petition), and if they are second- or third-generation immigrants, I do not know their country of origin. In my methodology, I used the term "Middle Eastern" as a category to include individuals with names that sound Arabic or Muslim, including individuals from North Africa or South Asia. I did not include in this category African Americans with Muslim names. I distinguished among these petitioners because very few African Americans with Muslim names sought to erase those names; instead Muslim African Americans almost always took on Muslim names (I deduced their racial

identity as African Americans typically from other clues in the petitions, including the names they decided to erase). I understand that this methodology, like my methodology in determining Jewish names, is imprecise. However, just as with Jewish names, this methodology focuses on the historical contingency of names—the "sound" of the names as Muslim or Arabic in the historical context of the post-9/11 world shaped both these individuals' decisions to eliminate their names and my own perception (as a non-Muslim, non-Arabic person) of those names as Muslim or Arabic sounding.

26. For more on this legislation and its impact on New York City, see Tyler Anbinder, *City of Dreams: The 400-Year Epic History of Immigrant New York* (Boston: Houghton Mifflin, 2016), 513–70; Nancy Foner, ed., *New Immigrants in New York*, rev. ed. (New York: Columbia University Press, 2001); Foner, *From Ellis Island to JFK: New York's Two Great Waves of Immigration* (New Haven, CT: Yale University Press, 2000); Arun Peter Lobo, Joseph Salvo, and Ronald J. Ortiz, *The Newest New Yorkers, 1990–1994* (New York: Department of City Planning, 1996); Frederick M. Binder and David M. Reimers, *All the Nations under Heaven: An Ethnic and Racial History of New York City* (New York: Columbia University Press, 1995), 225–62.

27. Campbell Gibson and Kay Jung, "Table 33: New York—Race and Hispanic Origin for Selected Large Cities and Other Places: Earliest Census to 1990," in "Historical Census Statistics on Population Totals by Race, 1790–1990, and by Hispanic Origin, 1970–1990, for Large Cities and Other Urban Places in the United States," Working Paper No. 76, Population Division, US Census Bureau, February 2005, www.census.gov.

28. White population here refers to non-Hispanic, Anglo whites; black population refers to non-Hispanic blacks; and Latinos refers to Hispanics of all races. City of New York, Department of City Planning, *NYC2010: Results from the 2010 Census: Population Growth and Race/Hispanic Composition* (New York: City of New York, Department of City Planning, 2010), 12.

29. For the point that New York's immigration patterns after 1965 did not produce one or two dominant ethnic groups, see Anbinder, *City of Dreams*, 516–17.

30. Marianne Bertrand and Sendhil Mullainathan, "Are Emily and Brendan More Employable than Lakisha and Jamal: A Field Experiment on Labor Market Discrimination" (working paper, National Bureau of Economic Research, November 18, 2002), www.chicagobooth.edu. The paper was republished as Bertrand and Mullainathan, "Are Emily and Greg More Employable than Lakisha and Jamal: A Field Experiment on Labor Market Discrimination," *American Economic Review* 94, no. 4 (2004): 991–2013. For academic citations to the Bertrand-Mullainathan study, see Social Science Citation Index, http://mjl.clarivate.com/. For some of the articles and blogs reporting or citing the Bertrand-Mullainathan study, see, for example, Michael Luo, "In Job Hunt, College Degree Can't Close Racial Gap," *New York Times*, November 30, 2009, www.nytimes.com; Jayne Matthews Hopson, "The Name Game: Are Emily and Greg Chosen over Lakisha and Jamal?," *Balti*

more Times, October 11, 2013, http://baltimoretimes-online.com; Katie Sanders, "Do Job-Seekers with 'White' Names Get More Callbacks than 'Black' Names?," *PunditFact*, March 15, 2015, www.politifact.com; Nick Gillespie, "Emily and Greg and Lakisha and Jamal," *Hit and Run* (blog), *Reason*, September 10, 2003, http://reason.com.

31. See, for example, Mahmood Arai and Peter Skogman Thoursie, "Renouncing Personal Names: An Empirical Examination of Surname Change and Earnings," *Journal of Labor Economics* 27, no. 1 (2009): 127–47; Anthony Edo, Nicolas Jacquemet, and Constantine Yannelis, "Language Skills and Homophilous Hiring Discrimination: Evidence from Gender- and Racially-Differentiated Applications" (Documents de travail du Centre d'Economie de la Sorbonne 13058, Université Panthéon-Sorbonne (Paris 1), April 2014); Latanya Sweeney, "Discrimination in Online Ad Delivery," *Communications of the ACM* 56, no. 5 (2013): 44–54; Katherine Milkman, Modupe Akinola, and Dolly Chugh, "What Happens Before? A Field Experiment Exploring How Pay and Representation Differentially Shape Bias on the Pathway into Organizations Journal of Applied Psychology," *Journal of Applied Psychology* 100 (2015): 1678–1712. For the wide press coverage of the Milkman study, see Leonard Davis Institute of Health Economics, University of Pennsylvania, "Katherine Milkman's Mentoring Bias Study Gets Wide Media Pickup," April 2014, http://ldi.upenn.edu. For a dissenting perspective on the Bertrand-Mullainathan article but one that still places the economists' work on African American names and discrimination in the popular eye, see Steven D. Levitt and Stephen J. Dubner, *Freakonomics: A Rogue Economist Explores the Hidden Side of Everything* (New York: William Morrow, 2005), 179–207. See also Roland G. Fryer and Steven D. Levitt, "The Causes and Consequences of Distinctively Black Names," *Quarterly Journal of Economics* 119, no. 3 (2004): 767–805.

32. Michael Luo, "'Whitening' the Resume," *New York Times*, December 5, 2009, www.nytimes.com; BuzzFeedYellow, "José vs. Joe: Who Gets a Job," YouTube, September 18, 2014, www.youtube.com. Thanks to Sara Fingal for the latter citation.

33. See US Census Bureau, "Profile of General Population and Housing Characteristics, 2010, New York City, New York," accessed March 8, 2018, www1.nyc.gov.

34. Petition N342-2002.

35. Petition N292-2002.

36. Petitions N281-2002 and N260-2007.

37. Petition N1431-2002; see also Petitions N258-2007, N511-2002, N641-2002, N751-2002.

38. See, for example, Petitions N1-2002 and N641-2002.

39. For a critique, see, for example, Yvonne M. Cherena Pacheco, "Latino Surnames: Formal and Informal Forces in the United States Affecting the Retention and Use of the Maternal Surname," *Thurgood Marshall Law Review* 18, no. 1 (1992): 1–40.

40. Petitions N241-2002 and N1003-2007. For other Latino petitioners dropping mothers' maiden names to conform to American naming culture, see Petitions N1-2007, N31-2007, N121-2007, N561-2007, N661-2007.

41. Christian Blauvelt, "Producers to Middle Eastern Actors: Don't Tell Anyone Your Real Name or You'll Never Work Again," *Entertainment Weekly*, October 7, 2011, www.ew.com.

42. Neil MacFarquhar, "U.S. Muslims Say Fear Hampers Their Right to Travel," *New York Times*, June 1, 2006; Susan Sachs, "A Nation Challenged: For Many American Muslims, Complaints of Quiet but Persistent Bias," *New York Times*, April 25, 2002.

43. "Muslim? Change Your Name like Me!," BBC News, June 10, 2005, http://news.bbc.co.uk.

44. For nonfiction, see Walid Jahad, "Anything to Fit In: The Struggles of an Arab American," *Al Arabiya News*, December 12, 2014, http://english.alarabiya.net. For fiction, see, for example, Ayad Akhtar, *Disgraced: A Play* (New York: Little, Brown, 2013), 12–13; Waldman, *Submission*, 26–32.

45. MacFarquhar, "U.S. Muslims Say Fear Hampers Their Right to Travel."

46. See, for example, Moustafa Bayoumi, *This Muslim American Life: Dispatches from the War on Terror* (New York: NYU Press, 2015), 124–25; Irum Shiekh, *Detained without Cause: Muslims' Stories of Detention and Deportation in America after 9/11* (New York: Palgrave Macmillan, 2011), 99.

47. See, for example, Jahad, "Anything to Fit In"; Sana Saeed, "American Muslims Stumble through Stereotypes and Double Consciousness," *Alakhbar English*, January 19, 2014; Sachs, "Nation Challenged." For detailed arguments about Muslim and Arab racialization after September 11, see, for example, Louise A. Cainkar, *Homeland Insecurity: The Arab American and Muslim Experience after 9/11* (New York: Russell Sage Foundation, 2009); Bayoumi, *This Muslim American Life*.

48. "Muslim? Change Your Name Like Me!"; Sachs, "Nation Challenged."

49. Cainkar, *Homeland Insecurity*, 168, 174, 176–77, 179.

50. Note that these general population figures include African American Muslims, which my calculations do not; the numbers of non–African American Muslims and Arabs emerging in the name-change petitions is thus even more disproportionate than this data suggests. See US Census, "The Arab Population—2000: A Census Brief," accessed September 22, 2015, www.census.gov. For the Muslim population of the entire United States being around 0.8 percent, see Pew Research Center, "Muslim Americans: No Sign of Growth in Alienation or Support for Extremism," August 30, 2011, www.people-press.org.

51. Petition N410-2002.

52. Petition N3-2002.

53. Petition N1206-2002.

54. See also Petitions N1031-2002, N114-2002, N1204-2002, N1356-2002.

55. Petition N479-2002.

56. Petition N535-2002.

57. Petition N721-2002.

58. See also Petitions N1274-2002, N1483-2002, N187-2002, N415-2002, N497-2002.

59. Petition N1727-2012.

60. Petition N91-2007.

61. Petitions N614-2012 and N783-2002.

62. Louise Cainkar, for example, suggests that a wave of hate crimes directed toward Arab and Muslim Americans immediately after September 11 subsided somewhat in the years afterward. She offers much evidence, however, of continued insecurity among Arab and Muslim Americans during the years after the attacks. See Cainkar, *Homeland Insecurity*, 190–95.

63. Matt Apuzzo and Adam Goldman, "With CIA Help, NYPD Moves Covertly in Muslim Areas," Associated Press, August 23, 2011, www.ap.org. See also Apuzzo and Goldman, *Enemies Within: Inside the NYPD's Secret Spying Unit and bin Laden's Final Plot against America* (New York: Touchstone, 2012).

64. Matt Apuzzo and Adam Goldman, "NYPD Keeps Files on Muslims Who Change Their Names," Associated Press, October 26, 2011, www.ap.org.

65. For a broader national context for the chilling nature of government surveillance in the Arabic and Muslim communities, see, for example, Cainkar, *Homeland Insecurity*.

66. Petitions N611-2002 and N311-2002; see also Petition N1001-2002.

67. Petition N1115-2007. For other examples of individuals reclaiming mother's maiden names, see Petitions N1125-2007, N1717-2007, N1767-2007.

68. Petitions N931-2002, N1371-2002, N1484-2002; see also Petition N1077-2002.

69. Petition N611-2007; see also Petitions N1747-2007 and N1206-2007.

70. Petition N621-2002.

71. Petition N211-2002.

72. See, for example, Stephen A. Crockett, Jr., "Keisha Ditches Her Black Name and Becomes Kylie," *Root*, November 2013, www.theroot.com; "Keisha: What's in a Name? Bigotry," *Kansas City Star*, November 5, 2013, www.kansascity.com.

EPILOGUE

1. Trish Kent, telephone interview by author, digital recording, June 26, 2017. See also Dove Kent, telephone interview by author, digital recording, May 24, 2017. Joanna Kent Katz emphasizes that it was not solely the need for a job that led her maternal grandfather to change his name; bitterness that his father had deserted the family also played an important role. See Joanna Kent Katz, telephone interview by author, digital recording, July 25, 2017.

2. Ironically, Litowitz's professor was probably Edward Acheson, the brother of Dean Acheson, who later went on to become secretary of state. It is possible that Acheson's family connections may have given him a better sense of the discrimination extant in the federal government.

3. Trish Kent, interview.

4. Ibid. Kent's full name is Patricia, and she has had many different nicknames throughout her life. She now chooses to be called Trish, although this was a name she took on later in life, after most of the events described.

5. Ibid.

6. Ibid.; Joanna Kent Katz, interview.
7. Dove Kent, interview.
8. Joanna Kent Katz, interview.
9. Dove Kent, interview.
10. See also, for example, Israel, email communication.
11. See, for example, Gold, interview; Nuland, *Lost in America*, 140–46; Clayton, "My Father's Humiliation"; Blum, interview.
12. For similar emphases on the emotional pain of racial reconstruction, see Hobbs, *Chosen Exile*; and Goldstein, *Price of Whiteness*.

INDEX

ABOUT THE AUTHOR

Kirsten Fermaglich is Associate Professor of History and Jewish Studies at Michigan State University. Her previous publications include *American Dreams and Nazi Nightmares* (2006) and the Norton Critical Edition of Betty Friedan's *The Feminine Mystique*, coedited with Lisa Fine (2013). She is coeditor of the journal *American Jewish History* with Adam Mendelsohn and Daniel Soyer.